Stout Fellow

Stout Fellow

◆

A Guide Through Nero Wolfe's World

O.E. McBride

iUniverse, Inc.

New York Lincoln Shanghai

Stout Fellow
A Guide Through Nero Wolfe's World

iUniverse, Inc.

For information address:
iUniverse, Inc.
2021 Pine Lake Road, Suite 100
Lincoln, NE 68512
www.iuniverse.com

ISBN: 0-595-27861-2 (pbk)
ISBN: 0-595-65716-8 (cloth)

Printed in the United States of America

To my mother

and, of course,

Rex Stout

Contents

Foreword

This book is dedicated in part to my mother because she tried. She tried to do many things for me, to show me many things, to tell me many things, to teach me many things. Since she was eminently human and thus, like us all, fallible, some of those things were right and some were wrong, even though well intentioned. Since I am also human, some lessons stuck with me as I matured, some I modified to my taste and some I cast aside. Such is the destiny of women who raise boys to become men.

Like most kids, some of the behaviors I saw in her, I emulated and some I adopted the exact opposite. She was a voracious reader and this is one of the behaviors I adopted. Spending my earliest formative years in a home that drew entertainment from radio instead of television (as horrible a deprivation as later generations might imagine that) stimulated my imagination, forcing me to develop and exercise the ability to visualize the implications of the spoken word in my mind. I can't remember ever seeing a picture of *Bobby Benson and the B-Bar-B Riders* or any of the characters in *Gangbusters* but, after several decades, I can still call up my mental image of them. When I did see Superman, Sgt. Joe Friday, Marshal Matt Dillon and others portrayed on television years later, It was amazing how closely they fit my previously conceived mental images. What a feat of mental accommodation this was is evidenced by the fact that the television Dillon, James Arness, was at least a foot taller than William Conrad, Dillon's radio voice. It is only a short step from this to visualizing the written word and deriving similar entertainment from it.

I can vividly remember the puzzlement I found in watching my mother sit for hours looking at books (with no pictures in them!), turning pages, frowning in concentration, smiling with satisfaction and erupting in gales of laughter. I could watch her live the stories. She explained this to me and I also discovered the wonder of it.

I later discovered from her that many of these books were the works of Rex Stout, specifically the Nero Wolfe series. Her lifetime was contemporary with the series. She was 25 years old when the first Nero Wolfe adventure, *Fer-de-Lance*, was published. Four decades later, she died the year before Rex Stout and, sadly, never had the opportunity to enjoy the culmination of the series in *A Family*

Affair. I hope Rex Stout was wrong in his agnosticism and somewhere, somehow, he is still writing and she is still reading, to their mutual satisfaction.

Rex Stout was writing the fifteenth book in that series during the first year of my life. Eventually, 59 of the 74 Wolfe adventures would be written during my lifetime. My mother would re-sell some of her books. Others she loaned, traded or packed away. These, however, she kept on shelves, reading and re-reading them until the bindings literally shredded. These were the books with the broken backs, the frayed spines, the dog-eared pages. I still have the entire collection, 46 books containing 74 stories, ranging from old paperbacks with a price of twenty-five cents printed on the cover to a $27 large-print hardback, altogether some three and one-quarter million words.

Besides entertainment, she learned things from these books and taught things from them as well. From my earliest memories, she never used "baby talk" around me. She spoke to me in an adult vocabulary even as a pre-schooler and showed me how to plumb the mysterious but logical depths of huge books called dictionaries and thesauruses. When I asked her about a word I didn't understand, she would invariably reply "Look it up." Long before the word "phonics" was ever invented, she would show me how to spell an unfamiliar word by sounding it out, then show me how to find it and the meaning. When I got the drill down, she no longer helped. It became a lifelong habit.

Also from the Nero Wolfe books came lessons in the subtleties and nuances of humor, sarcasm, deduction and logic, not to mention the erudition imparted by exposure to foreign words and phrases, *Haute Cuisine*, the Phylum *Orchidaceae* and some of the baser criminal motivations of mankind. Where else might I have learned what a Mogok ruby was?

So I began reading the Nero Wolfe canon. All read and re-read lovingly, just like mother did. I was still in grade school when I joined her in the annual anticipation of the publication of the next Wolfe book, even daring to hope that maybe two would be written that year. I was not a prodigy by any means, just inspired and addicted. The series of triple and quadruple novella collections written at that time were also gentler on a young boy's attention span until I developed the mental discipline to get through the novels.

Perhaps I learned my lessons too well. Nero Wolfe, Archie, Saul, Fred, Orrie, Fritz, Theodore, Cramer, Purley, the brownstone and the other details were too entrenched in my psyche to be displaced or modified. Had my mother lived to see the first television efforts, I feel certain she would have uttered an openly derisive "Pfui", said something scathingly Goodwin-esque about imitation not always being the sincerest form of flattery, shut the damned thing off and settled down with one of the canon to get the taste out of her mouth.

Therefore this book has probably been fermenting in my imagination for decades. But make no mistake about it, I have no intention of competing with Rex Stout so, for both our sakes, please, no comparisons. They are neither intended nor invited. This is my paean, my homage to the man and some of his enduring creations with a little cataloguing, summarization and analysis thrown in for good measure. It is not an original idea or effort. A previous excellent work was produced by William S. Baring-Gould but that was more than a quarter century ago and could not be complete since Mr. Stout was still alive and cranking the stories out. Therefore it preceded some of the cases not yet written, some of the information in unpublished accounts that didn't come to light until after Mr. Stout's death and the outstanding biography by John McAleer, characterized by his unprecedented access to and candor from King Rex.

In fact, it was Mr. Baring-Gould's work that precipitated me to start this volume. First came my reading of his wonderful volume *The Annotated Sherlock Holmes* which I believe merits a slight digression on the connection, at least philosophically, between Holmes and Wolfe.

I find it very difficult to believe that anyone who is a fan of the greatest fictional detective of the Nineteenth Century could fail to equally appreciate the greatest one of the Twentieth even while fully appreciating their differences which are at least as much as those of their creators.

Much has been said about the potential connections between the two great detectives. For a much more thorough examination than will be attempted here, I would again refer the reader to the McAleer biography and his more than two dozen references to Wolfe v. Holmes.

In McAleer's work, Rex Stout said that if there was any deliberate link between Wolfe and Holmes, it was "purely unconscious." While I hesitate to suggest any revisions in Mr. Stout's use of the English language, I think "subconscious" would have been a better word. I fail to see how anyone could read both canons and not see the convergences.

Wolfe has the mental acuity common to both of the Holmes brothers while his corpulence, obsession with routine and veneration of mental activity over the physical surely remind one of Mycroft. Their talents for deductive and inductive reasoning are on a similar plane although Wolfe's talents tend to lean more toward dealing with people and their motivations rather than Holmes preoccupation with forensic evidence, doubtlessly influenced by their respective tolerances for physical exertion.

The similarities extend to the other characters as well. As a chronicler, Archie is a tougher, more energetic and more perceptive Watson. It takes both Fritz and Theodore to supplant Mrs. Hudson. Saul, Fred and Orrie make infinitely more effective Baker Street Irregulars. Cramer and Stebbins alone rise to the level of Scotland Yard Inspector Athelney Jones while Rowcliff and the rest of the NYPD wallow among the perpetually disoriented with Inspectors Gregson and Lestrade.

Only Rex Stout could prove or disprove these theories and there is no reason to doubt his veracity or candor in his prior statements with regard to this subject. Besides, to disprove him would take someone with at least Professor Moriarty's grasp of higher mathematics to interweave combinations and permutations with theories of probability, chaos, coincidence and God knows what else. Enough digression.

Upon reading Baring-Gould's *The Annotated Sherlock Holmes*, it immediately occurred to me that it would be wonderful to have such a volume available for the Nero Wolfe canon but I decided it was beyond my endurance to produce such a work. Next followed a re-reading of his *Nero Wolfe of West Thirty-Fifth Street*. I noted that it had been written in 1966 and published the next year following his untimely death. My knowledge of basic crime statistics and the first line in the Foreword—"There are about six hundred murders a year in New York City"—brought home how long it had been since the volume was produced. I found a few errors in it that detract only minutely from its value as a reference source and also felt that a lot of information could be added. The continued reprinting of the stories and the number of Internet websites devoted to Wolfe told me there were new generations interested in him and his exploits. Thus I embarked on this quest.

Therefore, understand that many of the words in this work are not mine, they were and are Rex Stout's. He is the one who put many of them together in the order they appear in the first place. For that reason, I have chosen to differ in several important respects from the format of Mr. Baring-Gould's aforementioned volume. This is not intended in any way as a criticism of that excellent work. Rather, it is an expression of my personal idiosyncrasies that I find a surfeit of quotation marks, footnotes or accreditations distracting when reading a work that is not historical. In that also I will differ, at the risk of being branded a heretic. This work is not biographical or historical because (forgive me!) these are fictional characters dealing with circumstances that never happened. Many drawn, as we shall see, from the author's life experiences but nevertheless, fictionalized. That understood and duly credited, I will not forego the aforementioned tools entirely but will in many places. Just remember, it isn't plagiarism—Rex Stout said it first, his characters said it next and I said it last. Similarly, I don't intend to accredit every statement I repeat to the story it came from, either by title or abbreviation. I will most usually date a statement by the year in which the story was set (NOT the year it was published) rather than by the story's name. If you want to know where Stout or Wolfe or Archie or whoever said a particular thing, read the books. I think you'll enjoy it more that way, anyway. I did.

Another way I will differ from Mr. Baring-Gould's work is I will not provide a summary of each story. In documenting the various aspects of the stories as well as the sketches of the characters, I will endeavor not to give enough of the story away to significantly diminish a first-time readers enjoyment.

Similarly, I will not include information contained in the continuation of the series written by Robert Goldsborough even though I highly recommend them. Although they are excellent in their own right and especially satisfying for those of us who wish the Nero Wolfe series would never end, they are not the works of Rex Stout and that is the only reason for their omission.

On those occasions where I attempt any analysis or state any personal opinions, they will be mine and mine alone, doubtlessly very biased and opinionated. They are offered for your examination. Please read the books and form your own opinions, under no circumstances allowing mine to influence you.

Because of some crossover between the subject matter and the way the chapters are organized, there is some repetition of information in different areas of the book. I apologize for the redundancies but felt they were necessary within the context of the chapters.

So I do hope you enjoy it. But I will undeservedly adopt a smattering of Mr. Wolfe's arrogance by admitting that I didn't do it for the readers, I did it for myself and it was a labor of love. If you are a devotee of the series, I hope it adds to your future enjoyment of it. If you are a novice initiate, I hope it gives some manner of comprehensive overview of what lies ahead of you. If, by some miracle, this is your first acquaintance with the Nero Wolfe extended family, I hope they hook you like they hooked me, it whets your appetite for the adventures to come and I envy you the tingle of that first reading of each case.

I hope you find it satisfactory.

The Creator—Rex Stout

While this book is about Nero Wolfe, his companion characters and their adventures, it would be illogical to start the narrative anywhere except by briefly examining the man in whose mind, personality and life experiences they were born.

Rex Todhunter Stout was born on December 1, 1886, in Noblesville, Indiana, but the family soon moved to rural Kansas. The sixth of nine children of John Wallace Stout and Lucretta Elizabeth [Todhunter] Stout, he had five sisters and three brothers. Over the next nine decades, he would outlive all but two of them.

The seeds of a prodigious writing career were sown at the age of 17 when he sold a poem to a magazine for $12. In 1912, he began writing short stories and in the last month of that year, he published his first crime story, *A Professional Recall*, in The Black Cat magazine. The next year, he published his first novel, *Her Forbidden Knight*.

Writing, however, was not his life, just part of it. He served in the U.S. Navy on the Presidential yacht under President Theodore Roosevelt. While in the Navy in 1907, he was shot during hostilities in Santo Domingo. He met some of the literary giants of our time such as G.K. Chesterton, George Bernard Shaw and Edgar Rice Burroughs, and lunched with Mark Twain and Booth Tarkington.

He would eventually write 51 novels, 75 novellas and short stories, and numerous other essays and articles. At the age of 46, he would create Nero Wolfe and his retinue. Eight of those characters would appear in the first novel in 1934, the last novel more than four decades later and more or less consistently throughout the series—Nero Wolfe, Archie Goodwin, Fritz Brenner, Theodore Horstmann, Purley Stebbins, Saul Panzer, Fred Durkin and Orrie Cather. Thirty-three of Stout's novels, 39 novellas and two re-written novellas comprise the 74 Wolfe tales written over a span of 42 years considered in this volume. The series and the characters are permeated with his personal preferences, prejudices, politics, acquired knowledge and life experiences.

As a boy in Kansas, he had once been chased by a bull. His memories of that experience were recreated in *Some Buried Caesar*. The chicken and dumplings of his paternal grandmother, Sophia Swingle Stout, were the direct inspiration for Mrs. Miller's fricassee and dumplings served at the Crowfield County fair in the same novel. His maternal grandmother, Emily McNeal Todhunter, always had a book of some kind in her hands, and she kept a huge dictionary and an equally massive atlas close at hand. Remind you of anyone? At the age of 11, he was spelling champion of Kansas, Nebraska and Illinois, a talent and title later transferred to Archie Goodwin. Stout once reconciled differences with his father by making him a yellow nightshirt. What is Nero Wolfe's favorite color?

In April of 1905, an 18-year-old Rex Stout had his Victor record player and collection of records stolen from his home in Topeka, Kansas. The next month, his property was recovered and, a few days later, Stout claimed his property from Topeka's 42-year-old Chief of Police—A.G. Goodwin. And thus the seeds of a legend were planted.

Chief Goodwin (we don't know what the A.G. stood for) was a bachelor and evidently a very physically capable man, being over six feet tall and 200 pounds. John McAleer states that Goodwin "was the first policeman anywhere to use an automobile in police work." If accurate, it was probably a Veracity. These cars were produced from 1903 to 1905 by the Smith Automobile Company owned by Dr. Clement Smith of Topeka. Formerly known for manufacturing artificial limbs and trusses, Dr. Smith continued to produce the cars through 1911, thereafter known simply as the Smith. Chief Goodwin's car would have been a simple two-cylinder buggy with a planetary transmission and chain drive.

As a young man in his early 30's in New York, Stout often ate at the Brevoort and at Louis Martin's restaurant. At the Brevoort, he first ate *oeufs au beurre noir* (eggs prepared in a black butter sauce), which would become a staple on Wolfe's breakfast tray. Louis Martin's became the model for Marko Vukcic's Rusterman's Restaurant.

Like Wolfe, Stout was a man of routines and he disliked holidays because they disrupted them. The only books Stout kept in his bedroom were an Aventuros edition of Casanova's *Memoirs*. Wolfe also has a set on his bookshelves. Like Archie, Stout disliked synthetic fabrics and owned only cotton socks and pajamas. In fact, under the listed likes and dislikes of Nero Wolfe and Archie Goodwin, you might as well be reading those of Rex Stout.

For the most part, that is. Stout didn't ascribe all of his qualities to his characters and didn't adopt all of theirs. Unlike Wolfe, he liked scented geraniums—apple, apricot, nutmeg and lemon. Hyacinths, tulips and cactus also inhabited his gardens. Unlike Wolfe, Stout had no prohibition on taking care of business during meals and did it frequently.

Concerning Stout's likes and dislikes, it is also interesting to learn his views about his own writings and those of others. He once said that *Some Buried Caesar* was his favorite among his Wolfe novels. *The Next Witness* was his favorite among the novellas. He also named his favorite detective stories for interviewers, once in 1942 and again in 1973. On the second list, he included one of his own Wolfe stories:

1942

The Moonstone by Wilkie Collins
The Maltese Flacon by Dashiell Hammett
The Benson Murder Case by S.S. Van Dine
The Documents in the Case by Dorothy L. Sayers & Robert Eustace
The Innocence of Father Brown by G.K. Chesterton
Call Mr. Fortune by H.C. Bailey
The Bellamy Trial by Frances Noyes Hart
The Cask by Freeman Wills Crofts
The Murder of Roger Ackroyd by Agatha Christie
Lament For A Maker by Michael Innes
A Coffin For Dimitrios by Eric Ambler (added in 1951)

1973

Murders In The Rue Morgue by Edgar Allen Poe
The Hound of the Baskervilles by Arthur Conan Doyle
The Moonstone by Wilkie Collins
The Maltese Falcon by Dashiell Hammett
The Murder of Roger Ackroyd by Agatha Christie
The Daughter of Time by Josephine Tey
Strong Poison by Dorothy L. Sayers
The Brothers Karamazov by Fyodor Dostoievski
The League of Frightened Men by Rex Stout
And "one of a dozen or so Maigrets" (by Georges Simenon)

For anyone who has ever written or tried to write a book, an example of Rex Stout's work ethic, self-discipline and precision is instructive. He did all of his writing on manual Underwood typewriters. He first bought a used one in 1912 for $16.50. It was replaced with new ones in 1920, 1937 and 1956. He typed one and only one version of his stories, an original and two carbon copies. He never revised them which is to say he never second-guessed himself, went back and changed things. He did rewrite different versions of two of the novellas but those were expanded versions done under unusual circumstances. He never wrote more than twelve pages in a single day. To avoid clouding his faculties in any fashion, he didn't drink alcohol when he was writing but, in later years, he would smoke up to two Gold Label Barcelona cigars (90 cents each) during a writing session.

This has been but a short synopsis of the fascinating life and career of an extraordinary man. It goes without saying that there is much more to be said about such a long and interesting life of such an interesting man and most of it has already been said. For anyone whose interest has been piqued, I would highly recommend the outstanding posthumous biography *REX STOUT* by John McAleer, Little, Brown and Company, 1977.

The Creation—Nero Wolfe

Montenegro is a former province of Yugoslavia. A small, mountainous country about the size of Connecticut, it is probably a safe bet that for most of its existence, most of the world's students couldn't locate it on a map. The seeds of World War I were planted with an assassination in the city of Sarajevo, only a few hours walking distance north of its border. In one of the more volatile parts of our world, it is sandwiched in between Albania, Serbia, Bosnia-Herzegovina and Kosovo, names that have become increasingly familiar during the last decade.

Aficionados will tell you that Nero Wolfe was born in a small, simple house on a dirt road in Montenegro, near the River Cijevna, and about ten kilometers southeast of the city of Titograd, a mere two kilometers from the Albanian border.

If he is assumed to be fifty-eight years of age at the time of the time setting in the first novel, *Fer-de-Lance*, in mid-1933, he was born in the latter half of 1875 or the first half of 1876. Others have placed his birth year as 1892 or 1893. But, as we shall see, that is moot. Actually he was born in the first week of October of 1933 in the mind of Rex Stout. So were most of his eventual retinue of retainers (Archie, Fritz, Theodore, *et al*), competitors (Cramer, Stebbins, Rowcliff) and the first of what would become a long line of adversaries.

Coming within the same week as the birth of Stout's first daughter, the birth of his most enduring literary creation would be of shorter gestation but a longer labor. He first started writing about Wolfe on October 18, 1933, the day after his new daughter came home from the hospital. Unlike Barbara Stout, Nero Wolfe was born fully developed with an intellect, a personality, talents and foibles, routines, likes and dislikes, and more than his share of near obsessive-compulsive behaviors.

Wolfe has another advantage over Barbara Stout. He was endowed with immortality by his creator and was able to ignore the passage of time over the four-plus decades of his adventures. Rex Stout once told an interviewer that Wolfe was fifty-six years old and later told his biographer that he liked a permanent age of fifty-eight for Wolfe.

Much is known about Wolfe and yet, much is not. His closest friend, associate and essentially an adopted son (some would also argue with the "adopted"), Archie Goodwin, admits that much of Nero Wolfe is an enigma even to him and that Wolfe has "at least fifteen or twenty pasts." This is a synopsis of one of them. Be prepared for contradictions.

He was named for a mountain near his birthplace—*Monte Nero*, in Italian, The Black Mountain—and not the Roman emperor. The actual mountain, Mount Lovchen, is 5,770 feet high and is roughly centered in what was once the independent province of Montenegro.

His name was actually a reflection of how the mind of his creator worked. Rex Stout thought that the rhythm of a two-syllable first name worked best with a single syllable surname.

"Rex" is Latin for "king" and Nero was a Roman emperor. An animalistic turn of the name "Stout" conjures up the image of a bull and, by implication, "large." "Wolfe" produces the image of a wolf, one of which suckled Romulus and Remus, the founders of Rome.

Nero Wolfe spent his boyhood in the arid, mountainous region of his birth. He says he has known Marko Vukcic all his life and hunted dragonflies in the mountains with him. As a youth, he crossed the Adriatic Sea at least 80 times and left his home at the age of sixteen. For the next fourteen years, he traveled the world, becoming acquainted with most of Europe, much of Asia and a little of Africa in a variety of roles and activities.

He became a secret agent for the Austrian government and later joined the Montenegrin Army when World War I broke out. Thinking all misguided or cruel people should be shot, he shot some. He was allegedly in Albania in 1915 and in Zagreb, Yugoslavia, in 1916. He walked 600 miles to join the Allied Expeditionary Force when the United States entered the war in April of 1917. After the war, he returned to the Balkans and adopted a daughter in Montenegro in 1921. In the same year, he was in Bari, Italy, where a man named Telesio saved his life by knifing two Fascists who had him cornered. He soon left the adopted girl with people to care for her and went to America. In 1933, he says he owns a house he has never seen in Egypt and it was given to him ten years before. He has fond memories of the Rhages and Veramine tiles on the doorway. These are types of colorfully painted, glazed tiles from ancient Persia named after the respective cities (Vermin and Rhages or Rey) in ancient Medea where they originated.

In 1934, he hints that he was married but his wife tried to poison him with cold compresses on his head that contained "a penetrating poison…distilled from an herb." While working for the Austrian government in some clandestine capacity, he admits he was once jailed in Bulgaria. In 1974, after spending two days and nights in the New York City Jail, he says he'd spent more time in a much dirtier jail in Algiers.

In 1936, Wolfe mysteriously tells Archie that he's an uncle and sends monthly checks to Belgrade. That may imply the existence of siblings although he never mentions them or it may be a deliberate misstating of his role as an adopted father.

In 1937, he tells Archie that a quarter of a century earlier (then 1912), as a "youngster" on another mission for Austria, his travels led him through Figueras, Spain, to Port-Vendres, France and eventually to Algiers and Cairo. By our contrived timeline, he would have been in his mid-thirties then but as we have seen, that is pointless conjecture. In 1938 he says that twenty years before he had been an athlete. By Wolfe's current standards, that might have meant merely mobile but that is unfair in the context of the timeline because walking 600 miles is no mean feat for anyone, anytime. In the same year he tells an FBI agent that he was born in America but, given Wolfe's future opinions of and relations with that agency, it isn't inconceivable that he's lying and he later contradicts that statement on more than one occasion. One reason for the FBI agent's questions is that Wolfe has contributed money to the anti-Fascist loyalists in Spain and the League of Yugoslavian Youth. Wolfe probably felt his roots were none of the FBI's damned business especially while being read chapter and verse from the United States Code. He also made trips to America during these earlier periods, apparently more than one.

Eight years after he left his adopted daughter in Yugoslavia, Wolfe says he returned to look for her, was unsuccessful and was forced to leave the country. This would have been in 1928 or 1929 according to her age in the story in which she appears, *Over My Dead Body*. In 1957, he says that he came to America in 1930 (not penniless), bought the brownstone on West Thirty-Fifth Street (evidently outright—we never hear of Archie making mortgage payments) and started his private detective business. In 1951, he says that he became a naturalized American citizen 24 years before, that is in 1927.

In 1938, we are told that Wolfe keeps a metal box on a shelf in the safe which he alone has a key to and never opens in Archie's presence. May we speculate on what he might keep in it? Old ferrotype photographs of his parents? Or unacknowledged siblings? Or friends? Papers and/or photographs of his adopted daughter? Mementos of women from his past (admittedly unlikely)?

Rex Stout served in the U.S. Navy for two years, enlisting at 18. Initially rejected for inflamed tonsils, he spent two of the three dollars he possessed to have them removed in a barber's chair, recovered overnight lying in a vacant field and successfully enlisted that day. A remarkably resolute young man. It was on Navy cruises that he first saw orchids and even managed to get himself shot in the leg during an uprising of rebels in Santo Domingo. War being a young man's enterprise, Stout was a little long in the tooth for partaking in either of America's great wars. He was 30 when America entered World War I and 55 on the eve of World War II. In early 1945, six weeks after his fifty-eighth birthday, Stout managed to finagle a trip to the European war zone as a war correspondent. Near Aachen, Germany, he took a shot at a distant German soldier but "apparently missed."

Nero Wolfe, like his creator, is thoroughly imbued with a patriotism for democracy for all people and a virulent hatred of everyone and everything that threatens that ideal. Would it not be more likely that his private box would contain some mementos from his struggles against those oppressors?

We know he served as a secret agent for the Austrian government. We don't know his rank but the Austrian government awarded the Military Order of Maria Theresia to officers who showed great courage in the face of the enemy and the Medal for Bravery to enlisted soldiers. Might Wolfe have received one of these awards?

We know he served in the Montenegrin Army at the beginning of World War I. Montenegro's highest military decoration was the Milosh Obilich Medal, named for a 14th Century Serbian warrior who died fighting the Turks. They also offered the Order of Danilo I and the Military Bravery Medal. Serbia offered the Order of the White Eagle, the Order of St. Sava, the Order of the Star of Karageorge and the Obilich Medal for Bravery. Italy offered the Military Order of Italy and the Medal for Military Valor. Many of these decorations were awarded to Allied soldiers of different nationalities during World War I. Might Nero Wolfe have been awarded one or more of these medals after shooting some of those "misguided and cruel people?"

We know he served with the Allied Expeditionary Force in World War I. He would have, at a minimum, been eligible for the World War I Victory Medal. Is it in the box? There was also an Army of Occupation of Germany or Austria-Hungary Medal conferred upon occupying troops between 1918 and 1923. He may have been eligible for it. He says he killed 200 Germans during the war, a pretty significant accomplishment for any soldier in any conflict. He is not on the official rolls of recipients of the Medal of Honor (but then he is fictional). The Distinguished Service Medal was usually reserved for higher-ranking officers but might he have been awarded the second-highest combat decoration for heroism, the Distinguished Service Cross? Or the Silver Star? Might he have been wounded and awarded the Purple Heart? Although not officially instituted until 1932, the award could have been made retroactively.

He was of service to several different nations during that conflict. The British were stingier than most nations about awarding decorations especially to foreigners but were nevertheless known to confer some of their plethora of medals upon Allied compatriots. The French awarded their Croix de Guerre, Legion of Honor and Medaille Militaire to some Allied soldiers. Likewise, the Belgians awarded their Order of Leopold, Croix de Guerre, Military Cross and Military Medal to others.

Surely with the wartime record ascribed to him, Nero Wolfe was endowed with some of these awards but we'll never know.

We do know that while Wolfe himself might decline the title of a powerful and important man, he knows some important men. Besides handling cases for some of the wealthier industrialists in America, he has dealt with ambassadors, Secretaries of State, high-ranking military officers as well as the Secret Service and the FBI, although his ability to call in favors from the last two mentioned organizations might be questionable. In 1951, Archie says Wolfe knows important people in Washington D.C. who owe him favors and he uses some of that leverage to help the Vardas's with a call to a "Mr. Carpenter." That may or may not have been the same as Lieutenant General Carpenter that he was well acquainted with during the war and in four previous cases. That influence is ongoing because he calls in some favors from various Governors and Attorneys General as late as 1968.

Physically, Wolfe is a big man. Dora Chapin calls him "fat" in 1934 but Wolfe tells her he prefers the word "gargantuan." He is five feet, eleven inches tall. In 1937, Archie snidely estimates his employer's weight at "something between 250 and a ton." When preparing a description of Wolfe for a radio series in 1949, Stout listed his character's weight as 272 pounds but it fluctuates. The most frequently given weight in the saga is one-seventh of a ton which is a fraction over 285 pounds. An average size for a modern lineman in the NFL (although they're generally half a foot or so taller) but, in the first half of the Twentieth Century when the average American man was about five feet, nine inches and 160 pounds, Wolfe would have cut a truly imposing figure as his creator obviously intended.

One researcher has even tried to hypothesize whether Archie meant "a short ton [2000 lbs.] or a long ton [2240 lbs.]." Considering what we know of Archie's sense of practicality, I think it safe to assume he was speaking of the commonly accepted definition of a ton, 2000 pounds. In 1944, evidently somewhat deprived by yielding to wartime rationing of commodities and having virtually given up his detective business for the duration of the war with the inevitable effect upon the bank balance, Wolfe has melted down to "260-something." Celebrating the defeat of Fascism and Japanese militarism, by 1948 he's blossomed up to one-sixth of a ton (333 pounds). His apparent peak is 340 pounds in 1947. In 1950 he lost 117 pounds during his self-imposed exile from home plotting against Mr. X. Imagine. If Wolfe was still at his maximum of 340 when he took flight, he ended up at a lean and mean 223 pounds. But if he had been at his normal seventh of a ton, he would have been an emaciated 168 pounds! Twelve pounds lighter than Archie!!! No wonder Archie didn't recognize him.

Not to worry. Back under the thrice-daily ministrations of Fritz and in his favorite chair, like a gas, his volume expanded to fill all of the available space. Within five months after his pursuit of Mr. X ended, he was back up to one-seventh of a ton. By 1952, he's down to a modest 4,000 ounces, if accurate, a relatively svelte 250 pounds.

Periodically, Wolfe decides he weighs too much which Archie says is like the Atlantic Ocean deciding it's too wet. On two occasions Wolfe has taken unilateral steps to remedy this situation with what he called "exercise." This word has a special meaning for the man who once described a golf swing as "ungovernable fury."

In 1935, his "exercise" was darts or, as Wolfe preferred to call them, "javelins." He put up a dartboard in the office and maintained that he was exercising when he played. His exercise period was from 3:45 to 4:00 P.M., the quarter-hour preceding his afternoon session with the orchids. The board was "two feet square, faced with cork, with a large circle marked on it, and 26 radii and a smaller inner circle, outlined with fine wire, divided the circle's area into 52 sections. Each section had its symbol painted on it, and together they made up a deck of cards; the bulls-eye, the small disk in the corner, was the Joker." Thus each five throws from a distance of ten or fifteen feet made up a poker hand. He even preferred the darts with the yellow feathers.

In later years, it was pool or billiards. Marko Vukcic talked him into buying a pool table for a room in the basement. Wolfe had one of his special chairs placed down there also. Every Sunday morning thereafter, Wolfe would spend the morning in the kitchen with Fritz preparing something special. Vukcic would come for lunch at 1:30, then he and Wolfe would adjourn to the basement to have a five-hour session at the pool table. Wolfe was adamant that this was not play for him but exercise. Archie was invited to join them a few times but stopped going when Wolfe pouted whenever Archie ran up a long string of balls.

In spite of Wolfe's size, he is not terribly handicapped by it, with the possible exception of finding a comfortable chair in foreign surroundings. As Archie puts it, he may weigh one-seventh of a ton but, when necessary, he can move like it's only one-twelfth of a ton (166 pounds or so). In 1948, he tells us that he watches Wolfe with every expectation of him being awkward or clumsy but his movements are always "smooth and balanced and efficient." This should be no great surprise to anyone who has ever watched a fat man comport himself on a dance floor. This strength and grace of movement is very much in Wolfe's best interests. By 1944, Archie estimates that at least 22 people have threatened to kill Wolfe in the last decade. Wolfe says it is at least 100. Some have even tried.

In 1937, he is grazed by a bullet on one cheek in an attempted assassination. The next year Wolfe is attacked in his office by a murderer with a dagger but succeeds in defending himself by using two beer bottles to crack his assailant's skull and break one wrist. In 1954, after traveling halfway around the world, he is shot ten inches above the left knee in New York harbor. His survival instincts don't seem to erode much with time. Two decades later, he rocked back in his chair and kicked Elaine Usher in the chin when she tried to jump over his desk to get a piece of paper from him. Wolfe also has five canes, one in a stand in the downstairs hall near the front door and the other four in a rack in his room. Since he doesn't need them for walking (which he amply proves on a number of occasions), they are probably intended as a rather innocuous weapon for self-defense and his actions prove that on at least one occasion. One is a redthorn but the biggest, toughest one is topped with a fist-sized knob made of Montenegrin applewood.

The rest of Wolfe's description comes from his author. He has a "mass of dark brown hair, very little greying, is not parted but sweeps off to the right because he brushes with his right hand. Dark brown eyes are average in size, but look smaller because they are mostly half closed. They are always aimed straight at the person he is talking to. Forehead is high. Head and face are big but do not seem so in proportion to the whole. Ears rather small. Nose long and narrow, slightly aquiline [Sherlockians, take note]. Mouth mobile and extremely variable; lips when pursed are full and thick, but in tense moments they are thin and their line is long. Cheeks full but not pudgy; the high point of the cheekbone can be seen from straight front. Complexion varies from some floridity after meals to an ivory pallor late at night when he has spent six hard hours working on someone. He breathes smoothly and without sound except when he is eating; then he takes in and lets out great gusts of air. His massive shoulders never slump; when he stands up at all he stands straight. He shaves every day. He has a small brown mole just above his right jawbone, halfway between the chin and ear." John McAleer notes that Rex Stout had a similar mole.

Nero Wolfe is also a very opinionated man, very sure about who and what he is, what he does and does not like. For instance:

Likes:
-all things yellow
-beer
-books
-breakfasting alone
-chess
-crossword puzzles
-good form, good color and fine texture. He has good taste in those matters.
-the look and feel of silver table cutlery
-orchids
-the performance of stainless steel
-reading
-sharpening his own pencils and knives

Dislikes:
-arguing on the telephone
-babbling women
-bare floors
-being bounced or jostled in moving vehicles
-being called "Boss"
-being read aloud to
-being touched
-being compelled without warning to make quick movements
-bells and chimes
-canned soup
-carrying things
-cats
-cinnamon rolls
-credit cards
-dandruff
-diamonds
-discussing business at meals or in cars

-doughnuts
-eating from a tray which is an insult both to the food and the fed. This doesn't apply to breakfast in his room.
-eating with strangers
-facing a hearth fire or an open window
-fastened manuscripts
-genteel manners
-gin. Both the taste and smell.
-gin drinkers
-highballs before meals
-ice water
-interruptions
-jellied consommé'
-loud noises
-men who marry money
-more than six at a table
-movies
-moving vehicles of any kind
-paper dishes
-people who quote although this doesn't apply to himself
-people on vacation
-plastic covered furniture
-practical jokes
-pressure cookers
-pug noses, especially on women or a pronounced incurve anywhere along the bridge
-rain
-reading lying down
-shaking hands with strangers
-speed reading
-spray cans
-telephones
-television
-the colors red and purple
-the word "contact" used as a verb
-the word "newscast" as a contraction for "news broadcast"
-timetables
-trains

-travel
-truisms
-unctuousness
-unemptied ashtrays
-waste
-Webster's International Dictionary, Unabridged, Third Edition
-working

In most of these specific preferences and prejudices, he mirrors Rex Stout. Most but not all. I doubt if anyone ever implied that Stout had an aversion to working, possibly only a different definition of what working was.

It appears that Wolfe approaches obsessive-compulsive behavior in his routines. Approaches but does not actually exhibit because when his routines are disrupted, as happens frequently during the saga, he continues to be fully functional, he's just grumpy as hell about it. Perhaps his routines are so much more regimented than the rest of us because he is able to do it and thus does.

He rises at 8 A.M. every morning regardless of when he went to bed the night before and some of the adventures allow for some very long nights. He rarely varies from this and then under only the most extreme circumstances. Fritz brings his breakfast tray to his bedroom promptly at 8:15. It will contain some combination of peaches and cream, bacon, eggs (*oeufs au beurre noir*), ham, sausage, griddle cakes with wild thyme honey and hot chocolate (no coffee at breakfast). In 1958, after a particularly long, harrowing night, he orders four eggs and ten slices of bacon for breakfast which we are told is twice the normal portions.

On rainy or gray mornings, he eats in bed but in sunny weather he has it at a table next to a window while reading his two morning newspapers on a reading rack. On those occasions when Archie comes up, Wolfe refuses to speak until he has had his orange juice and he refuses to gulp orange juice. Archie gets to tell us on several occasions what a glorious sight he is at these times, decked out in several acres of bright yellow pajamas reflecting the sunlight coming through the window, his hair tousled and his feet bare, and a scowl betraying the effect on his digestion if Archie is in the room on business, which is essentially the only reason Archie would invade his den that early. Archie says on one occasion that it takes eight yards of material to make one pair of these pajamas and on another he says ten yards so you can't be certain when he's being facetious. Wolfe sleeps with the windows cracked open year round (and in the later years, under a yellow electric blanket, just like Rex Stout) and eventually has a gizmo installed that automatically closes them at 6 A.M. so the room is warm when he gets up. If it's still cool, he wears yellow slippers with turned-up toes and one of five yellow wool dressing gowns with thin, black stripes. Usually this sight is reserved for only Archie and Fritz but Inspector Cramer gets to see him in this condition in 1944.

Following his breakfast, Wolfe bathes (he doesn't use showers, probably for obvious reasons), shaves with an old-fashioned straight razor that he sharpens himself and grooms himself. Like Archie, he gets his hair cut regularly. Considering his predispositions, naturally he wouldn't go to anyone who deemed themselves a "hair stylist" and it would never be a female. His original barber was a man named Fletcher on Twenty-eighth Street. Fletcher retired and Wolfe tried going to Archie's barber, a man named Ed Graboff at the Goldenrod Barber Shop on Lexington Avenue. Archie had been getting haircuts from Graboff for six years by 1951 but Wolfe didn't like his work and switched to a barber named Jimmie Kirk in the same shop two years before that. That relationship didn't work out either and Wolfe ended it somewhat uniquely. We aren't told who he settled on after that. For all we know, he may have had Fritz giving him trims in the basement.

Wolfe hates geraniums but uses a geranium-scented soap. Go figure (a modern phrase that would repel him). Perhaps it's an appeasement to the fact that Rex Stout does like geraniums. Wolfe dresses every day in a three-piece suit with a vest and tie. He used to carry a large platinum watch in a vest pocket but it fell into disuse. He has a clock on the wall to the right of his desk but sees no reason why he should turn his head when he can simply ask Archie the time. He never wears a wristwatch but had to get used to one in 1950 when he temporarily divested himself of all his luxuries. He uses two freshly laundered yellow dress shirts every day. Like his shirts, pajamas, sheets and pillowcases, his socks (and presumably his underwear) are always canary yellow. He is fastidiously clean even when unseen or in private. This habit eventually provides a murderer with a weapon in 1959 when a murderer has the gall to strangle a victim with one of Wolfe's ties.

Continuing his inflexible and ritualistic behaviors, Wolfe takes the elevator two flights up to the plant rooms promptly at 9 A.M. every day except Sunday. After playing with the orchids for two hours, he descends to the office at 11. He always greets Archie with a "Good morning" whether it is or not and regardless of how much interaction (*not* contact) they have already had that morning. He is always carrying a freshly cut spray of orchids which he places in a vase of water on the right front corner of his desk. He then gets himself situated in his favorite chair and rings Fritz for beer, two short buzzes and one long from the buzzer on his desk.

Wolfe loves beer. His usual brand is Remmers although when the first story opens in June of 1933, Wolfe has been buying it from bootleggers, disdainful of Prohibition. The Twenty-First Amendment is in the process of being ratified by the states and Fritz has just returned from an extended shopping trip, bringing Wolfe one bottle of every brand commercially available. He is allegedly trying to cut down from six to five quarts daily which Archie thinks is futile. They are always brought to him unopened and he keeps count of his intake by keeping the caps in his desk's middle drawer (as if it made a difference). That is also where he keeps the solid gold beer opener he uses. It has an unknown inscription on it and was a gift from a grateful client who couldn't afford it. He has another gold opener given to him by Marko Vukcic but it doesn't work very well so the other one does the majority of the work.

He even has a specific method for drinking beer. He pours until the foam is exactly one-quarter inch below the rim of the glass and then drinks the glass empty in one motion. After allowing the foam to dry on his upper lip, he likes to use his tongue to lick it off and then dab it dry with his handkerchief. He graciously omits the tongue part when company is present.

Now fortified, he tears yesterday's date sheet from his desk calendar and discards it, goes through the morning mail that Archie hasn't already discarded as unnecessary, checks his pen on a scratch pad to be certain it's working, signs the necessary checks to pay the bills and inspects the current bank balance. He then dictates letters or memos to orchid hunters or other correspondence. He then reads orchid catalogs, his current book or does crosswords puzzles until lunchtime. He prefers the difficult puzzles in the London Times and the London Observer. Occasionally he will listen to the noon news on the radio unless the broadcaster offends him which probably occurs often. Once a week he will pass some time by sharpening the penknife he always carries even though he hardly ever uses it, using the oil can and oilstone he keeps in his desk.

Lunch is at 1 or 1:15. He and Archie (if present) adjourn to the dining room and Fritz serves. Lunch usually takes an hour to an hour and a half. Then it's back to the office for more of the usual routine unless there's business to pester them.

At 4 P.M., it's back to the plant rooms for another two hours tweaking the orchids. He returns to the office at 6 P.M., rings for beer and, unless there's business, reads until dinnertime. The usual evening beer toll is one or two and three is a big beer night. To forestall any friction, he and Archie get two copies of the evening papers delivered.

Dinner is at 7:15 P.M. in the early adventures but is later advanced to 8 P.M. An hour and a half is usually allotted for the meal and no business talk is allowed at the table although even this rule is not sacrosanct and is broken for the first time in the 1939 case. Non-business conversation is encouraged at Wolfe's table and may even be considered mandatory to good digestion. He is liable to expound at length upon any conceivable subject and he does not expect the conversation to be one-sided. These interactions have definitely improved upon Archie's two weeks of college education over the years.

Following dinner, they adjourn to the office for coffee. Wolfe hates to have to work for an hour after dinner. He will if it's necessary but the effort tells on his mood. If there is no business at hand, they may continue their dinner conversation, listen to the radio (Wolfe likes the Joy Boys which Archie thinks is pretty damn vulgar and he prefers the band at the Hotel Portland's Surf Room) or, if Archie has a date with Lily Rowan or tickets to some sporting event, Wolfe will read until bedtime. He rarely goes to bed before midnight and always turns the phone on to his room when he retires if Archie's not home yet.

His late hours are good training because business forces him into them quite frequently. He isn't thrilled about going past the midnight deadline for business but won't shrink from it. In 1935 he is up until 2 A.M. on one occasion and 3 A.M. on another. In 1937 he's up all night although that may not count because he's on a moving train. Later he is also up until 4 A.M. and then pulls another all-nighter. This doesn't diminish with the passing years. In 1953, he's up until 4 A.M. again.

Wolfe is a lifelong non-smoker but he will tolerate it from Archie, Inspector Cramer and assorted clients and guests depending upon the individual and the circumstances. Both Archie and Cramer smoke in the early adventures but both eventually quit. Cigarette and pipe smoke don't particularly bother Wolfe but he pinches his nose when a cigar is lit, to prepare it for the impending assault. This is one of those counter-habits since Rex Stout smoked cigarettes for decades before switching to cigars which he kept up until just a few months before his death.

Wolfe once refused to allow a surprise guest to light his pipe after dinner but that was probably retribution because Wolfe had to share his portion of beef with him. In 1953 he refused to let Paul Kuffner smoke in the office but that relationship was very adversarial. Wolfe will not tolerate a used ashtray with remains in the office. He will walk all the way to the bathroom to empty one.

Wolfe doesn't snack between meals but occasionally will go on binges lasting from a few days to two weeks. The binges may swing from one extreme to the other. He once went to bed for several days, living on bread and onion soup. On another occasion, he spent every day sitting in the kitchen telling Fritz how to cook things and eating magnanimously. He once ate half a sheep cooked twenty different ways in two days.

Oddly enough, he even manages to turn these experiences into professional assets. In 1946, he spends two and one-half days in bed, feigning a nervous breakdown while hiding from the cops. He blew all the rules for that one, abandoning the office, dining room, plant rooms and kitchen for all that time. It was excruciating.

Although presented with many opportunities, Wolfe rarely curses and never on the level of, say, a longshoreman or a Marine drill instructor. Perhaps it is an example of the axiom that "profanity is what one says when one doesn't know what to say." Nero Wolfe very rarely doesn't know what to say. Even his style of profanity is literate. "Bah", "Egad" or "Confound it" are his most common eruptions. "Great hounds and Cerberus" is close to the limit of his frustrations. In spite of his agnosticism, he is never blasphemous and comes closest when someone says something slanderous about food and once said "Good God!" when he guessed wrongly about which seasoning was missing from a dish. In the last case in 1974, he said "By God!" under extreme pressure.

In one sense, Wolfe is a dedicated misogynist but, in another sense, a gentleman who makes allowances for women or at least certain women. He once made Archie apologize when he said "Damn" in front of a woman. He also understands these attributes in others. He once deduced that Fred Durkin had an unseen woman with him from hearing the respectful tone of Fritz's voice in the hall. Archie missed it completely. Conversely, Wolfe is the only man Archie ever met who uses exactly the same tone of voice to a man as he does to a woman.

Like most men's opinions of women, Wolfe's may be the result of past experience, in his case, most of it negative. In 1938, he tells Archie that he has physically skedaddled once in his life and it was from a Montenegrin woman. In 1974, he admits that he was married once in the Balkans and his wife tried to poison him. In a 1966 interview, Rex Stout said that it "was thought" that Wolfe murdered his wife although, considering the prior poisoning attempt, an element of self-defense could be reasonably assumed.

Wolfe may or may not rise from his chair for a woman. When he does, it is an extraordinary concession. At various times, he grants it to Evelyn Hibbard in 1934, Neya Tormic and Carla Lovchen in 1938, Julie Alving, Nancylee Shepherd and her mother in 1948, Meg Duncan in 1960 and Laura Fromm in 1953 although the last wasn't much of a compliment since it was within minutes of lunchtime. For his exact reasons for rising or not, you'd have to ask him and even he may not be able to verbalize them. They definitely have nothing to do with perceptions of status, power, money or titles. In the first case, he stood up for a fairly ordinary woman but once refused to rise for the wife of an English duke worth $20 million.

His opinions of women are fairly consistent. When Lily Rowan tells him she wants him to like her, he tells her he rarely dislikes women and never likes them. He thinks they are all dotty, devious or both. When considering them as suspects of murder, he has stated that they do not require motives that are comprehensible by any intellectual process. He also believes they do not faint unless sufficiently clubbed, they are just putting on an act. Nevertheless, Archie keeps smelling salts in his desk. The mere implication of a stranger that he (Wolfe) might have a wife is enough to cause him to visibly shudder at the horror of the thought, much to Archie's amusement.

Wolfe will panic when women cry in his presence. He maintains that their moments of calm are merely recuperative periods between outbursts. When that happens, he rapidly becomes desperate and flees the area if Archie cannot control the situation. He once abandoned his own plant rooms when Beulah Page erupted upon learning of her father's murder.

Wolfe doesn't disapprove of women except when they try to function as domestic animals. He thinks they are sometimes splendid creatures when they stick to vocations for which they are best adapted such as chicanery, sophistry, self-adornment, cajolery, mystification and incubation. In 1935, Clara Fox is the first woman in many years to sleep under his roof.

Wolfe will sometimes pinch his nose with a thumb and forefinger when women are present, whether it's just one or a covey of them, because the air is tainted with perfume. He can't stand skinny women or anyone he thinks doesn't eat enough. He is much more likely to judge a woman from her appearance than a man and is especially sensitive to the formation of their noses. He has been begged more than once by a prospective client but it's bad tactics. His reaction to an emotional appeal from a man is rarely favorable and from a woman…never. He won't do divorce or marital work (his vanity bristles at the mere offer) or industrial surveillance.

Wolfe prefers never to shake hands with strangers but makes allowances sometimes. At one time or another, he has shaken hands with gangsters, Nazi agents and, by 1945, at least forty murderers. He has shaken hands with John Barrett, Mrs. Jasper Pine, Dr. Michaels and Laura Fromm. He refused to shake hands with Sarah Rackham but Archie says he was just being lazy. In 1952, he refuses to shake hands with Priscilla Eads because she invaded his house without his permission but he probably regrets that. His refusals are sometimes arbitrary. In 1958, he refuses to shake hands with Edwin Laidlaw but then invites him to a sumptuous lunch of clams hashed with eggs, parsley, green peppers, chives, mushrooms and sherry. In 1961 he shakes hands with Ralph Purcell and leaves him wiggling his fingers to get the circulation back which causes Archie to comment that when Wolfe takes a hand, he really *takes* it.

There are nine or ten people Wolfe will willingly shake hands with without wincing. One is, of course, Archie. Wolfe rarely comes downstairs until after his morning session with the orchids but he makes an exception when Archie returns from a very successful investigative trip to California in 1951. He even greeted him with a handshake to honor his intrepidity in the line of duty by risking his life on a transcontinental airplane flight. We can probably assume he includes Fritz and Theodore in this club. He shakes hands with Saul Panzer, Fred Durkin and Orrie Cather when he hasn't seen them for a few weeks. Others in this select company include Marko Vukcic, Nathaniel Parker and Dr. Edwin Vollmer. That's nine. If there's a tenth, Lewis Hewitt may qualify, certain distinguished chefs (especially if they've got a recipe he wants), some of the staff at Rusterman's Restaurant or some of his overseas contacts. You decide. Similarly, Wolfe says that there are only four people on earth he would ask a favor of. One of them is definitely Archie and one is definitely not Orrie Cather. The other three (my guess) are probably Marko Vukcic, Fritz Brenner and Saul Panzer.

Wolfe is, by his own admission, a born actor, dramatic by nature and insufferably conceited. He has a healthy ego (a gross understatement), is a self-proclaimed genius and has proven it many times. He says he has no equal as a detective but, in 1946, comes close to contradicting that statement by saying "There was a man in Marseilles once—but he is not available and doesn't speak English." Like Sherlock Holmes, he has a very selective memory. Archie says that a list of the things Wolfe doesn't know that any two-bit dick does would fill a book. He lives in the largest city in the world, which he may be aware of, but has to ask Archie if the Secret Service has an office in New York. He does, however, know something about law. In a rage, he once threatened to dislocate Cramer's nose with a *habeas corpus ad subjiciendum*. This is Latin for "you should have the body for submitting." It is the full legal title of the well-known writ of *habeas corpus* to force authorities to justify holding someone in custody. He also once impersonated a defense attorney tearing up one of Cramer's arguments before an imaginary jury, doing an excellent job in the process.

For any observer of body language, Wolfe is an intricate study but probably only Archie can really appreciate the full treatment. He likes for people to sit in his presence because he likes their eyes at his level. When he must speak while standing, he is always curt. When Wolfe is forced to answer his own telephone, he always answers it by saying "Yes?" or "Yes, whom do you want?" Archie's told him a hundred times that's a hell of a way to answer a phone but he's too damn pigheaded and Archie can't break him of it.

His eyelids lowering slowly and rising slowly means his approval of whatever he's just seen or heard. Half closed eyes mean he's watching you like a hawk. When Archie reports and Wolfe keeps his eyes open, it means part of his mind is on something else. When he's briefing Archie, Saul, Fred and/or Orrie, Wolfe keeps his eyes on Fred and Orrie because he knows Archie and Saul are getting it right. When his eyes are wide open, it means he's sleepy, indifferent, irritated or distracted. When his eyes are only slits, he is at his most attentive and most dangerous. At those times, he doesn't miss the slightest twitch of a muscle, the slightest nuance of word or expression.

When he rubs his cheek with the tip of a forefinger, slowly and rhythmically, it means he's irritated but attentive. Rubbing his nose with one finger shows inner tumult and rubbing his chin means he's boiling inside.

He is not normally overtly physically demonstrative but can be when the occasion demands. His voice can crack like a whip, stopping Inspector Cramer or almost anyone else in their tracks and his bellow would stop a tiger ready to spring. He can and does grunt, growl and snap but Archie doesn't have his chuckle tagged. It could be anything from a gloat to an admission that someone got something over on him to genuine amusement. Holding up his hand with the palm out is "a pretty violent gesture" and striking the arm of his chair with his palm is so violent that it's the next thing to hysterics. A few times he hits his desk with his fist which is a convulsion for him. In 1959, he succumbs to the fourth of these fits, beating on his desk with his closed fist and bellowing in Serbo-Croat but the conditions are extraordinary. He is faced with three murders and no clues so he swears off of meat and beer until he solves them. He skips a meal of squabs marinated in light cream and rolled in flour seasoned with salt, pepper, nutmeg, cloves, thyme, crushed juniper berries, sautéed in olive oil and served on toast spread with red currant jelly. The sacrifice might have killed him.

When he murmurs, Wolfe's at his worst although he never likes to speak above that tone for half an hour after lunch unless he must. He also murmurs when he's at his maddest. In 1938 he makes the gesture of spitting when he's talking of the political intrigues of the Balkans prior to World War II and Archie's only seen him do it one other time. Forming his lips for a whistle and pumping air in and out but making no sound is a sign Wolfe has surrendered to his emotions. If he moves the tip of his right forefinger on the arm of his chair in small circles the size of a dime, he's fidgeting. If the circles are slightly larger, he is momentarily flummoxed. If the circles become much larger, he's becoming speechless with fury. Tapping gently on his chair arm means he's dodging meteors and comets, i.e. he's confronted with a thoroughly unforeseen development that enormously complicates the work that has gone before. Moving the same finger in the same motion but on his desktop means uncontrollable fury. This is what greeted Inspector Cramer when he arrived with a search warrant in 1944. He tore it up without serving it.

The position of Wolfe's reclining chair also figures into these observations. If he closes his eyes without leaning back in his chair, he's suffering. If he leans back, he's thinking. Sitting up straight in his chair means he's ready to pop with fury.

Wolfe's mouth is particularly expressive. When two of the folds in his cheeks open a little, he thinks he's smiling. One corner of his mouth twisted a little out of line means he's suffering acute pain. Archie finds that the most exciting mouth action is when Wolfe leans back in his chair, closes his eyes and his lips start pushing in and out. When that happens, things are going real fast inside him. It means Wolfe thinks he's found a crack somewhere and he's trying to see through it. When he starts that, he's oblivious to everything in the outside world. It means his brain has crashed the sound barrier and the process is not to be interrupted. By 1936, even Cramer realizes the significance and waits expectantly. It can last anywhere from a few minutes onward. It has lasted as much as half an hour in 1944 and up to an hour in 1956. One thing is certain, when Wolfe's lips start their acrobatics, something's getting ready to pop.

Some of his body language is positive if reserved by most people's standards. To soften the blow of not rising or shaking hands with women, he will occasionally bow his head—sort of. Inclining his head one-sixteenth of an inch is, for him, an emphatic nod. An eighth of an inch is a bow. Shaking his head a full half-inch left and right is for him a frenzy of negation. His most exaggerated nod is half an inch and his most lavish bow is two inches.

In three cases between 1934–1936, he winks at Archie four times in fits of conspiratorial satisfaction. Wolfe humming and moving a finger to keep time while Beulah Page sang was practically drunken revelry for him. He throws his head back and laughs heartily about once a year. It is mentioned specifically in 1948. Archie says that Wolfe is the best listener he knows. During Archie's verbatim reports, Wolfe usually listens with his elbow on the chair arm, chin resting on his fist and his eyes half closed or leaning back in his chair with his eyes closed. In the latter state, he is the most attentive. Wolfe's highest praise for anyone, usually reserved for Archie, Fritz or one of the operatives, is "satisfactory." It never fails to make Archie's heart beat a little harder for a few beats. Archie got a "*very* satisfactory" from him in 1962.

His language is not always so flowery or complimentary, to Archie or others. One of his favorite words is "Pfui" which is NOT the same as "Phooey" either in pronunciation or meaning. Since much of this interpretation is left up to the reader, I have always imagined it not so much as the exclamation of a word as a disdainful, somewhat exasperated expulsion of air through the upper teeth clamped loosely over the lower lip.

When Wolfe is staging one of his "charades" in the office to denounce a murderer, his natural taste for the dramatic comes out again. He invites those willing or eager to come and for those who are not, uses various ruses, threats or enticements to insure their presence. Usually these invitations are handled by Archie, only occasionally by Wolfe personally and, in the case of the most recalcitrant, he contrives to have the NYPD do the "inviting."

Archie lets the guests in, seats them according to Wolfe's instructions or, absent that, his own preferences and offers them refreshments. Archie has tried to deduce a pattern in Wolfe's seating of guests according to which one is the murderer but, if there is one, he can't figure it out. He does believe that Wolfe occasionally will have him alter the seating arrangements when there is a female with an especially good set of legs present so Wolfe will have a good view of them from the comfort of his chair.

Wolfe stays in the kitchen until everyone is present, then Archie buzzes him on the house phone (one long, two short, the reverse of the signal for beer). Then, and only then, does Wolfe enter the office. But he doesn't just enter, he makes an entrance, designed to demonstrate and reinforce his omnipotence in this arena to all those present.

In one sense other than the dramatic, his tactics in this area do have a logical basis. His entrance usually brings about a vocal eruption from some of the guests, either from having been forced to come or forced to remain. Also Wolfe (as well as Archie, Cramer, Stebbins, and/or the operatives, even if they don't know who it is) is fully cognizant of the fact that at least one of the guests is a murderer who is usually in the position of a trapped chess piece, unable to move anywhere Wolfe doesn't want them to. If Wolfe was astride his throne as the guests filtered in singly or in groups, they would begin the cacophony immediately and all would be chaos before everyone arrived.

When he does arrive and seat himself, sometimes there are questions to be asked but usually it is a monologue of what Wolfe has already figured out. Sometimes when he is confronted by a group containing an as yet unknown murderer, Wolfe will lean back in his chair and shut his eyes. Occasionally one of those present will accuse him of having gone to sleep until Archie assures them that isn't the case. Momentarily unencumbered by visual distractions, Wolfe is merely absorbing their words and "tasting" their tones of voice. When his eyes open, he examines their expressions and tries to balance them against their words in an attempt to see if they are being truthful or camouflaging guilt.

He has other idiosyncrasies concerning food, orchids, books and other areas but we will consider those in due course.

As an end to this chapter of the generalities of Nero Wolfe, it might be instructive to conduct a short examination of the inside of his head by going through his mouth. While hardly dissecting this complex a character, it may give us some insight into his dogma, his opinions, how his mind works and the impact his emotions (or lack thereof) have on those workings.

Wolfe admits his genius and says he is also very dramatic by nature, thus explaining his penchant for his "charades" that gather all the principals in a case together to reveal the solution and name the murderer. Archie has said he couldn't understand how, with Wolfe's beer intake, he could still work his brain so fast and deep no other man in the country could touch him. Wolfe contended he didn't work his brain, just his lower nerve centers. On the occasion of one such remark by Archie, Wolfe refused to acknowledge the flattery since "if sincere, [Archie] was a fool and if calculated [he] was a knave".

Wolfe dispassionately states that he is not a coward but admits to being "insufferably conceited." He has a remarkably low opinion of international financiers. He says that if one was confronted by a holdup man with a gun, he would automatically hand over not only his money and jewelry but also his shirt and pants because it would never occur to him that the robber might draw the line somewhere.

He once states that his favorite professional philosopher is Protagoras and his favorite amateur is Montaigne. A few quotes from Wolfe on a variety of subjects provides some insight into his personal philosophy;

"Probably no man will ever corral truth but Protagoras came closer to it than Plato."

"A pessimist gets nothing but pleasant surprises, an optimist nothing but unpleasant."

"The subconscious is not a grave, it's a cistern."

"A man who hires another man to forge distinction for him deserves as little as he gets."

"You can't know what a woman is like until you see her at her food."

"Never marry a woman until you have seen her eat an egg sandwich with her fingers and drink from a bottle."

"Innocence has no contract with bliss." (To Archie's threat to propose to a remarkably chaste female.)

"All music is a vestige of barbarism."

"The brain can be hoodwinked but not the stomach." (After insisting upon feeding a client.)

"There is nothing in the world as indestructible as human dignity."

"Debts are preposterous…the envious past clutching with its cold dead fingers the throat of the living present."

"We are all vainer of our luck than of our merits."

"I am an artist or nothing."

"Nothing is more admirable than the fortitude with which millionaires tolerate the disadvantages of their wealth." (Stated sarcastically.)

"All murder is melodrama because the real tragedy is not death but the condition which induces it."

"Few of us have enough wisdom for justice or enough leisure for humanity." (Upon a female appealing to his higher principles.)

"Nothing is simpler than to kill a man; the difficulties arise in attempting to avoid the consequences."

"A guest is a jewel resting on the cushion of hospitality."

"Proscriptions carried too far lead to nullity."

The Amanuensis—Archie

It is probably safe to say that Nero Wolfe could not function as he does without Archie Goodwin functioning as he does. His unique, self-described job description includes titles such as chief assistant detective, bookkeeper, secretary, bodyguard, guardian, goad, goat, stenographer, the flea in the elephant's ear, the balance wheel, chauffeur, errand boy, doorbell answerer, factotum, prod, lever, irritant, accomplice, flunky, combination accelerator and brake, Secretary of War, hireling, comrade, man Friday, Saturday, Sunday and so forth.

That is not to say Wolfe is totally dependent upon Archie nor vice versa. Both prove they aren't for several consecutive months in 1950 but then, neither is functioning as they normally do when acting in tandem. Archie will also admit that Saul Panzer could do his job at least as well as he does and maybe better, and Saul could have Archie's job if he wanted it. But he doesn't and probably wouldn't as long as Archie is ready, willing and able to perform his duties for Wolfe. Even if that were the case, Saul might take the job out of loyalty to Wolfe but he wouldn't be at his happiest or most satisfied. Fred, Orrie, Johnny and Bill are not even worth discussing in this context, Orrie's and Johnny's opinions notwithstanding.

Also there are some aspects of Archie's duties, unwritten but nevertheless essential, for which Saul would be totally unsuited. Such as needling Wolfe to work when the bank balance is healthy or even barren, in that eventuality. That just isn't Saul's style. Saul's charisma with females could never match Archie's nor would he try. Lastly, we don't know anything about Saul's writing talents but we could probably not depend upon Saul to record Wolfe's adventures for readers like Archie does and certainly not with the same talent for a sardonic turn of a phrase. Enough said. Now that we have dealt with his virtual indispensability, let's get to know him a little better.

Mrs. Jasper Pine has him investigated in 1947 and is told he was born in Canton, Ohio, in 1914. His father was James Arner Goodwin, his mother's maiden name was Leslie and he has two brothers and two sisters. But we don't know the caliber of the private investigator she hired to obtain this information.

Archie (NOT Archibald) Goodwin celebrates his birthday on October 23rd. The year is unnecessary because, like Wolfe and the other primary characters, he doesn't age and is forever 34 years old. His own version of his biography is that he was born in Chillicothe, Ohio, to Mr. and Mrs. Titus Goodwin and spent his boyhood on a farm there. Is it coincidental that his father's Christian name is that of a Roman emperor? Like Nero?

As of 1945, his father is dead and his mother is living as are a sister and three aunts. One aunt (Margie) makes incredible fried chicken and another (Anna) makes a delicious chicken pie. He once claimed to have been the spelling champion of Zanesville, Ohio, at age 12 but he said it to a beautiful woman so we can't take it to the bank. Chillicothe and Zanesville are about 100 miles apart in southern Ohio. They are about the same population so it doesn't make much sense that the spelling championship was moved to the slightly larger town but perhaps he moved for a while. There was a picture in his old dining room of people in a sleigh throwing a baby out to the wolves that were chasing them. Possibly he was waxing allegorical but there was an identical picture in one of Rex Stout's homes.

Archie's own synopsis of his pre-Wolfe life is that he attended public school in Ohio, was pretty good at football and geometry, graduating "with honor but no honors." He also says he graduated at 17 but again, he's telling a woman so we can't be assured of his sincerity. In his youth, he could run 100 yards in 10.7 seconds. He attended college for two weeks (deeming it childish), quit, went to New York City, got a job guarding a pier, shot and killed two men, got fired, was recommended to do a chore for Wolfe, did it well, was offered a job, took it and still has it.

Rex Stout's description of him in 1949 was; "Height six feet. Weight 180 pounds. Age 32 [this was when he described Wolfe as being 56 and, maintaining a 24-year difference in their ages, before he later settled on permanent ages for them of 34 and 58 respectively]. Hair is light rather than dark, but just barely decided not to be red; he gets it cut every two weeks, rather short, and brushes it straight back, but it keeps standing up. He shaves four times a week and grasps at every excuse to make it only three times. His features are all regular, well-modeled and well-proportioned, except the nose. He escapes the curse of being the movie actor type only through the nose. It is not a true pug and is by no means a deformity, but it is a little short and the ridge is broad, and the tip has continued on its own, beyond the cartilage, giving the impression of startling and quite independent initiative. The eyes are gray [and hard], and are inquisitive and quick to move. He is muscular both in appearance and movement, and upright in posture, but his shoulders stoop a little in unconscious reaction to Wolfe's repeated criticism that he is "too self-assertive." He wears size 9 shoes and exercises every morning.

In 1941, an angry woman called him "a ten-cent Clark Gable who thought he was so slick he could slide uphill if he wanted to." Archie disagreed and thought if he resembled any movie star, it should be Gary Cooper, not Clark Gable. He thinks his nose is too flat but Mrs. Rita Sorrell thinks he's very handsome. His speaking voice is a fine baritone.

During the early adventures, he was a cigarette smoker and smoked both in the office and his bedroom with Wolfe's forbearance. Undoubtedly he was considerate about it due to Wolfe's sensitivities and never appeared to be a heavy smoker. He smoked consistently from 1933 through 1949, at least after meals. By 1957 he seldom smoked but still kept an ashtray on his desk although perhaps from sentimentality. It was jade, six inches across and was a gift from a client. In 1958, he lit a cigar at the dinner of the Ten for Aristology but mostly to be sociable. In 1965, he says he doesn't smoke anymore.

He drinks alcohol moderately and has fairly broad tastes that do not include wine (it makes him sleepy). In the early adventures, he drinks rye whiskey and keeps a bottle in his bedroom. In 1935, he drinks bourbon. In 1958, it's scotch and water. In 1959, he has a gin and tonic after discovering a decomposing body. He has another one in 1974 to deal with the stress of a bombing. He likes orange juice at room temperature for breakfast, coffee with Wolfe after dinner but his most consistent drink is milk.

Archie has a great appreciation for Fritz's cooking and Wolfe's epicurean tastes but he also has more egalitarian tastes. He usually indulges them when he is out of the house on an errand and won't offend the more sophisticated palates. He likes corned beef sandwiches, beef stew, sliced tomatoes and blueberry pie at Matt's Diner on Eleventh Avenue. He is also not above going around the corner on Tenth Avenue to eat beans at Bert's Diner or to Ost's Restaurant for pig's knuckles and sauerkraut or pork and beans. Wolfe would probably shudder with revulsion and Fritz would probably get his feelings hurt so Archie doesn't advertise these ventures. He also likes rhubarb, apple, green tomato and chocolate pies, once eating five pieces on a stakeout in 1958.

Archie says he was "born neat" and his normal attire proves it. If only for his sartorial tastes, he could never have been a FBI agent under J. Edgar Hoover when the regulations demanded conservative suits and ties with white shirts. He seems to have a preference for colored shirts. A June uniform in one of the early adventures is a dark blue suit, blue shirt and a tan tie. In 1949 he wears a Pillater shirt with a tropical worsted suit by Corley. In 1950, a mixed tweed jacket, off-white shirt and maroon tie. In 1953, a brown tropical worsted suit, light tan striped shirt, brown tie and tan shoes. In 1959 he gets complimented on a fashionable Peter Darrell suit. He doesn't normally wear a hat before Thanksgiving because he believes rain and snow are good for hair but, in season, has been known to wear a Panama hat and a straw hat.

His sense of neatness extends to all his habits in addition to his clothing. After checking the cash and locking the safe, the last thing he does every night is clean off his desk because he can't stand to face a cluttered desk in the morning.

Like Rex Stout, he needs eight and one-half hours (510 minutes) of sleep a night and prefers nine hours. Naturally, working for Wolfe, that isn't always possible but he isn't at the top of his game without it. Like Wolfe and Rex Stout, he sleeps with the windows open and, in later years, under an electric blanket.

Barring business complications, the clock-radio on the table next to his bed is normally set for 7:30 A.M. and Fritz has his breakfast ready at 8:10. He prefers to eat at a table with a telephone on it in the kitchen with Fritz. He reads his morning papers (first the Times, then the Gazette) on a reading rack while he eats. A normal breakfast involves some combination of ham, bacon, sausage, waffles, griddle cakes with wild thyme honey, eggs, muffins, orange juice at room temperature, cold milk, hot coffee, grapefruit or an omelet but occasionally he will indulge in some of Fritz's specialties like figs and cream or kidneys. For a late night snack, he often likes doughnuts, blackberry jam and milk. This is a special treat for him because Fritz must make them specially for him because Wolfe hates doughnuts.

Archie usually doesn't go into the office until the morning mail comes between 8:45 and 9:00 A.M. As an aside to the last two generations, believe it or not, mail used to be delivered twice a day! Between then and when Wolfe comes down from his morning session with the orchids, he dusts the office, empties the wastebaskets, removes the previous day's orchids and changes the water in the orchid vase on Wolfe's desk, fills Wolfe's fountain pen and tests it (in spite of the fact that Wolfe tests it himself every morning), sorts the mail and puts it on Wolfe's desk unopened, writes necessary checks for Wolfe's signature, balances the expense book, as well as types and files the orchid propagation and germination records that Theodore puts on his desk every evening. If there are any reports undone on any current investigations, he types the notes he takes in his own special brand of shorthand. He uses a manual Underwood typewriter and can type ten pages an hour in a real pinch, the average is six or seven and he moseys along at four or five. In between these chores, he answers the phone. It is

"Nero Wolfe's office, Archie Goodwin speaking" until 6 P.M. and after that, it's changed to "Nero Wolfe's residence."

When Wolfe comes down from the plant rooms, he always wishes Archie a good morning upon entering the office no matter how many times they've talked before that. If there are any checks in the morning mail, after Wolfe has seen them, Archie endorses them with a stamp and walks to the Metropolitan Bank and Trust Company on Thirty-Fourth Street to deposit them. When he returns, if they don't have a current case and, in his estimation, need one, he proceeds to handle one of the touchier parts of his job.

One of Archie's most important functions is to badger Wolfe into earning fees by taking jobs that he would prefer to reject, a premise that Wolfe recognizes and agrees is sometimes justified. In 1938, Wolfe says that his [Wolfe's] only true fault is lethargy and he pays Archie to help him circumvent it. One of the reasons Wolfe puts up with Archie is his verbose badgering. Another, conversely, is his brevity at the proper times, using one word instead of fifty. Wolfe admits why Archie puts up with him is "beyond conjecture."

One of the ways he badgers Wolfe is to sharpen pencils that don't need it because the sound of the sharpener gets on Wolfe's nerves. He got Wolfe to agree to give Hattie Annis two minutes of his time that way in 1959. He also rattles papers to achieve the same effect.

He also badgers Wolfe verbally which requires true courage. And he isn't at all gentle about it. He and Wolfe have insulted each other a million times, more or less. He unabashedly calls Wolfe "fat" to his face in 1934. Seeing Wolfe without his yellow silk pajama top, Archie remarks that enough hide was exposed to make shoes for four platoons. Returning home from an errand following a strained discourse, he asks Fritz "How's the pet mammoth?" Seeing Wolfe bending over to fish something out of a wastebasket, Archie asks him if he hurt himself. Wolfe has told him that someday, when Wolfe finds him no longer worth tolerating, Archie will have to marry a woman of very modest mental capacity to find an audience for his wretched sarcasms. In one of the early cases, Wolfe tells Archie to go to a location and "search and bring back any items that seem to you unimportant." This was said in front of the client to put him in his place.

Another way they go at each other is that Archie resigns or Wolfe fires him. The first time he quits is prior to the beginning of their recorded cases. He got beat up and phoned Wolfe from the hospital. Wolfe came to the hospital personally and took him back to the house. Wolfe's concern impressed him so much he "unquit." It was not to be the last time he quit or the last time Wolfe sent him in harm's way.

By 1960, Archie estimates he has resigned and been fired about the same number of times, 30 or 40. He resigns again that year because Wolfe highhandedly cancels an appointment Archie made for a prospective client. In the last month of that year, he considers resigning for the forty-third time because Wolfe refused to see a witness.

This isn't just a phenomenon of the later years. It started right off the bat. Wolfe fired him in 1937 for riding him on the way to West Virginia while he was suffering a train trip. Something about how to get him undressed for bed without turning the train over. Wolfe fired him again before 1944 for "contributing a note of skepticism when Wolfe was in one of his romantic moods." Archie resigned in 1938 in mock prudery after accusing Wolfe of having a child out of wedlock. He did it again in writing (albeit facetiously) in 1939. He resigned in 1948 by telling Wolfe he was "entirely too conceited, too eccentric and too fat to work for." Another resignation was in the New York Giants locker room at the Polo Grounds in 1952. Other threatened resignations were in 1945, 1946, 1950 and 1958, the latter accompanying a demand for a month's severance pay. Occasionally Archie instigates a case on his own without consulting Wolfe, causing Wolfe to remark that Archie is subordinate only when it suits his temperament and convenience (which we already knew).

Since firing him is fruitless and always exceedingly temporary, Wolfe has other methods of torturing Archie. When Wolfe talks to someone on the phone, a standing order is that Archie stays on the other line unless told to get off. Wolfe does this occasionally by telling him that "no record will be required." A less frequent method for keeping Archie (and thus the reader) in the dark is for Wolfe to give Saul a chore Archie isn't allowed to know about and have him report to Wolfe in his bedroom in the morning. Archie used to get peeved at that but, by 1955, it just irritates him because he can't guess what the chore is. The last resort for Wolfe is to send Archie to bed when someone is coming late at night and Wolfe doesn't want Archie present. By 1949, this has only happened twice in five years. The most recent occurrence was a guest that Wolfe didn't want Archie to see or hear, a "Mr. Jones", who is a mysterious specialist of some kind who provides a service to Wolfe we are never told about (and neither is Archie).

Archie is his own man in spite of his closeness to Wolfe. Not necessarily less opinionated but perhaps broader in some of his tastes (probably due to his increased mobility), he has a somewhat more abbreviated list of likes and dislikes;

Likes:
-being read aloud to (according to Lily Rowan)
-betting on sports
-billiards
-the Brooks Brothers fragrance called Stag at Eve
-chess
-colored shirts
-dogs
-fishing
-good food
-holidays in Montana
-hot beverages served at moderate temperatures
-nine hours of sleep nightly
-neatness
-the New York Giants baseball team and, later, the New York Mets
-opera
-plays starring the Lunts
-prize fights
-theater

Dislikes:
-beer
-breakfasting alone
-button-down collars on shirts
-desk drawers left partly open
-functioning before breakfast
-horseradish
-long telephone calls
-men named Eugene
-noiseless typewriters
-not falling asleep instantly
-sleep interrupted or shortened below nine hours
-southern California
-talking while driving
-television

Again, he shares most of these traits with his creator, Rex Stout.

The month after Pearl Harbor, Archie joined the Army. Specializing in Military Intelligence, he apparently went in as a Captain and was promoted to Major only two months later. In America's unprepared state at the beginning of World War II, this was not particularly unusual for people in specialized fields like law, medicine, nursing and, apparently, detective work. Although he was making only a third of what Wolfe paid him, this isn't a particular problem since Archie isn't very materialistic, at least not enough to threaten his integrity. Over the years, he has turned down proffered bribes from $5 to $60,000, back when that was real money.

He was soon stationed in an office in Military Intelligence Headquarters on the tenth floor at 17 Duncan Street. He soon returned to Wolfe's residence on special assignment to assist in special projects entrusted to Wolfe (for which he received no pay). Archie was discharged as a Major in October of 1945 and returned to his permanent duties.

In their first recorded case, Archie says the only girl he was ever soft on found a better bargain which is how he met Wolfe. He gives no further details.

Most of Archie's love life is left to our imaginations but there is little doubt that he is aggressively heterosexual and quite attractive to women. He has an ironclad rule about women—if their ankles are more than half the diameter of their calves, he is definitely not interested.

Archie likes to combine his appreciation for women and sports. He will settle for a Yankees game if the Giants are out of town but he is primarily an avid Giants fan. He apparently abandoned them when they abandoned New York for San Francisco in the late 1950's and transferred his allegiance to the Mets. His favorite recreation on most Saturday nights (when Wolfe isn't exposing some killer) is to take some person of "an interesting sex" to a hockey or basketball game or a prize fight at Madison Square Garden.

He isn't above placing a bet on sporting events which leads up to another of his pastimes, poker. He enjoys it and is good at it. By 1961, he and four other men engage in a poker game every Wednesday night at Saul Panzer's apartment. The game lasts until 2:00 A.M. and Archie usually comes away with more money than he started. Saul Panzer is almost always a winner and Lon Cohen is another of the four who usually does well. By 1969, poker night has been moved to Thursdays.

Another of his favorite sports is dancing and he's good at it also. Dinner and dancing is always high on his list for activities on a night off. In 1947, he likes to take girls to Frisbie's where the shad roe is three dollars. Not taking things too seriously, he also makes a date with three women for the same time at Rusterman's Restaurant. He has been known to take women to Ribeiro's, a Brazilian restaurant on Fifty-Second Street east of Lexington Avenue, Sardi's, Colonna's in the Village, Mohan's Bar, Pete's Bar and Grill, Charlie's Grill and the bar at the Churchill Hotel.

Speaking of the Churchill, it's also one of his favorite dancing spots especially the Calico Room and the Silver Room. He also likes the Bobolink but his definite favorite is the Flamingo Club. Outside of the fact that he and Lily Rowan spend many nights there, Archie has taken many other ladies there including one future murder victim and one murderess.

This also shows the fact that his personal and professional lives sometimes merge. Wolfe thinks Archie's judgement of women under the age of thirty is infallible. He will often defer to Archie as to the truthfulness of their statements and the workings of their minds which mystify him.

In 1934, Archie tells us that Wolfe is terrified of guns but tolerates them in his home because he recognizes them as an occasionally necessary tool of his trade but they are not for his own use, they are strictly Archie's province. Don't waste your time trying to reconcile this statement with a man who has allegedly killed at least 200 men in wartime. Like Wolfe's cars, with rare exceptions, the makes of his weapons are fictional.

Archie keeps the guns in his second desk drawer, unloaded, and he routinely cleans and oils them. In 1954 the weapon is in the back of the third desk drawer. He prefers a shoulder holster rather than a waistband holster. In their first recorded case in 1933, he carries an unspecified .38. In the second case in the Fall of 1934, Archie is carrying a Colt pistol. He doesn't specify whether it is an automatic or a revolver. About three months later, in February of 1935, some unrecorded incident occurred than convinced Archie he should never leave the house on business involving murder without carrying a gun. Archie mentions it but doesn't give any details.

In 1936, his weapon is an automatic. He always makes it a point to carry a gun when he and Wolfe are going out of town and mentions this habit during their first interstate excursion in 1937 but doesn't specify the weapon. When they're out of town in 1938, he's carrying a Worthington .38 automatic, owned by Wolfe, serial number 63092T. In 1943 he is carrying a gun in a shoulder holster while in his Army uniform. He knows this is against Army regulations but makes the exception because he's driving a murderer around. In 1946 he is once armed with two guns, one in a shoulder holster and one in his pocket. In 1947 the "arsenal" consists of two revolvers and a Wembly automatic. After this, he develops a preference for Marley revolvers in either .22, .32 or .38 calibers, the caliber usually suited to the circumstances. In 1953, for instance, he chooses a

Marley .22 as a pocket gun for a formal occasion because a .32 in a shoulder holster would ruin the lines of his tuxedo.

Wolfe's acceding to the necessity of owning the weapons is proven valid on a number of occasions. In 1937, Marko Vukcic tells Constanza Berin that Archie has saved Wolfe's life three times and it becomes four before that case is over. In 1941, Wolfe tells Cramer that Archie saved his life "once" and Archie takes umbrage at the "once."

Nevertheless, Archie's ability with guns serves them both well. In September of 1940, Archie shoots the gun out of a man's hand. He also killed a man in 1941 but he didn't mean to and wasn't aware of it for a while. In 1950, he and Fred Durkin get shot at in a mix-up with some fur hijackers. In that same year, he gets shot in the left shoulder with his own gun in the course of trapping a murderer. In 1953 he defends his decision to go armed by stating he once spent a month in the hospital after having a bullet dug out of his chest and later has to shoot the guns out of two men's hands. In 1954 he takes a Marley .32 overseas and later acquires a Colt .38. During this case, he is forced to kill three men in the process of saving Wolfe's life (and his own) again.

Archie's knowledge of the underworld also comes in handy periodically. In 1950, he is called upon to acquire a "cold" gun (i.e. one that cannot be traced or identified) to Wolfe's exacting specifications—one with the size and weight of a .22 but with the power of a .45. He settles on a Carson snub Thirty. In the same case, Archie loses his favorite Colt to Zeck's bodyguards but replaces it with a Grisson .38. In 1952, he has a snub-nosed Farger and a rubber silencer that can also be used as brass knuckles.

Archie has other specialized knowledge that isn't available to everyone. He says he wouldn't qualify as a lock expert on a witness stand but he can tell a Hotchkiss from a Euler and can open your suitcase with a paperclip, given enough time.

Archie begins the adventures as a somewhat hardboiled antithesis of Wolfe's intellectualism, more muscle than brains, if you will. As time goes by, he gains more sophistication but his physical talents never go completely out of style. Even so, he managed to get through the first two recorded cases without having to strong-arm anyone. That ended in the third case when he threw two cops out of the hallway when they tried to rush in the house.

In 1938, he knocked out a loan shark and took some blackmail evidence from him on Wolfe's orders. Two years later, he knocked Phillip Tingley out and hog-tied him but Archie would always have a soft spot in his heart for him because later, with two burly detectives within arm's reach, Tingley sprang at Archie fearlessly to try to start Round Two. Archie was forced to stiff-arm another combatant in 1941.

These efforts were not with impunity. Although he never got any official Purple Hearts during his wartime service, Archie almost sprained a wrist and got his shins kicked in 1944 helping Purley Stebbins wrestle a murderer out of the South Room. Archie has a special antipathy for kickers and he met another one two years later. He was throwing Don O'Neill out of Wolfe's office and ducked his first punch when O'Neill kicked him so Archie plugged him good. Archie gets bitten on the arm in 1956 and pistol-whips the offender.

In 1947, Archie's best punch is to the right kidney, turning his whole weight behind it. Harold Anthony withstands three of them on the sidewalk in front of Wolfe's stoop. He later says Archie's right would "dent a tank" and an admiring cab driver tells Archie he's good enough to fight at the Garden.

It's a good thing Archie exercises every morning because he needs to stay in shape. He's attacked from behind in 1951 but perseveres and whips Daniel Gale when he threatens Archie with sulfuric acid in 1952. Three years later, he handles Johnny Arrow after Arrow had already proved his prowess by beating Paul Fyfe and was getting ready to prove it again, breaking one of Wolfe's yellow chairs in the process. He takes on two men at once in 1960 and ducks a too-slow punch from Andrew Busch the same year. A year later, he's ducking more punches in the office and has to handle two suspects at once when they jump him. Archie's physical contests decline in the later years but he's always ready, willing and able. It must be nice to be an eternal thirty-four.

With all this combat going on, it is inevitable that Archie runs afoul of the law periodically. Oddly enough, it's not usually his shootings or fights that gets him arrested, it's lying to the cops or not telling them the truth about Wolfe's dealings which the cops view as one and the same. Not that he couldn't help them with the information they seek. Archie is used to repeating verbatim conversations to Wolfe that sometimes covers hours. He says that the only difference between him and a tape recorder is that a tape recorder can't lie.

His first recorded arrest is in Crowfield County in 1938 for material witness, a charge with which he is to become intimately familiar. In March of 1942, Purley Stebbins arrests him on the same charge but it was based upon Archie framing himself. Archie managed some leaks to a reporter and the resulting headlines spurred Wolfe to stop training for the Army and get back into the private investigation business. He goes to jail for material witness again in 1951, 1952, 1960 and 1961 (twice-once in Westchester County and once by Cramer).

In 1952, Archie tells Purley Stebbins that he's only been arrested nine times but, considering their relationship, you can't bank on that number being accurate. The same year he sets a record by being arrested twice in the same case. In 1960, Stebbins arrests him again for Impersonating A Police Officer which he technically didn't. In 1961, he is named on a warrant from Westchester County for removing half a million bucks from the Vail's country home. The next year he spends 21 hours in jail as a material witness and costs Wolfe a $20,000 bond. That arrest accounts for his fingerprints being taken for the nineteenth time.

Archie might be a tough guy but he does have a sentimental side. He keeps a number of professional relics as souvenirs in a drawer in his room. Among them are the toothbrush and soiled handkerchief of a girl who occupied the South Room for a few hours before she was murdered. One of his most precious possessions is a leather identification case in which he carries his police and fire ID cards. It is engraved in gold with tiny Colt automatic pistols on one side, *Cattleya* orchids on the other and is personalized "A.G. from N.W." Archie says he might trade it for New York's five boroughs if they threw in a few interesting suburbs. He actually cried when it was stolen from him in 1934.

Wolfe's most frequent and most complimentary instruction to him is to act "according to your intelligence guided by experience." From their earliest days right up to the end, his heart still does an extra thump whenever Wolfe says "Satisfactory, Archie."

The Family

Fritz Brenner

After Nero Wolfe himself and Archie, Fritz Brenner is first among equals when it comes to the characters of the saga. He is first mentioned in the second sentence of the first book in 1933.

He is first and foremost the resident chef (NOT cook!). He is also house-keeper, house manager and supervisor of household comforts. In the hierarchy of Wolfe's egocentrism, only Archie outranks him. As housekeeper, he is responsible for cleaning all of the house except the plant rooms (Theodore) and Archie's room and the office (Archie). In later years, a cleaning man is hired temporarily and when that didn't work out, evidently the duty was farmed out to various commercial companies.

Fritz comes from "the part of Switzerland where they speak French." Because of its location and history, Switzerland considers French, German and Italian all official national languages. Of the 22 Swiss cantons (states), five are primarily French-speaking; Geneve, Vaud, Neuchatel, Fribourg and Valais. All five are clustered around the city of Geneva in southwestern Switzerland. This then is Fritz's homeland.

According to Archie, Fritz has a sweet faraway smile, catches jokes but doesn't return them and is usually precise in his speech, perhaps a habit acquired from his years with Wolfe which predate Archie's employment. About the only slang he ever uses is "And how." He rarely curses and then only mildly. He said "Grand Dieu" (Great God) in 1938 when Archie carried an unconscious woman in the front door. When someone poisoned a guest in Wolfe's office in 1955, Fritz called him a "Cochon" (swine).

In the first adventure, Fritz lived in a room on the third floor of the brown-stone across from the plant rooms. Not long afterwards, he moved to a den in the basement, presumably because it was more convenient to his primary battle station in the kitchen but it was also much larger. His den in the basement is as big as the office and front room combined. It is furnished with a king size bed, five chairs and tables stacked with magazines. In later years it has a television and stereo cabinet. No mention is made of his tastes in music but I suspect it is almost exclusively classical. He can play the piano and when he occasionally takes a turn at the one in Wolfe's front room, he usually plays Chopin.

The room is decorated with the head of a wild boar he once shot in the Vosages Mountains in northeastern France, two large cases of ancient cooking vessels (one of which he thinks was used by Julius Caesar's chef) and busts of Escoffier and Brillat-Savarin.

Georges Auguste Escoffier (1846–1935) was a famous Parisian chef known as "The King of Cooks." He served as the chef at the Reine Blanche in Paris, the Savoy, Carlton and Ritz Hotels in London, and the Grand Hotel in Monte Carlo. Anthelme Brillat-Savarin (1755–1826) was a noted French gastronomist who wrote *The Physiology of Taste*. Fritz also has an engraving of him on the wall. The rest of the wall space that isn't taken up with framed menus consists of bookshelves. He has 289 cookbooks and the number is up to 294 by 1967. His room is probably the most cluttered area in the house, another example of the autonomy Wolfe affords him because of his talents.

Fritz rises at 6:30 A.M. and goes to bed at 11 P.M. unless he is asked not to or Wolfe is still up. He never goes to bed until after Wolfe does. In a 1948 case, he stayed up past 4 A.M. with everyone else.

He usually has Archie's breakfast ready in the kitchen at 8:10 and delivers Wolfe's tray to his bedroom at 8:15. Archie eats in the kitchen while Fritz cooks and reads his morning papers. He always glances through the editorials in three newspapers, one of which is The Gazette, and he also reads a newspaper printed in French.

After Archie goes to the office and Wolfe heads upstairs for his morning session with the orchids, Fritz removes Wolfe's tray from his bedroom and then eats his own breakfast in the kitchen.

Fritz is apparently eternally unaware of the bank balance's condition, is always fretting that they are teetering on the edge of starvation and is Archie's biggest cheerleader when it comes to goading Wolfe into working and earning money. To allow Wolfe and Archie to discuss or conduct business (hopefully), he usually answers the door after 11 A.M. unless he is involved in preparing lunch. He also answers the telephone from 9 A.M. to 5 P.M. when Archie and Wolfe are both busy. No doubt he is happy to do it because the only time that is likely is when they're working on a case. He also answers the door whenever Archie is out of the house but you really have to be somebody to get past him. When Archie returns, he uses a special code when ringing the doorbell to let Fritz know it's him since the bolt is always on. In 1938, the code is two short rings and one long, By 1944, it has changed to three short rings.

When Fritz answers the door, he usually introduces people to Wolfe as "There's a gentleman (or lady) at the door." There are only two kinds of people he doesn't call gentlemen: someone trying to sell something and policemen, uniformed or not. He can smell them.

Fritz is always stiffly formal when ladies are in the house, not from a sense of propriety but fear. He is always apprehensive when any female is in the house until she leaves. He thinks every woman that crosses their threshold wants to take over the entire house, especially his kitchen. Nevertheless unfailingly polite, he always "sir's" Archie in front of company and Archie can't get him to stop.

Fritz is a Master Chef but refuses to fry eggs or chicken so Archie has to get those treats elsewhere. He always blushes profusely under compliments from Wolfe or Archie. Prior to 1940, Marko Vukcic offered Fritz "a fantastic sum" to work at Rusterman's but was scornfully refused by both Wolfe and Fritz.

Fritz has lunch ready at 1:15 and dinner at 7:15, 8:15 in later years. He probably eats his lunch after Wolfe and Archie finish theirs and he eats his evening meal about 9 P.M. in the kitchen.

He likes to wear his slippers after dinner because of things left on his toes and feet by the war to remember it by, therefore he is presumably a veteran of World War I.

Fritz is a gentle man (in 1954 he has a pet turtle) but during the early years, he occasionally took a more active part in the cases as warranted by circumstances. In 1935, he stationed himself in the hallway with an automatic pistol while Archie threw two cops (who hadn't identified themselves) out after they tried to force their way in the house. He held a gun on other people in 1944. The next year, he pulled Colonel Percy Brown's feet out from under him and then worried about dinner being late just because a woman had been strangled in the office. Fritz always has his priorities straight.

Theodore Horstmann

The resident gardener, the tender and defender of Wolfe's 10,000 orchids is Theodore Horstmann. Theodore is a little guy who weighs about 135 pounds (about half as much as Wolfe), has a pug nose, sleeps in the plant rooms and eats in the kitchen with Fritz. He has Sundays off and often goes to visit his married sister in New Jersey. He is not one of Archie's favorite people because he babies Wolfe which Archie knows is bad for them both.

Theodore walks a lot because he thinks it's healthy. His mother lives in Illinois but becomes ill in 1948. Theodore having to go care for her brings about a case when Wolfe tries to seek a temporary replacement.

Both Theodore and Fritz are either mentioned in virtually all of the cases or, if not, may be considered to be omnipresent.

Charley

Although his deserving of a place in this area is very questionable, Charley the cleaning man makes a single appearance in the saga in 1946. It was his only appearance and he disappeared with no further mention. Stout later told his biographer that Charley stole an orchid and was fired.

Carla Britton

Carla Britton, *nee'* Wolfe, alias Lovchen, probably deserves her place in this section somewhat more than Charley and somewhat less than Lily Rowan. She appears in two of the cases. Wolfe adopted her in Montenegro in 1921 when she was three years old. Hardly anyone's idea of a single dad, he made provisions for her to be cared for there and began his worldwide adventures. When grown, she came to New York and became involved in one of his cases in November of 1938. In spite of the successful conclusion of that case and all that she owed him for that, Carla upheld Wolfe's estimation of Montenegrin women and they remained as incompatible as matter and antimatter.

She got a job at a Fifth Avenue travel agency in 1938 and married the American owner, William R. Britton, a year later. She and her adopted father were estranged and remained so. Twice a year, on her birthday and New Years Day, Wolfe sent her a bushel of orchids from his best plants and went to her husband's funeral in 1950. As a fervent but not intelligent Montenegrin nationalist and anti-Communist, she became involved in his *Black Mountain* case in 1954 when Marko Vukcic was murdered.

Marko Vukcic

Marko Vukcic makes his first appearance in the saga in 1937. He appears in seven of the cases and is mentioned in six others.

Marko is Nero Wolfe's oldest and closest friend. They were boys together in Montenegro and hunted dragonflies in the mountains. Some researchers have tried to make the case that they were brothers. Perhaps. They have some of the similarities of brothers—Marko has a dense tangle of hair and is huge, not fat, just huge, like a lion upright on its hind legs. Also like brothers, they have opposing qualities—Marko smokes cigars and has a great appreciation for women—many women, some of whom he marries. Certainly the two men could have been no closer if they had been brothers. Wolfe has unabashed affection for and trust in him. Marko is one of only two men other than employees that Wolfe calls by their first names and he is one of only three men who call Wolfe by his first name.

Marko is a Master Chef in his own right, owns Rusterman's Restaurant in New York City and is personally responsible for its reputation as having the best grub in New York outside of Nero Wolfe's kitchen. He is a member of *Les Quinze Maitres* in 1937 and his influence drags Wolfe across four states on a 14-hour train ride for a meal and a murder. This together with the fact that he tried to hire Fritz away from Wolfe and it didn't damage their relationship is adequate evidence of their closeness. He also got Wolfe into another case in 1948.

He dines once a month at Wolfe's home and Wolfe and Archie dine once a month at Rusterman's. Vukcic bought a suitably sized chair exclusively for Wolfe's use in the soundproofed private dining room on an upper floor of Rusterman's. To guarantee the ultimate in privacy without sacrificing service, the table is specially equipped with a button to signal waiters when to bring food and remove plates. When Wolfe wasn't using the chair, it was kept in Vukcic's personal den. The beginnings of a plan to embarrass the FBI was hatched in that room over a meal of Squabs *a la Moscovite*, Mushrooms *Polonaise*, *Salade Beatrice* and *Souffle' Armenonville*.

Since his last divorce, Marko will also occasionally drop by Wolfe's for an evening snack and some conversation. He is the one who talked Wolfe into installing a pool table in the basement and Sunday lunch and pool games became a tradition in Wolfe's home.

When Wolfe took a temporary "retirement" in 1950, Marko had his power of attorney, hired Fritz for the duration and put the brownstone up for sale. He was deliberately unsuccessful at the latter. During that trying time, Marko was the only one in touch with Wolfe including Archie.

Marko was murdered in front of his house on East Fifty-Fourth Street about 7:30 P.M. on March 18, 1954. Wolfe goes to the morgue to identify the body, gently puts dinars on his eyes and this is only the beginning of paying his debt to this man. Wolfe is named the executor of Marko's estate and this duty continues to the end of the series. Neither Wolfe, Archie nor any of their guests are ever allowed to pay for anything at Rusterman's. That tradition continued after Marko's death.

Lily Rowan

Lily Rowan makes her first appearance in 1938 and her first meeting with Archie, over the horns of an angry bull, sets the tone for their relationship. Serious but not life-threatening. Her pet name for him becomes *Escamillo*, the name of the bullfighter in Bizet's opera *Carmen*. She quickly evolves into Archie's best girl and primary love interest. Never slated for marriage, from either direction, they have an understanding and a lot in common. She eventually appears in 19 of the cases and is mentioned in six others.

Lily is blonde, has dark blue eyes and the top of her head comes about to the bottom of Archie's chin, the perfect height for dancing which is just as well. She is bright, quick-witted, witty, sophisticated but not patrician, an excellent dancer and likes to party (preferably at the Troubador Club at the Churchill Hotel and the Flamingo Room—Archie says the latter has the best band in town).

Lily is also rich, lazy and Democratic, about equally on all three counts. Her father was James Gilmore Rowan, an immigrant, and her mother was a waitress. Her father became a Tammany Hall district leader for 30 years, made $8 million building sewers and pavement and ultimately left her $17 million.

In early 1942 she had her own tower at The Ritz. Later she lives in a penthouse on the roof of a 10-story building on East Sixty-Third Street between Madison and Park Avenues. The apartment contains a 19x34 Kashan rug, a garden pattern in seven colors that cost $14,000 and original paintings by Renoir, Cézanne and Manet. Archie has a key to her apartment. She also owns the Bar JR Ranch in Lame Horse, Montana. Archie was there for a month's vacation in 1958 and on a murder case a decade later. She and Archie also took a vacation together to Norway in 1950. In 1953, she also has "a 14-room shack" in Westchester County called The Glade.

She and Archie frequently go out to dine, dance and then adjourn to her apartment. On those nights, he may get home as late as 3 A.M. So they definitely have an understanding. Every week Archie sends her a couple of Wolfe's orchids of the kind that can't be bought anywhere. Nevertheless, he's not her slave. In 1957, he walked out on one of her parties when he found out she'd invited people she knew he didn't like.

Since they met on a murder case, it is only fitting that Lily has a continuing presence in both Wolfe's and Archie's professional lives. In 1942, she instigated one of Wolfe's cases because the potential client was a friend of hers and indeed, Lily actually instigated the murder unknowingly. She later became a suspect herself and even provided a temporary alibi for the murderer.

In 1950, she validated Archie's faith in her and even impressed Nero Wolfe (against his better judgement) with her acumen. In the process of that case, she squirted some $60-an-ounce perfume on Wolfe and became the only woman in America who had "necked" with him. When Archie chided her for it, she said "he has a flair."

Perhaps all that needs to be said about her is that Nero Wolfe never shakes hands with women—but he does, unflinchingly, with Lily Rowan.

The Extended Professional Family

Nero Wolfe, by the God-given right of his genius, primarily occupies himself with dabbling with orchids, salving his palate and absorbing knowledge from books. He must, unfortunately, solve murders to pay for these luxuries but he expects to get paid several thousand dollars every time he pushes his lips in and out in deep thought in this process. Before the lips can move, however, he needs information and that information can frequently not be had just by summoning people to his lair. It also cannot always be provided by the single pair of arms, legs, eyes and brain lobes Archie Goodwin provides. He can also not always depend upon finagling the NYPD into loaning him the efforts of their thousands of minions dedicated to his needs. Therefore he requires a substantial retinue of outside able assistants.

First and foremost must come the private investigative operatives Wolfe uses when the work expands beyond Archie's capabilities to be in more than one place at one time. This isn't hard to do when you're dealing with cases that immediately confront you with a dozen or more suspects. In the second case, in 1934 Wolfe uses investigators from the Metropolitan Agency. In that case also is the first mention of the Del Bascom Detective Agency. Evidently a large, reputable and effective firm, they are the primary agency Wolfe relies upon when he needs manpower to rival the NYPD. The Bascom Agency is mentioned in nine of the cases ranging from 1934 to the last case in 1974 including one referral as the "Larry" Bascom Agency.

Wolfe hires a free-lance operative named Rattner for a case in 1951 and has him supervised by Fred Durkin. Little else is known about Mr. Rattner but by the time you get through with this chapter, that fact alone will tell you all you need to know about his capabilities and his position in the relative pecking order of private detectives. Various others pop up from time to time, usually on assignments that stretch out of the city, state or even the country but they are minor characters usually relegated to a single appearance.

Since Wolfe can be expected to use only the best he can find, he has a rather small circle of free-lance investigators he favors with most of his work. Therefore we have a cast of five private detectives who populate Wolfe's cases in varying degrees of frequency. Saul Panzer, Fred Durkin and Orrie Cather comprise an "inner circle" of the most effective of the lot with Johnny Keems and Bill Gore acting strictly as bit players. I will list them here in the order of the relative value they are to Mr. Wolfe which is, not coincidentally, practically the same order as the frequency with which they appear in the cases.

Saul Panzer

In Wolfe's first recorded case, Archie, Saul Panzer and Fred Durkin are all evidently getting paychecks from Wolfe every week, Archie for his normal duties and the other two on an apparent basis of constant usage or stand-by. When times get tight, Archie's and Saul's paychecks are cut down and Fred's is stopped altogether. For these reasons and others—namely, the obvious respect and, yes, affection both Wolfe and Archie have for him, and the trust both frequently place in him which is never misplaced—Saul Panzer is always accorded a position superior to the other operatives. This is a position he has earned through consistent performance rather than ingratiation. In fact, he is almost accorded a status similar to Archie's, almost as Archie's adopted step-brother and Wolfe's other adopted son (I'll forego the psychological implications here if you don't mind). More than the others covered here, Saul should probably be afforded a place in the previous chapter on The Family since he deserves it more than any of the people in that chapter except the actual residents of the house. Nevertheless, Saul himself has chosen his position within the Wolfean hierarchy and here he shall reside, as a first among equals.

Saul Panzer is five feet seven inches tall, weighs 140-145 pounds and comes to the middle of Archie's ear. Archie describes him as "a slight build, wiry, undersized, homely, sagging shoulders with one of them half an inch higher than the other, and with a face that's all nose." He has sharp gray eyes that are the best eyes for seeing on the face of the globe. With one glance, those eyes can permanently add you to the picture gallery he carries around in his head. After admitting over 200 guests to Wolfe's home, Saul was able to place a single name and face together which Inspector Cramer didn't believe until he saw it. Even so, Cramer arrested Saul, for a few moments anyway, during the *Christmas Party* case.

Saul's general appearance is that of a cab driver; that is, unremarkable, forgettable and anonymous. The perfect appearance for a spy—or a private detective.

He always looks like he needs a shave and looks one-fifth as strong and one-tenth as smart as he really is, more obvious advantages in his line of work.

Archie's opinion of him is as high as Wolfe's. Archie says Saul is the best man in the world for everything that can be done without a dinner jacket. He can do almost everything better than anyone Archie knows including talk. He's the only person on earth who's better than Archie at tailing someone. But he's not just a bird dog. Even Archie admits that if Saul wanted Archie's job, he'd get it. Although he might sit in for Archie on occasion, Saul doesn't want anything to do with permanently replacing him, probably knowing that he'd have to force himself to accomplish some of the more esoteric duties that Archie relishes such as goading Wolfe into working when he doesn't want to.

In spite of that, they are close friends and the only competition between them seems to revolve around poker. Saul, Archie, Lon Cohen and an unnamed fourth man have poker games at Saul's apartment one night a week for years. In 1954 it is on Saturday nights but eventually moves to Wednesdays and then to Thursdays. Saul almost always wins. A quiet but very competitive guy.

His sartorial tastes (or lack of them) assist him in those ventures. His normal attire is an old brown suit and an equally aged brown wool cap that he wears from the first of November through mid-April. It is reversible, light tan on one side and plaid on other, able to be swept off the head in the blink of an eye and crammed in a pocket, thus changing his appearance ever so slightly to avoid being spotted by someone he's following. Ignoring New York winters, he never wears an overcoat.

Although Saul owns two houses in Brooklyn, he lives alone on the fifth (top) floor of a remodeled house on East Thirty-Eighth Street between Lexington and Third Avenues. In 1937 his telephone number is Liberty 2-3306. At the beginning of the series he is a bachelor. In 1950 we are teased with the indication that he may possibly have a wife and children but no further information is forthcoming.

His apartment consists of a big living room lighted with two floor lamps and two table lamps, a bedroom, bathroom and kitchenette. One wall is solid with windows, another is solid with books on bookshelves and another has shelves cluttered with everything from mineral chunks to walrus tusks. A grand piano rests in a far corner of the living room and it isn't just for decoration. Saul can play it and is the only person besides Fritz who plays the piano in Wolfe's front room. His repertoire has been known to stretch effortlessly from ragtime to Debussy. Wolfe has been there more than once. He hid from the law there for a while in 1954 and concocted one of his infamous charades there in 1956. Wolfe says it's a good room. That should tell you something.

Saul smokes a cigar in the second case but soon switches to Egyptian Pharaoh cigarettes. As you may have already gathered from his musical talents and the furnishings of his home, Saul Panzer is a lot more than the sum of his parts. He is a man of cultured tastes and a Renaissance man after Wolfe's own heart. Although we are never told, we are led to believe he is Jewish. Yet, in 1939, he speaks fluent Italian. He has been known to take a bourbon and soda but he also likes fine brandy and champagne. In 1956, the Broadway play *The Lark* starring Julie Harris comes up during a case as part of someone's alibi. Not only has Saul seen the play, he remembers exactly when the first act ends which turns out to be of considerable help.

That is only one example of the comprehensively curious and attentive brain behind those gray eyes. Saul has no office for the same reason that he never takes any notes, because he doesn't need to. He is the only operative in New York who routinely gets double the average market for his services. Over time, that eventually becomes triple the market. He's worth ten of Fred and Orrie and is consistently worth twice what he charges. His fees are $30 a day in 1946, move to $10 an hour for most of the Fifties and Sixties, and move to $15 an hour toward the end of the series. At least that's what he charges Wolfe and he has never been known to turn Wolfe down unless he's on something where he absolutely can't shake loose.

His working relationship with Wolfe is special. On the rare occasions when he doesn't come up with results for Wolfe, Saul always offers to forego his daily pay rate and just work for expenses. Wolfe always refuses the offer and pays him the full rate anyway. By 1948 that has only happened three times but Wolfe never gets riled at him.

Saul also rarely gets riled. Usually his strongest exclamation is "Lovin' babe." He never swears except under extreme duress. In 1956 he did say "Jumping Jesus!" when he and Archie walked in on a murder and he said "Goddam!" in 1947 after he lost a tail on a man which kept him from witnessing (or preventing) the man's murder.

When having meetings in Wolfe's office, Saul never sits in the red leather chair during the day. Although he could probably appropriate it, he always prefers one of the yellow chairs. This isn't from false modesty, it's because he doesn't like to sit facing a window. Probably for the same reason Wolfe doesn't like open fires. In 1956 and 1974, he does sit in that chair at night.

We are never told Saul's habits or choices in firearms. He may or may not always be armed but he always has a gun when he needs one. Nor is he a novice with them. In a gunfight with a murderer in Wolfe's office that involved two gangsters and Saul, it was Saul's bullet that pierces the murderer's heart.

Wolfe himself admits that he trusts Saul farther than might be thought credible. In 1952 he sends Saul all the way to Peru on a case. One of Stout's favorite artifices for keeping Archie (and thus the reader) in the dark is to periodically have Wolfe get secretive (cute, Archie calls it) about certain strategies and developments in a case. These almost always involve having private visits and/or phone calls with Saul that specifically exclude Archie.

Saul's first appearance is in the first case and his last in the last case. In the interim, he appears in 55 of the 74 tales and is mentioned in one other. He is the only one of the inner circle (Saul, Fred and Orrie) in 17 of the tales. None of the others are featured by themselves in any case. Therefore when he needs one and only one, Wolfe inevitably calls on Saul. Suffice it to say that Saul is always entrusted with the most sensitive, difficult and sophisticated assignments, and many things are entrusted to Saul that are not to Fred and Orrie.

Fred Durkin

Fred Durkin is big (one inch shorter than Archie and two inches broader), burly, bald and Irish. He looks like a piano mover, moves like a bear and you would expect him to be clumsy but he isn't. He has deep-set little eyes and a heavier beard than Archie.

He is the first of the operatives mentioned in the series because he brings the first recorded case to Wolfe. The client was a friend of Fred's wife, Fannie. Fannie is Italian. When all the operatives meet together in Wolfe's office, Fred gets the red leather chair by right of seniority (and because Saul doesn't want it).

Fred is "all right up to the neck—as honest as sunshine but unimaginative—not a genius but has good eyes." Archie's short description of him is "thick" (meaning mentally), apparently with justification. Not five pages into the first story, Fred reported a date two days earlier wrongly to Wolfe by looking at the next year's calendar. In 1935, Fred screwed up an assignment, assaulted a police officer and allowed himself to be followed to Wolfe's front door. Wolfe berated him publicly, told him to go to the kitchen and have Fritz prepare him a cyanide sandwich. Not improving, Fred gets himself arrested later in the same case. When he enters the office, Fred has a habit of throwing his hat and trying to hook it on Archie's chair (when Wolfe isn't present, of course). He always misses.

In spite of these shortcomings, as a surveillance man Fred is second only to Saul and Archie. Wolfe trusts his integrity implicitly if not his head. That trust extends to funds because Fred never wastes money. That fiscal trust does not extend to Orrie, Johnny or Bill.

His personal and professional relationships with Wolfe vacillate somewhat. When the operatives dine at Wolfe's home, Saul and Orrie are allowed to eat in the dining room with Wolfe and Archie but Fred has to eat in the kitchen. This is because Fred put vinegar in a brown roux with squab in 1932. Wolfe fired him for a month and, when re-hired, he was forever banished to the kitchen.

Of all the operatives, Fred is the most in awe of Wolfe. Fred worships him, thinks he can prove anything he wants to, hangs on his every word and won't take his eyes off of him during a meeting. In the beginning, Fred drinks straight rye with no chaser and later becomes a bourbon and water man. He thinks beer is "slop" but always drinks it when Wolfe offers because he thinks it would offend Wolfe if he didn't.

Fred carries a Smith & Wesson revolver in a shoulder holster and occasionally needs it. He and Archie get shot at in the first months of 1950 by some fur hijackers. In 1966, Fred gets shot in the leg by a sniper while working on a case trying to get Orrie out of jail.

By 1953, he and Fannie have started a family and it eventually grows to four daughters. In 1969, his oldest daughter, Elaine, is smoking marijuana and Fred is perplexed by it.

In 1939, Fred is paid one dollar per hour. For the first two decades, he makes about half what Saul does which is about what he's worth. By 1959, Saul is making $10 an hour (worth $20), Fred makes $7 an hour (worth $7.50) and Orrie makes $7 an hour (worth $6.50). Fred eventually progresses to $8 an hour before the end of the series.

Like Saul and Orrie, Fred makes his first appearance in the first case and his last in the last case. Altogether he appears in 33 of the cases and is mentioned in six others.

Orrie Cather

Orrie Cather is a little over six feet tall, half an inch taller than Archie, weighs 180 pounds, is tall, trim, dressy, muscular with no flab, and looks like an auto salesman. He has confident dark brown eyes, wavy lips and Archie says he's handsome. By 1945, he'll be able to get along without a hairbrush in a few years.

In 1953, we are told that his first name is Orvald but in 1957 we hear from his own lips that it's Orville. He carries an old Smith & Wesson .38 and is a good detective but has an ego that his talents can't match. He is smarter than Bill Gore and probably thinks he's smarter than Fred Durkin. That may or may not be but he doesn't have Fred's instincts and aptitudes. Orrie is usually paid the same rate as Fred and that probably offends him because he thinks he's worth more than Fred but he isn't. Orrie's strong suit is getting people to tell him things, not by his questioning technique but just by the way he looks at them. Orrie's primary liability is that he pushes the limits too much. Wolfe also questions his integrity. The baser things in life, like stealing an orchid, Wolfe would never suspect of Archie, Saul or Fred, but he might suspect of Orrie. His judgement is later proven right. Orrie exhibits a number of character defects toward the end of the series that cause Wolfe professional difficulties and even get Orrie thrown in jail, falsely accused of murder. The whole group has to work like sled dogs to get him out of the mess he got himself into.

He smokes a pipe in the office in 1949 but later quits smoking altogether. He drinks beer with Wolfe on occasion but that may be out of deference like Fred. He later prefers gin fizzes or vodka and tonic.

Another of Orrie's downfalls is that he constantly competes with Archie. He thinks he should have Archie's job but no one else does. Actually, for Orrie to even aspire to Archie's job is egomania that borders on megalomania. Archie admits there is one little detail of detective work that Orrie can do better than he can but he refuses to tell what it is so he won't name it. When Orrie comes to the office while Archie is out, Orrie likes to plant himself in Archie's chair because he knows it irritates him. That finally backfires on him in 1957 when Archie, in a foul mood anyway, pulls him bodily out of his chair and drags him across the floor. Presumably there was no recurrence.

Orrie has a good singing voice and once camouflaged an interview for Archie by singing "Git Along Little Dogie" so lawmen couldn't overhear the interview.

Orrie is quite a womanizer and his ethics and moral standards in that area are part of the reason Wolfe questions his integrity. In May of 1966, Orrie marries Jill Hardy, an airline stewardess for Pan Am on international flights. She is beautiful and petite with big gray-blue eyes. She thinks Archie looks a little like Orrie but Archie doesn't.

Orrie made a suggestion to Wolfe about his assignments for the operatives only once but it was notable. Orrie's tenure also runs throughout the series, starting in 1933 and ending with the last case in 1974. He appears in 35 of the cases and is mentioned in five others.

Johnny Keems

John Joseph Keems looks like a Princeton boy with his face washed. He puts slick stuff on his hair and wears spats. He does exercises every morning and buys gum at every slot vendor for an excuse to look in the mirror. He's a smirker and desperately wants Archie's job. He sits in Archie's chair every chance he gets but he isn't as blatant about it as Orrie, at least not risking physical expulsion. He never carries a notebook because he thinks his memory is as good as Archie's but it isn't.

A gentleman from his skin out, he errs by telling Wolfe things he already knows. He thinks he's especially effective with young women, a big mistake when competing with the likes of Archie and Orrie. Early on, he offends Wolfe by using "contact" as a verb and then trying to defend it with the dictionary definition, which is ignored under Wolfe's roof.

Johnny has a plethora of professional problems in Wolfe's employ. Stridently conservative, he does not approve of labor unions. He once lied to a witness in Wolfe's name and got caught at it. Wolfe had him pay $8.40 for cab fare on his own without putting it on expenses, severely chastised him publicly and told him to quit trying to imitate Archie because he'd never make it. Wolfe then dismissed him perfunctorily. Johnny wasn't available during the 1936 case because he was freelancing for Del Pritchard's agency which had already failed to solve the case before Wolfe got it.

Johnny was a pretty good operative but had to be handled. Wolfe has known him to overstrain his talents and he does so most notably in April of 1956.

Johnny debuted in the second case in 1934, appeared in six cases and was mentioned in four others.

Bill Gore

Bill Gore is described as "full size, 200 pounds and no fat, and unpolished." In 1946, Archie predicted he'd be bald in five years. Saul, Fred, Orrie and Johnny Keems missed all the World War II cases because they were in the military but there is no mention of Bill in this regard.

In 1946, Bill makes $20 a day, about two-thirds what Saul makes. He's not too smart to live but he hangs on. Archie said something funny to him in 1948 and he laughs every time Archie speaks.

Bill makes his first appearance in 1934 and his last in 1956. He appears in only four of the cases and is mentioned in two others. Rex Stout later told his biographer that he probably dropped Bill from the series because he "bored him."

All five of the primary operatives, Saul, Fred, Orrie, Johnny and Bill, appear in only one of the cases together: *Too Many Women* in 1947.

Dol Bonner

Not really one of the inner circle of Wolfe's operatives, Ms. Bonner rates a place here simply because she is unique in the saga.

Theodolinda (Dol) Bonner is about Archie's age, very attractive and has long black eyelashes over caramel-colored eyes. A young socialite whose family's fortune was wiped out in the Depression, she's the female counterpart of Wolfe. Her fiancée jilted her so she hates all men.

Dol operates her own detective agency at Fiftieth Street and Madison Avenue, the only female owner/operator of a detective agency in New York. She has become successful enough to afford to become a fashionable and expensive dresser. She's it as female dicks go and she must be because she's the only female detective Wolfe can stand. At one time, Archie considered that she may have had her eye on Wolfe and thought it would be entertaining to see how Fritz reacted to her. He found out when Wolfe invited her to breakfast once and Fritz was *very* jumpy. Wolfe uses her assistance in cases in 1956, 1957 and 1962.

Since his line of work intimately involves newsworthy stories like murder and the law, it makes sense that Nero Wolfe would have a need for specialists in journalism, the law and medicine. Naturally, he uses only the best.

Lon Cohen

Lon Cohen is a high-up muckety-muck in the New York Gazette. No one seems to be quite sure of his title but by 1949, he's second in command of the Gazette's City Desk. He knows more facts than the NYPD and the Public Library combined, and what he doesn't carry in his head is quickly available from his resources. His office is on the Twentieth Floor of the Gazette Building on Forty-Forth Street, two doors down the hall from the publisher's corner office. He has the only desk in that 9x12 office which barely leaves enough room for his feet which are also 9x12. There are three telephones on his desk and he is always talking on at least one of them. He comes to work late, about noon, and always stays until at least midnight.

He is very dark complected, has dark skin, dark brown deep-set eyes and almost black hair, slicked back and up over his sloping dome.

Besides their business relationship, Archie and Lon are close personal friends. Lon is one of the regulars at Saul Panzer's weekly poker games and he is the second best poker player Archie knows, second only to Saul. Besides having been a guest at Wolfe's table, Lon has had drinks (B&B) with Archie at Yaden's Bar and dined with him at Pietro's, Pierre's and Rusterman's. Lon is also one of the people on a list who receive orchids from Wolfe. For years, the receptionist on the third floor of the Gazette Building got orchids from Wolfe twice a year.

Lon first appears in 1946 and, in 1949, says he has 19 years to go before he can retire. Too valuable to dispense with, he remains in the series to the end in 1974. Along the way, he appears in 37 of the cases and is mentioned in one other.

Nathaniel Parker

As much as Archie and Wolfe deal with killers, kidnappers, thieves, extortionists and other malfeasants, not to mention their trips to jail, they need a good lawyer.

The first one shows up in the third case in 1935. Henry H. Barber is the lawyer they count on for everything but fee-splitting. His main job in that case as getting Fred Durkin out of jail.

They manage to get along without legal counsel for the next decade but in 1946, Nathaniel Parker makes his debut. He is mentioned as the source for bail to get Wolfe out of jail but, as it turns out, he isn't needed.

Nathaniel Parker is six feet, four inches tall, thin, and middle-aged in 1960. In 1955, his telephone number is LIncoln 3-4616. The next year it is EAstwood 6-2605 and a few months later, it has changed to PHoenix 5-2382. Wolfe doesn't have it memorized but Archie always does. It's a good thing.

Parker's esteem rises quickly. He is one of only eight men (not counting Archie) that Wolfe consistently shakes hands with. In 1950 he gets Archie out of jail in Westchester County on Easter Sunday. But the situation soon gets confusing.

Between 1951 and 1953, Wolfe and Archie vacillate between what is apparently two lawyers. Henry George Parker makes his debut in 1951. If he is a relative of Nathaniel, we aren't so informed. He gains a reputation as the only lawyer Wolfe would admit to the bar if he had his way. He gets Archie out of jail after 18 hours for carrying an unregistered weapon and material witness. He is no dilly-dallier, knows the employer-employee relationship, and knows when to stop giving legal advice and do what he's told by the man paying the bills. He sued Harry Koven for $1 million and in 1953, Wolfe phoned him to counter a possible replevin order on a fee after his client died.

Nathaniel Parker fades in and out of the scene periodically. In 1952, he's the only lawyer Wolfe has ever sent orchids to and would give Wolfe his right eye, if asked. By 1954, when Wolfe leaves the country, Parker has the authority to sign checks for him and is Wolfe's only lawyer. He arranges an injunction against Softdown Inc. and dates a homicide victim (Parker's a bachelor). He's gotten Archie out of jail three times by 1955. The next year he bails them both out. He is also the only lawyer Wolfe has ever invited to dinner although that changes in 1956 when Albert Freyer, Peter Hays' attorney, is invited to dine at Wolfe's.

Parker is very conservative in dress, has his clothes made by Stover and wears a homburg hat. From the 1950's to the 1970's, he progresses from a scotch and water drinker to a vodka on the rocks man. Nobody ever said working for Wolfe was easy. Archie likes the half-glad, half-sad way he says "Yes, Archie?" when he answers the phone. Parker knows that chores for Wolfe will be interesting but often tough and ticklish.

He is also somewhat cosmopolitan and speaks French with Wolfe in 1955, to the frustration of an eavesdropping state trooper. The same year, he sued Inspector Cramer and six other people for $1 million each at the behest of one of Wolfe's clients. He gets Archie out of jail in 1957, 1960, 1961 and 1962. In 1974, he's bailing out Wolfe, Archie, Saul, Fred and Orrie and getting their suspended private detective licenses reinstated.

Between 1946 and 1974, Nathaniel Parker appears in 17 of Wolfe's cases and is mentioned in one other. There is little doubt that he earned all his fees.

Doctor Vollmer

Doctor Edwin A. Vollmer is a sad-looking little guy with lots of forehead, a narrow lean jaw, a round face and round ears, short legs, a slight paunch and spectacles. His combined house and office is half a block (200 yards) east of Wolfe's house, down Thirty-Fifth Street towards Tenth Avenue. Other directions from Wolfe's front stoop tell us to turn right towards Ninth Avenue and halfway there, turn right into Vollmer's vestibule. Thus we have some confusion at to whether the first street to the right or east of Wolfe's house is Ninth or Tenth. More will be said about that when we examine the location of Wolfe's brownstone later.

At any rate, Vollmer's house is the same size, color and age as Wolfe's and is a one-minute walk away. His secretary is Helen Gillard. His medical offices are on the lower floors and Vollmer lives on the third floor. He has three phone numbers to the house including an unlisted one on the third floor. Wolfe has all of them.

Vollmer's proximity to Wolfe's residence is only part of his attractiveness. Another part is that he makes house calls. In 1934, he makes house calls for

Archie and Dora Chapin. The next year he treated a bullet wound in Wolfe's left arm. He was charging $5 for a house call when he pronounced one of Wolfe's clients dead from poisoned aspirin in 1936. He made several other house calls, treated a cut infected with tetanus germs and pronounced a woman dead in Wolfe's house before the war.

Their relationship became more personal in 1941. A crook named Griffin tried to frame Vollmer on a malpractice suit. Wolfe fixed it and Vollmer told him that whatever he wanted or needed in the future, all he had to do was ask. Wolfe did, numerous times, and the good doctor lived up to his word. Archie persists in calling him "Doc" but Wolfe has told him a dozen times it is an obnoxious vulgarism, dismissive of Vollmer's professional and educational credentials. Wolfe himself always calls him "Doctor."

The year after the war ended was a busy one down the block. He treated scratches on Archie's face (from a woman, naturally, but business, not pleasure), pronounced a girl dead on the stoop and declared Wolfe insane for a while to allow him to hide out from the cops.

Over the next few years, Vollmer pronounces at least two people dead in Wolfe's house, goes to Westchester County to conduct a mini-autopsy, treats a man who just had a gun shot out of his hand by Archie, takes 22 stitches in Archie's side from a knife wound and treats a guest in the South Room. Since the late 1940's, he always has a beer with Wolfe when the house calls are in the evening.

We never meet Mrs. Vollmer (perhaps he's a widower?) but we know he has a son, Bill. In 1961 Bill is away at school, presumably college or medical school. Archie taught Bill how to take fingerprints when he was a boy.

The emergencies he figures into aren't just medical. In 1961, Archie and Wolfe move into Vollmer's house overnight to hide from the cops. In 1965, he is used as a go-between to deliver an anonymous phone message from a mysterious stranger and Vollmer actually started the case in 1969.

Medical assistance became necessary even before legal assistance. Doctor Vollmer made his first appearance in the series in 1934 and his last in the next to last case, in 1969. He appears in 16 of the cases and is mentioned in two others.

Homicide

The first recorded member of the New York City Police Department (NYPD) Homicide Squad to visit Wolfe was a Detective O'Grady—young, athletic and trustworthy. But he told Wolfe the only reason he wasn't a suspect in a murder was because it would take a boxcar to haul him around and Wolfe said O'Grady was "cerebrally an oaf." They didn't get along. Perhaps the police decided then and there that a mere detective would always be ineffectual when dealing with Wolfe because they rapidly escalated their response to Sergeant Purley Stebbins and, in the second adventure, a full inspector (Cramer).

To give the reader an idea of what that means, it might help to understand a little about the organization of the chain of command of the NYPD. It is loosely analogous to a military rank structure.

The NYPD is overseen by a Police Commissioner and several Deputy Commissioners who are civilians. The commissioner is like a five-star general and the situation is analogous to civilian control of the military. The highest-ranking police officer is the Chief of Police, equal to a four-star general. Under him are several Assistant Chiefs over various areas, usually referred to as "three-star" and "two-star" Chiefs. Deputy Chiefs are like one-star generals. Inspectors are analogous to Colonels. Under them are, in order, Deputy Inspectors, Captains, Lieutenants, Sergeants, Detectives and Patrolmen, the lowest rank.

So Inspector Cramer, while hardly all-powerful, still swings some weight. While Cramer's and Stebbins' (and certainly not Rowcliff's) cunning and intellect never escalated to the level of equality with Wolfe's or, for that matter, Archie's and Saul's, the two primary police protagonists weren't stupid, had integrity and their own brand of official ethics. Stout evidently felt the need for a Homicide representative with none of these redeeming features and in the third novel, *The Rubber Band*, Lieutenant Rowcliff makes his first, very memorable appearance.

The offices of Manhattan West Homicide are housed in the Tenth Precinct at 230 West Twentieth Street, conveniently located less than a mile from Wolfe's brownstone residence. One of their phone numbers is SPring 7-3100 but the one most frequently used is Watkins 9-8241. It changed to Watkins 9-8242 in 1946 but this was probably a rollover number and it went back to the previous number the next year. Both Wolfe and Archie have it memorized. As an interesting aside, the real telephone number for the old NYPD headquarters on Centre Street was Spring 3100 and that is still the name of the official NYPD news magazine.

Archie has frequent business dealings there on both a voluntary and involuntary basis. Since 1951, he is not allowed in there without an escort ever since he took a snapshot of a piece of paper the cops were saving although they couldn't prove it.

Wolfe does not look down his nose at the NYPD, only at some of their minions and some of their hidebound methods. On the contrary, Wolfe has a great appreciation for their talents and resources. He advises one client looking for a missing person to call the police because for a ten-cent phone call, in ten minutes they can have 10,000 men looking and Wolfe charges more for less.

Now let us look at the primary NYPD officers in Nero Wolfe's world in ascending order of rank.

Sergeant Purley Stebbins

Stebbins is the only law enforcement officer to permeate the entire corpus of the series, from first to last. In between, he appears in 57 of the stories and is absent from 17 of them although he is mentioned in one of those.

In the first adventure in 1933, Stebbins is a Detective with the District Attorney's Homicide Bureau. He is absent for the second novel but is back in the third, *The Rubber Band*, as a Detective working for Inspector Cramer at Manhattan Homicide West. The next year he is still a Detective in *The Red Box* but is absent for the next two novels because they take place out of his jurisdiction in, respectively, West Virginia and Westchester County, New York. When he returns in *Over My Dead Body* in 1938, he is a Sergeant. Purley evidently has no more interest in promotional tests because he keeps that position for the next 37 years through the final adventure in 1975.

Purley is big, strong and has a bull neck. He is an inch taller than Archie and two inches broader. He and Cramer weigh about the same, about 190 pounds with little or none of it fat but Stebbins has more muscle packed around the bones. He is not handsome, has a big, bony face and pig bristle eyebrows (Archie's opinion). His countenance is probably not helped by the fact that most of his communications with Wolfe and Archie consists of snarls and growls which may also account for the fact that when he does speak, he is usually hoarse. He has honest brown eyes which accurately reflect his character.

Homicide is serious business for Purley. The primary reason for his snarls and growls is he doesn't like all the stunts Wolfe gets away with and Archie's light-hearted attitude about it all. Wolfe and Archie frequently frustrate the cops with what they call the Hitler-Stalin technique in reverse. That is, instead of telling barefaced lies, they tell the truth in a manner that has them taken for lies. Archie's reputation as a gagster helps. Purley frequently calls him "a goddam clown." These frustrations probably account for the fact that in the early adventures, Purley bangs doors closed and Cramer doesn't. Later Cramer bangs them, too. Nevertheless, Stebbins is a good cop and an honest one. He is a proud man and Archie wouldn't go so far as to say he has nothing to be proud of.

Stebbins typifies the love-hate relationship between the police protagonists, Wolfe and Archie. By 1952 he has called Archie by his first name eight times over the years which happens about every two years. Archie attributes it to fits of absentmindedness. On a case in 1968, they start off calling each other "Archie" and "Purley" but it soon degenerates into Stebbins shouldering his way into the house, charging up the stairs to the plant rooms and eventually being ordered out of the house after being caught searching the desks in the office without a warrant. Purley never learns. But that's not true, either. Both Wolfe and Archie are complimentary of his brains on more than one occasion. It's just that his instincts overrule his brain sometimes when the boys are flimflamming him. So sometimes he shoulders his way in and searches desks. He knows better, he just can't help himself and he gets burned for it occasionally. In 1942 he is ignominiously ordered to telephone Fritz with orders to dust and air out the office, order three cases of beer and prepare a pan-broiled young turkey with all the trimmings for dinner at eight.

They do occasionally have a certain spirit of cooperation, however. In 1944, Stebbins helps Archie wrestle a murderer out of the South Room and gets slightly injured in the process. At one point, Archie says that their intimacy has never reached the point of having a joint meal but that's not true. In 1950, Archie buys him a lobster at Jake's. In 1952 they are colleagues for a short time when Archie works with Homicide including having a uniformed driver and credentials signed by a Deputy Commissioner! During this time, Archie buys Purley a double order of fried clams, apple pie with cheese & two steins of ale at Louie's. Ever the honest cop, Purley tries to pay for his own meal but Archie insists on paying since he makes at least four times more than Purley.

This spirit is always temporary. Stebbins has arrested Archie on several occasions for material witness and everything else he can think of. He is not malicious about it though. He arrested Archie in 1958 for obstructing justice on Lieutenant

Rowcliff's orders, then unarrested him after making a deal with Archie to appease Rowcliff. We get the distinct impression that Purley doesn't like Rowcliff either.

When Cramer and Stebbins come to the office, Cramer always prefers the red leather chair and Purley is naturally relegated to one of the yellow ones. On the rare occasions when Purley comes to Wolfe's office alone, he still sits in a yellow chair instead of the red one. Archie doesn't know why but it almost certainly is because he prefers it and not because he is in awe of Cramer.

Stebbins hates being ordered to attend the little charades Wolfe stages in his office to solve murders but this has happened in 54 of the stories and Purley is there to arrest the bad guy (or girl) in virtually all of them. Purley follows orders but he is not a martinet and very much has a mind of his own. He never sits with his back to anyone if he can help it including his police superiors. During these soirees, Purley likes to sit or stand at the rear of the gathering, sometimes placing himself next to the person who is his personal favorite among the suspects. On one occasion, he silently disagreed with Cramer and stood next to the person Wolfe identified instead of the one Cramer preferred. Stebbins' choice was rewarded by being correct.

Lieutenant Rowcliff

Lieutenant George Rowcliff serves the purpose of making Cramer and Stebbins look emotionally like puppies and intellectually like geniuses. We are initially told that his first name is George but in 1969, Wolfe calls him "J.M. Rowcliff." He is married and his wife's name is Diana. That becomes very relevant in a later comeuppance.

Archie says that if and when he gets his choice of going to heaven or hell, he'll only have one question; "Where's Rowcliff?" Archie thinks the world will never reach universal brotherhood as long as there are opinions like his of Rowcliff. In Wolfe's estimation, he's an imbecile but Archie would just like to twist his ears.

Archie describes him as six feet tall, strong, handsome and a pain in the neck but he doesn't really mean neck. Rowcliff makes his entrance into the series in the third novel in 1935 with a rather dramatic gesture. He serves the first recorded search warrant on Wolfe's brownstone but didn't find the woman he was looking for. Wolfe would endure other search warrants in the course of the saga but Rowcliff would always have a special animus for being the first to invade Wolfe's sanctuary. He was forever damned as "that man who searched my house." Cramer and Stebbins would go up and down in Wolfe's estimation but Rowcliff started at the bottom and went down from there. Wolfe carried the grudge eternally.

As a semi-constant irritant, Rowcliff appears in 17 of the stories, is absent from 50 of them but is mentioned in seven others. Their relationship reaches its nadir in 1946 when Archie says he hopes to help investigate Rowcliff's murder someday. If he did it himself, Archie wouldn't have to premeditate it because he already had. There aren't many murderers so vicious or inhuman that Archie would enjoy seeing them caught by Rowcliff. Probably the most cordial moment between them occurs in 1947 when Rowcliff invites Archie to go along on a search warrant but it should be noted that it was their third search of a murdered man's papers and the cops were totally lost but so were Wolfe and Archie.

Unlike Stebbins, Rowcliff wants a promotion to Captain so bad he can taste it. He's unlikely to get it because, also like Stebbins, Rowcliff occasionally oversteps his bounds but it's through stupidity and not professional zeal. On April 3, 1949, he is ordered by Police Commissioner Skinner to sign a written apology to Wolfe and Archie for some unrecorded offense.

Undeterred by this humiliation, Rowcliff continues to persevere and outdoes himself in 1952. He arrests Archie for impersonating a police officer, then pushes his way past Fritz, charges up to Wolfe's plant rooms, arrests him for material witness to a homicide and actually puts his hands on him. He then, in Wolfe's words, "brings [me] to the Police Department in a rickety old police car with a headstrong and paroxysmal driver." This earns him a new epithet as "the Police Department's champion ass."

In the face of this new affront, Archie begins a campaign of psychological warfare against Rowcliff. He discovers that when the good Lieutenant reaches a certain pitch of excitement (or more likely frustration and rage), he begins stuttering. Archie has it timed so he starts stuttering just before Rowcliff, thus triggering him into it and then accusing Rowcliff of mimicking him which just makes it worse. By 1957 his best time is eight minutes but by 1960, Archie once got him stuttering in a record two minutes and twenty seconds. He has a bet with Saul Panzer that he can get it down to two minutes flat in three more tries.

Inspector Cramer

When it comes to the cops in Wolfe's life, Inspector Cramer is The Man. He wasn't originally because he skipped the first story and made his debut in the second. But like any good cop, once he gets his foot in the door, he's hard to get rid of. He proceeds to become the most omnipresent member of the supporting cast. He appears in 64 of the stories and of the 10 he is absent from, he is mentioned in two of them. Of the 10 he isn't in, eight of them are out of his jurisdiction. But if it involves a dead body and it occurs in Manhattan, Cramer is in your face.

He may or may not be Irish. In 1940, we are told his first name is Fergus but, in 1946, Archie forged his initials as "L.T.C." He is a big man, broad-shouldered, weighs 190 pounds, not much of it fat but not as much muscle as Sergeant Stebbins. He has sharp little eyes that progress from blue to blue-gray to gray. He has eyes like a pig but that description comes from one of Wolfe's unhappy clients so it's probably far too unkind. His hair makes the same progression except we aren't told what the original darker color is. It is half-gray by 1957 but looks whiter at night. He has delicate little ears close to his skull and wrinkled pink skin. He has a big, round, red face that gets redder at night, during the summer or when perplexed by Wolfe which is almost every time they have contact. (Oops, was that a verb?) He wears size twelve shoes, wears an old felt hat year round, has known Wolfe longer than Archie and is an inflexibly honest cop. In 1950 he makes about $10,000 a year and takes a swing at Archie (he missed) when Archie hints he might be on the take. Years later, Archie apologized (indirectly) when he assured Cramer he knew he was "on the level."

Speaking of which, that is probably one of the thorns Cramer has in his side. Archie consistently is paid more than Cramer and it would only be human that Cramer is piqued that both Archie and Wolfe make so much more money than he does for doing the same thing with so many fewer resources and so much less apparent effort.

Lily rowan's father was one of his best friends, got him on the police force and got him out of a couple of tight spots in the old days. Cramer knew Lily before she could walk. Wolfe has a great appreciation for his power and resources which are ideal for checking alibis, tracing movements, establishing times and collecting evidence that requires persistence, time and manpower. Wolfe says Cramer is constantly leaping at the throat of evil and finding himself holding on for dear life to the tip of its tail. His phone number is one of only three Wolfe has bothered to memorize.

The question of Cramer's seniority on the NYPD vacillates somewhat. In 1936 he says he'll be ready (probably meaning able) to retire in another ten years. In 1960 he's been in charge of Homicide for 20 years and in 1965, he's been a cop for 36 years.

Even in the beginning adventures, his rank rates him an unmarked Police Department Cadillac with a detective for a driver. In the beginning, he is an avid smoker of both a pipe and cigars, smoking both in Wolfe's office but he soon settles on cigars. He smokes two of them in the 1935 story and four in the 1936 edition but begins tapering off. The last time we know him to light one is in 1945, ironically in a case where a victim's face is blown off by a booby-trapped cigar.

Maybe that did it for him. After that, Archie persistently tells us that he rarely sees him light one and eventually progresses to the point of saying that he's never seen him light one but you know how Archie exaggerates.

Although he quit smoking, Cramer never stops using the cigars. The cigars become a prop, a surrogate and occasionally a kind of therapy. He has a habit of squeezing his eyes shut tightly and then opening them, usually when he's concentrating. On the rare occasions he takes notes, he writes in a small, neat hand. He takes the cigar out of his pocket, rolls it between his hands while he's thinking (usually counting to ten, at least, before telling Wolfe what's on his mind), then sticks it in his mouth and chews it. This usually occurs when he is faced with an unpleasant prospect like asking Wolfe for a favor or giving in to one of his demands. Sometimes he squeezes them, usually in lieu of squeezing Wolfe's neck. When he exits in a huff, he often throws the mangled remains of his cigar at Archie's wastebasket, usually misses and has only been known to pick it up on one occasion.

Like Stebbins, his relationship with Wolfe is basically adversarial but it has its ups and downs. When they're not at odds, Wolfe has condescended to shake hands with him which tells you something. When allowed to follow his inclinations as the gracious host, Wolfe occasionally offers him beer and many times, Cramer accepts. Archie unkindly but perhaps not inaccurately says Cramer only takes beer when he wants it understood he's only human and wants to be treated accordingly but when he doesn't get what he wants, he turns red and stomps out, leaving the beer unfinished. He has also accepted bourbon and water from Wolfe's refreshment table.

In 1935, he slapped Archie on the back in an uncharacteristic spell of joviality and called him "son." In the same case, he admitted to Wolfe that he liked him and the next year, he winked at Archie conspiratorially during a case. In 1946, he called Archie by his first name but he was tired and it was after 4 A.M. in Wolfe's office during a tough case. Usually he only calls him Archie when he wants to peddle the impression that he's one of the family, which he isn't. The rest of the time it's Goodwin. By 1960, it has only happened twice and Archie says that the ratio of "Goodwin's" to Archie's" is at least fifty to one.

Cramer is held in general good repute and respect by both Wolfe and Archie. Archie wouldn't give you an unconditional guarantee on his brains but says there's nothing wrong with his guts. In spite of that, their professional relationship has more downs than ups. In July of 1939, Cramer tried to arrest Wolfe on a material witness warrant but Wolfe negated it. Archie keeps the warrant in his desk as a souvenir. In 1941, Cramer made the great tactical error of taking away a man Wolfe had invited to dinner. Archie had to sit through a totally silent meal and Wolfe had to take Amphojel twice before going to bed. In retaliation, Wolfe later refused entrance to Cramer, Stebbins and Rowcliff, bolting the front and back doors, disconnecting the doorbell and buttoning up the fortress. When they returned with a squad and a warrant, they were handed a flock of statements, a confession and a murderer. In 1944, Cramer arrived with a search warrant for Wolfe's house but circumstances forced him to tear it up without serving it. In a fit of uncontrollable fury, Wolfe told Cramer that his acceptance of his salary constituted a fraud on the people of New York and he was a disgrace to an honorable profession.

When Cramer's not threatening to take their private investigator's licenses, he's getting warrants. Sometimes he doesn't wait for the warrant. In 1948, he jailed Archie for more than 18 hours. In 1958, he pulled Stebbins' trick of charging up the stairs to the plant rooms in violation of an agreement with Archie. He had material witness arrest warrants for both of them in 1959 but didn't serve them. Circumstances again. He got a search warrant the same year but was beaten to it by a federal warrant. In 1961, he arrested Archie for material witness and, later in the same week, served him with a murder warrant, thus setting a record by arresting him twice in one week. Actually he changed his mind about serving the second warrant. Inspector's privilege. In a rage in 1965, he arrests both Archie and Wolfe for material witness and then, exasperated, walks out on them with Wolfe's voice trailing him, "We are under arrest!" He later buys Archie a carton of milk as a peace offering and, as a reward, has a FBI Special Agent In Charge humiliated in his presence.

In the first story in which Cramer appears, Archie develops a series of code names for him to warn Wolfe in the presence of others when Cramer shows up or calls unannounced. Originally, it's Mr. Purdy. Later he uses Mr. Bluff, Mr. Cross or "the man about the chair." By 1960, he's calling him Mr. Judd or any name with two "d"'s in it. In 1969, it has been modernized to Mr. Fuzz.

When Cramer comes calling, Archie can tell with a glance at his face if he's on the warpath. When he's boiling, he leaves his hat on. Otherwise he removes it upon entering the house. When he's allowed in, that is. He is often refused admittance. After four decades of aggravation, in the last case in 1974, Wolfe tells him to "Shut up!" for the first and only time.

Archie occasionally plays mind games with Cramer like he does Rowcliff but of a less harmful and more playful nature. Cramer is strictly a family man with very stern ideas about that, a genuine old-fashioned guy and a patriot. His son is a bombardier with the Army Air Corps in Australia during World War II.

Archie calls him "a terrible prude." Cramer blushes furiously when Archie baits him by telling him a female suspect stayed in his room the previous night. Archie occasionally deliberately gives Cramer the wrong impression about his gallivanting around with women. Cramer has cussed Wolfe and Archie numerous times but only once in the presence of ladies, when they were all locked in a fumigating room in Wolfe's plant rooms and thought they were about to be gassed with poison gas. In a much milder version of the Rowcliff/stuttering ploy, Archie sometimes raises one eyebrow at Cramer which annoys him because he can't do it. When he tells Wolfe about it, Wolfe also tells him it disconcerts him but Archie doubts it, saying he's never seen Wolfe disconcerted.

Cramer plays back, too. In Wolfe's presence, he always makes it a point to rise from a chair using only his leg muscles because Wolfe always uses both hands and arms when rising. Cramer imagines it irritates Wolfe which it probably does. Or it's Cramer showing Wolfe he can do something he can't.

When Cramer is admitted to the office, he usually prefers to sit in the red leather chair, regardless of the number of visitors, unless he wants to stay at the back of the crowd to head off a murderer. He usually sits forward in the chair with his feet planted flat on the floor. Archie's never seen him cross his legs. On at least two occasions he has been allowed to use the peephole behind the waterfall picture to spy on someone in the office. As with Purley Stebbins, Cramer is usually in the office when the murderer is denounced there and whether Purley or Cramer gets to them first is usually only a question of proximity. The suspect in one of the first adventures even committed suicide in front of him in that office.

He has a general habit of giving Wolfe's clients the benefit of the doubt because he's never known one to be guilty. He eventually becomes disabused of that notion but the effect lingers which is a subtle compliment to Wolfe's judgement.

Apparently in 1962 the Detective Bureau goes through some kind of reorganization because, in that year, Homicide West under Cramer's command becomes Homicide South although they're still located at the same address on Twentieth Street. It remains that for the final eight novels. By 1967, Cramer says he and his men are "following the new rules", a reference to the *Miranda vs. Arizona* court decision of 1966. Now they don't even ask a suspect if he's thirsty unless his lawyer is present.

Et Al

Dozens of other NYPD men make a single appearance in the course of the adventures but two of them deserve at least a short mention here.

In 1952, Wolfe is forced to handle a murder case while attending a World Series game at the Polo Grounds. I won't elaborate here on how Archie got him to the game but it has to do with food and I don't mean ballpark hot dogs. Since he is out of Inspector Cramer's jurisdiction, a new face is in charge for a change.

Inspector Hennessey is tall, straight and silver-haired with a bony face and quick moving gray eyes. It is apparently not their first acquaintance because two years earlier, he had told Wolfe that if he ever poked into a murder in his territory again, he would be dunked in the Harlem River. Well, Wolfe did and he wasn't but apparently even Hennessey understood that Wolfe was a captive of circumstances.

Earlier, in 1946, came the only NYPD man to rival Rowcliff in Wolfe and Archie's affections. Inspector Ash had been a Captain under Cramer between 1938–1943 and had since been promoted. He was tall, had plastic eyes and a bony face (a common condition among New York cops, it would seem). Terribly ambitious and very incorruptible, he had no sense of humor (also a frequent failing in his profession).

Inspector Ash had been in charge of Homicide in Queens until he replaced Cramer in Manhattan West when Cramer was temporarily discredited. Yes, he got a raw deal. Ash thus became mired in a case with Wolfe and Archie. Determined not to "soft-pedal" with them as his predecessor had, his first act was issuing a material witness warrant for Wolfe. Wolfe called him childish, a numskull and a hooligan. Ash then had the brashness to actually put his hand on Wolfe's arm to arrest him whereupon Wolfe slapped his face resoundingly and actually urged Archie to attack him. Apparently no one had told him the fat man didn't like being touched and, in spite of his corpulence, was quite capable of defending himself. Archie, ever guided by his experience and intelligence, kept his own counsel.

In the course of the case, Wolfe's respect and admiration for Cramer doubled, and not because he had been "soft-pedaled." It all eventually got worked out. Wolfe consistently came to Cramer's defense with the NYPD brass, made sure he got credit for the murderer's arrest and Inspector Ash got transferred to Richmond on Staten Island, never to be heard from again.

The Other Edifice—The Brownstone

Nero Wolfe is the center of his own self-created universe and, to the limits he can control it, all else revolves around him. The protective nucleus that surrounds him is his combined home and business office in New York City.

It is a traditional New York brownstone, so called because of the reddish-brown sandstone used to construct them. It is located on West Thirty-Fifth Street between Tenth and Eleventh Avenues. Exiting Wolfe's house to the right would lead to Tenth Avenue, to the left to Eleventh Avenue. It is about half a block from the Hudson River, a five-minute taxi ride or a fifteen-minute walk from Times Square. It is on the south side of the street and the primary entrance faces to the north. The west side butts directly against another building but there is an open space on the east side. Wolfe owns the house outright and does not have a mortgage on it. When Wolfe temporarily abandoned it in 1950 to pursue his personal Moriarty, Marko Vukcic used his power of attorney to put the house up for sale for $120,000, obviously grossly overpriced and not really intended to be sold.

House addresses are not usually transient but the precise address of Wolfe's residence is problematical. In the first mention of it in 1936, it is 918. Two years later, it is given as 506. In 1946 it is given as both 909 and 922, in 1947 as 924, in 1951 as 902, in 1952 and 1965 as 914, in 1957 as 918 again, in 1960 as 618 (twice) and 918 (once), in 1962 as 618 and as 938 in 1966. In 1946 Wolfe receives a letter there addressed to 909 W. 35th. The most frequently given address, however, is 918 West Thirty-Fifth and, in fact, Wolfe testifies to that in court under oath in 1954. Since it would be imbecilic to perjure oneself on a matter so mundane and easily proven, hopefully we can let the matter rest there.

In actual fact, if there were a 900 block on West Thirty-Fifth Street, it would be in the middle of the Hudson River. The last block of the real West Thirty-Fifth Street is the 500 block.

Telephone numbers can and do change much more easily than addresses. Wolfe's evolves from BRyant 9-2828 in 1933 to PRoctor 5-5000 in 1946 and to

PEnnsylvania 3-1212 in 1951. I'm sure the current one would be listed in the New York City directory. After all, a businessman must be accessible to those requiring his services.

The building is a double-width house, four stories high or five stories counting what is called the basement even though it is only three feet below street level. A stoop of either seven or eight steps leads up to the front door. Seven is the most commonly given number but we will return to the stoop presently.

From the sidewalk in front of the house, to the left or east side of the stoop as you face it, five steps lead down to a paved area under the stoop. Entering an iron gate leads to a small vestibule in which one of Wolfe's clients was beaten to death in 1946. From that vestibule, a heavy door leads into the basement of the house which is three feet below street level. This area contains Fritz Brenner's living quarters (which face the street), bathroom, a storage room and a game room with a pool table. Since Wolfe considers playing billiards a form of exercise, the game room contains a raised bench and a large, comfortable chair suitable for supporting him when he must take breaks or where he can be petulant when Archie runs up a long string of balls. The storage room contains boxes of case records and Archie's old notebooks, and a table with an old doubled-up mattress under it that Archie has used for test firing guns. The mattress, or a replacement, is also used to cushion a bomb in 1969. From a central hallway, a staircase leads up to the upper floors of the house and another at the rear of the house leads up to a back door and a court yard in the rear of the house. Returning to the sidewalk and mounting the seven steps of the front stoop, one is confronted with a formidable front door which a few clients and witnesses, many murderers and countless law enforcement officers have wished to batter in over the years but none have. Eventually one did manage to blast the glass out of it with a bomb and a few have breached it by subterfuge but it has served pretty well as a barrier between the jungle and Wolfe's inner sanctum.

At eye level in the door is a glass panel covered by a curtain on the inside. It is through this glass that visitors are observed, identified and either admitted or refused entrance. Archie used to have to finger the curtain aside to peek out but in 1947 it was replaced with a pane of one-way glass to prevent the observed from that awareness. There is a chain bolt on the inside of the door that is evidently adjustable, allowing the door to be opened from one to five inches. The allowable gap was five inches in 1938, was reduced to two inches the next year after the house was subjected to the ignominy of a search warrant and went down to one inch after Lieutenant Rowcliff dragged Wolfe out of the house in 1952. Since those experiences, the door is treated like a raised drawbridge and is almost always kept locked and bolted. Archie usually answers the door during business hours unless otherwise occupied and when Fritz is preparing meals. Since his meal schedule is different, Fritz usually answers it when Wolfe and Archie are dining, when Archie is busy or when he's out. When Archie answers, you might get in and might not. If Fritz answers, it is nearly impossible to get in unless he knows you or you're expected. If Wolfe answers, God help you. This has only happened once in the recorded tales and the door was determinedly pushed shut on Inspector Cramer with the force of one seventh of a ton behind it. When Archie goes out, even after using his key when he returns, Fritz has to take the chain off to admit him. Archie usually rings the bell with two short buzzes and one long one to allay Fritz's suspicions when he returns.

Before we enter the house proper, a word is required here about dimensions and architectural floor plans. I considered including a floor plan of the first floor of Wolfe's house in this book but decided it was futile. In a 1963 magazine article, Stout said the house's exterior dimensions are 34 feet by 86 feet. I have invested some hours trying to create a floor plan that fits all the nuances of Rex Stout's descriptions and have consistently failed. A number of ingenious efforts are available at various websites on the Internet but none of the ones I've seen fit all the descriptions either. One suggested that "old Rex wasn't all that sharp on distances" which I think is a little dismissive of a man whose IQ was once estimated at "185 or better" and, in retrospect, whose life achievements would seem to bear out that estimate. Others have suggested that Stout's descriptions were "wrong"—Archie's desk can't be to Wolfe's right, it has to be to his left and so forth and so on. The upshot of it all, I believe, is that Rex Stout wasn't writing his descriptions from a set of architectural plans but from a vision in his mind. That vision stayed fairly consistent but fluctuated somewhat from time to time to meet artistic circumstances. I don't know if Stout ever envisioned that his creations, like those of Conan Doyle, would be subjected to having their surroundings held up to the specifics of reality but I suspect, if he did, he didn't give a damn. Hopefully, someone more architecturally gifted than I will come up with a solution one day.

On the other hand, I, for one, have no desire to try to imagine an octogenarian Wolfe giving instructions to an Archie in his late fifties. Perhaps just as a certain suspension of the passage of time and the agelessness of the lead characters is necessary to the enjoyment of the stories, a suspension in the belief in the inflexibility of feet and inches is necessary to a mental picture of the brownstone. I have no doubt it all fit together quite clearly in Rex Stout's mind.

But back to the brownstone. Push the doorbell and it rings in four places; in the kitchen, the office, Fritz's basement room and Archie's room on the third floor. It can be turned off in any of those places or silenced altogether if Wolfe is circling the wagons and hiding under the covers. If admitted, one would be faced with a wide hallway that runs most of the length of the house. In 1934 it is rubber-tiled but in later years it is carpeted. To the right of the doorway is a massive coat rack, eight feet long, with a mirror. In the early years it is made of oak. In 1951/1952 it is walnut but is usually referred to as oak. A stand for umbrellas and one or more of Wolfe's walking sticks stands next to it. The hallway is evidently wide enough to have a bench and several chairs placed in it since some are occasionally taken from there for large meetings in the office. One chair is directly across from the coat rack. That chair is four feet from the door on the left that leads into the front room.

Proceeding down the hallway, the first door on the right side leads into the dining room. Like all of the rooms, it is carpeted because Wolfe hates bare floors. It is a large room because he had the partition removed between two rooms to create it, thus it is forty feet long. True, that would make for a truly cavernous dining room especially when considering the rest of the information about Wolfe's preferences for entertaining guests but it's his house. Two windows face out onto the street. Naturally the dominating feature is the dining table, centered in the room. Although usually serving only Wolfe and Archie, it is large enough for six which Wolfe considers the maximum number practicable for good conversation at a meal but it can be extended to serve more. Wolfe sits at the head of the table with his back to the windows (admittedly unusual for a man in a profession where paranoia equals survivability) and Archie sits to his right, facing the hall door. There is a door at the other end of the room connecting to the kitchen. It isn't specified but I would expect there to be a sideboard where dishes are kept and orchids somewhere in the room.

Back to the hall and proceeding down the right side, one comes to the stairs leading to the upper floors. The stairs are carpeted and wide enough to allow two people to use them side by side (but not two Wolfe's—although that isn't a problem; the only time he has been known to use the stairs was in 1942 when he was energetically training to kill Germans in World War II).

Just beyond the stairs is the elevator that spares them the ravages of Wolfe's tonnage. It was installed before 1942 at a cost of $7,000 and was originally three feet by four feet. By 1960 it has grown to four feet by six feet and is rated safe for six hundred pounds which Archie probably considers an ominous portent for Wolfe's future caloric plans. The elevator serves the dwelling from the ground floor to the plant rooms and Wolfe uses it exclusively, the hum of its motor announcing his approach or ascension. On the occasions he descends to the basement, he must use the stairs that descend from the kitchen.

At the far end of the hall is a swinging door that leads into the kitchen. It covers the entire width of the rear of the house's ground floor with three windows on the south and one on the east. No doubt containing all the dishes, pots, pans, tools and accoutrements of a master chef, its central feature is a large table in the center of the room covered with linoleum. Fritz prepares the meals on this table. A smaller table by one of the windows is where Archie eats his breakfast and reads his newspaper propped up on a rack every morning. Fritz and Fred Durkin routinely eat there also as well as the other operatives when the occasion warrants. Several stools are scattered about as well as one of the chairs specially suited to Wolfe's dimensions. He likes to sit there and either collaborate with or kibitz at Fritz about the food. The room contains two refrigerators, one cool and one cold. There is a telephone extension there as well as a house phone on Archie's kitchen table that connects the kitchen, office, plant rooms and Wolfe's bedroom. On the west side of the room is a pantry that connects the kitchen to the dining room through another swinging door.

On a direct line from the kitchen door is the rear door of the house. Out the back door, a small porch and some steps lead down to the basement. The back yard of the house is a small courtyard surrounded by a solid board fence between seven and eight feet tall. This is the back way into the house.

From Thirty-Fourth Street and Eleventh Avenue, go east for 92 of Archie's paces and turn up a narrow passage between a loading platform on the left and a wholesale paper products business on the right. After exiting the passageway, twenty more paces bring you to the fence surrounding Wolfe's rear courtyard. Entering the gate after opening the Hotchkiss lock takes you down a brick walk between rows of chives, tarragon and other herbs Fritz grows there. At the rear of the house you can descend four steps into the basement or ascend a dozen steps to the kitchen's rear door. Clients and witnesses are occasionally smuggled into or out of the house by this route.

Returning to the viewpoint from the front entrance, the first doorway on the left of the hallway leads to the front room. This room is fairly small with two north windows facing out onto the street. The furnishings show that Wolfe uses the room only for temporarily warehousing business guests and doesn't give much of a damn about the décor. It contains at least five chairs (yellow, naturally), one of them a big one by a window. Also present are a sofa with six velvet pillows (one of which gets a bullet hole through it during the course of the adventures) that faces the hall door and has a speaker behind it wired to a microphone in the office. There is also a table between the two front windows, a vase on the table that contains orchids or it wouldn't be there, a bench and a piano. Wolfe apparently doesn't play, neither does Archie and Theodore's virtuosity extends only to botany. The piano is played by only two people; Fritz and Saul Panzer. Fritz's limited repertoire consists of three Chopin preludes, Debussy's *Golliwog's Cakewalk*, *Malbrouck s'en va-t-en guerre* and *Believe Me It All Those Endearing Young Charms*. Saul usually wings it with improvisations but has been known to play some Debussy on the piano in his own apartment. Two of Wolfe's less talented operatives passed the time by playing checkers in this room in 1935.

The front room has an adjoining door to the office and a door to a bathroom between both rooms. All the doors and walls on the ground floor are sound-proofed. Since Wolfe doesn't like open fires (like Rex Stout, he finds them distracting), the front room also contains the only fireplace in the house. The only recorded time Wolfe has made use of this feature was in 1962 when he grimly incinerated Webster's New International Dictionary, Unabridged, Third Edition, piecemeal for high crimes and misdemeanors against the English language.

The second door on the left side of the hallway leads to the office. While some might argue for the kitchen or the dining room or the plant rooms, this is the true center of Wolfe's universe because all of the activities in the aforementioned are made possible from this room. If any further argument need be made, on a normal day he spends about three hours in the dining room, four in the plant rooms and nine in the office. The only room that rivals it by that standard is the bedroom where he sleeps, eats breakfast, bathes and dresses, none of which bring in any money to fund the activities in the other rooms. By another standard, he keeps a few dozen favored books in his bedroom. He keeps 1200 in the office along with his dictionary, atlas, globe and favorite chair. I rest my case.

Wolfe would prefer never to leave his house but, as we shall see, some excursions are unavoidable. He also prefers to finish his cases by calling a gathering of all the principles, suspects, witnesses and, if he's in the mood, cops, solving the case in a grand final denouement at a time and place of his choosing. The preferred time is always when it doesn't interfere with meals, orchids or sleep and the preferred place is always his office. He manages this with remarkable regularity. In 54 of the 74 stories, this is how and where the case is solved.

The office is nearly square, at least twice as big as any other room on the first floor and it is just as well. When Wolfe starts staging one of his charades (as Cramer calls them) and operatives, clients, witnesses, suspects, cops and lawyers start filing in, things can get crowded. Complicating matters is the fact that in and around the brownstone occasionally becomes a crime scene. Gatherings of a dozen or more are commonplace. The largest, in 1953, found 27 people in the office at once when most of the Homicide Squad and their commanders were interviewing half a dozen suspects until 4 A.M. You can imagine Wolfe's joy.

For those entering the office for the first time under more relaxed circumstances, one of the things first noticed is probably the rug. Wolfe is a connoisseur of fine rugs as much as he is of food or books and is as knowledgeable about them. In 1962, Wolfe admires a fine Tekke and an Eighteenth Century Feraghan in Lucy Valdon's house. Persian and Armenian carpets are generally named for the city or region where they were produced. Tekkes are red Turkmenistan rugs from the southern USSR and are among the most highly prized by collectors. Feraghans are Persian rugs from the Arak district of northern Iran. Most use the Herati design, rosettes surrounded by diamonds with small palmettes at the points and curving, tapered, serrated leaves that resemble fishes around the sides. They are extremely fine rugs and priced accordingly. Current day prices are about $500 *a square foot.*

Like many other furnishings, the rug in Wolfe's office changes periodically although the dimensions, 14x26, are consistent which gives us at least a minimum size for the room. Wolfe's original rug is a Kerman in yellow (naturally) and red (fortunately, since it has a murderer's blood spilled on it in 1935). Kermans are produced in an area of Iran where the wool is noted for being very fine and velvety. Known for their floral designs, their predominant color is usually a soft, rosy red.

In 1956 the rug is a Feraghan. In 1961, a visitor to the office asks Wolfe if his rug is a Kazak and he tells them it is a Shirvan given to him in 1932 by a man in Cairo. Both are Armenian rugs. Kazaks are woven in the area between Tiflis and Erevan in the southern USSR, usually consisting of large scale patterns and bright contrasting colors. Shirvans are produced south of the Caucasus Mountains and are characterized by a relatively short pile and fine knotting. Usually produced in blue and ivory colors, they are not as bold as Kazaks. Wolfe was disdainful of his visitor for not knowing the difference, at least since she felt compelled to try to impress him by commenting on it. He also has a 15x11 Kashan rug in the South Room. From a city in north central Iran, most Kashans feature Judaic symbolism like kiddish cups, menorahs or Stars of David and are usually considered to be the most conservative of all Persian carpets. In 1969, he told an Assistant District Attorney the rug was a Keraghan and it was a gift from the Shah of Iran which Archie thinks is twaddle.

The walls are hung with a variety of objects that attest to the owner's range in tastes. There is an engraving of Anthelme Brillat-Savarin, the French gastronomist whose bust resides in Fritz's quarters. Some framed maps are there along with some reproductions of Hans Holbein The Younger (1497–1543), a German artist best known for his portraits of Sir Thomas More and King Henry VIII. The office wall also holds an iconoclastic trio of oil paintings; portraits of Socrates, William Shakespeare and one of an unwashed coal miner by the Hungarian artist Zoltan Sepeshy (1898–1974). Wolfe says they represent man's three primary resources—intellect, imagination and muscle. Not coincidentally, Rex Stout had three similar paintings in his home for the same reasons. The two latter ones were identical to Wolfe's but the portrait personifying intellect was of Albert Einstein rather than Socrates. There are several other items on the walls that we will cover in due course.

The doorway from the hallway into the office opens roughly in the middle of the room's west wall. To the right or north of the door, deep bookshelves cover both sections of the wall in the northwest corner. The room has high ceilings and the woodwork stretches all the way from the floor to the ceiling. There are movable steps for reaching the upper shelves. The shelves contain the bulk of Wolfe's library of about 1200 books. Interspersed with the bookshelves are cupboards and compartments. In these are kept back issues of the Times and the Gazette, for three days, five days or five weeks, the size of the collection varying over time. Other compartments contain magazines, cameras, rubber gloves to prevent leaving fingerprints and a fingerprint kit for those without the foresight to use rubber gloves. In 1954, the camera is a Veblex. In 1957 it is either replaced or joined by a Centrex that is primarily used for taking pictures of flowers because it sharply differentiates between the various shades of color but is occasionally drafted into the detective business. In 1974 it is a Verblex.

In front of the bookshelves on the hall wall in this corner is a large globe in a stand. It is one of the few made by Gouchard and cost $500. Like many other things, its size fluctuates somewhat. In most cases, it is referred to as being three feet in diameter. In 1946 it was two feet, in 1962 Wolfe tells a visitor it is 32 3/8 inches in diameter and in 1965 it is 35 ½ inches. Several straight backed chairs upholstered in yellow are next to the globe and at least one other that is adequate for Wolfe since he uses it sometimes. Although Wolfe uses the globe to locate specific places, he will occasionally stand at it and absently turn it. Archie says that at these times, he is looking for places he wishes he were other than in the office. A table with a telephone on it is next to the globe. It usually has magazines on it but is also sometimes used as a sideboard when Wolfe's office guests are being served drinks.

At other times Archie stocks a portable cart covered with a yellow linen tablecloth in the kitchen and wheels it into the office for gatherings. Wolfe yields the hospitality of his home grudgingly but, once offered, it is not niggardly. Since he hates for a guest to ask for anything he doesn't have on hand, these carts are well supplied. At these occasions, Wolfe also insists that his guests have small stands or tables at their elbows.

Also on the hall wall is a two-ton safe. After opening the outer door, the inner door has a four-way combination known only to Archie and Wolfe. It is usually left unlocked when Archie is in the office but is always locked when he is not. Once opened, the safe drawer is partitioned in the center. A small amount of petty cash is kept on the right side and an emergency reserve of $5000 in cash in used tens, twenties and hundreds is kept on the left. A cash withdrawal book is kept in there where Archie and Wolfe record the cash given to Archie and the other operatives for business expenses. Wolfe also keeps a locked metal box in there which he has the only key to and its contents are unknown to Archie. Archie caught Wolfe once with the box open on his desk but he immediately put something back in it and shut the lid. Archie assumed it was mementos of Wolfe's youth but we shall never know.

The bathroom that serves both the office and the front room is situated in the northeast corner of the office with doors exiting into both rooms. The door that provides the office entrance to the bathroom faces the hall. A wide, well-cushioned couch that will comfortably seat four rests against the south outer wall of the bathroom. It is upholstered in yellow and as a result, has to be cleaned about every two months. Sometimes it has to be cleaned more often. In 1946, a man died rather memorably on that couch.

The office's east wall has two windows with yellow drapes. Facing the east wall is Archie's desk. When Archie is facing his desk, Wolfe's desk is eight feet to his right and at a right angle to it. Archie has to swivel his chair a ninety-degree quarter-turn to face him or a one-hundred-eighty degree half-turn to face the hall door or someone in front of Wolfe's desk. In 1957, Archie mentions that his swivel chair cost $139.95. He mentions it in the context that Wolfe's chair cost $650.

On Archie's desk are a desk lamp, a telephone and a faded, scuffed and scarred red leather box in which he keeps postage stamps. That red box, ten inches by four inches and two inches deep, was the subject of the 1936 case by the same name. Also on the desk is a jade ashtray six inches across which was a gift from a grateful client to him—not to Wolfe, to *him*. It is seldom used by 1957.

In the middle drawer on the right side, Archie keeps his weapons, usually two guns that belong to Wolfe and one that belongs to Archie. Ammunition, a shoulder holster and gun cleaning supplies are kept in the back of the drawer. The guns are kept unloaded until he readies them for use. Wolfe personally dislikes and fears guns but accepts their presence in his home only because he recognizes their occasional necessity in his chosen profession, although not in his hands. All in all, a remarkable example of adherence to principle for a man who has been shot at least three times. Or perhaps a reversal of attitude for a man who used guns to shoot some cruel, misguided people in his earlier years.

In the bottom right hand drawer Archie keeps small miscellaneous tools like a hammer and screwdriver. He also keeps unspecified personal items in that drawer. He also keeps maps of all five New York City boroughs in his desk.

His original desk apparently had a collapsible leaf to hold the typewriter so it could be concealed when not in use. Later he placed it on a portable stand with wheels so it could be rolled into place when needed and moved aside when idle. Although unspecified, it was probably a manual Underwood if he follows the inclination of Rex Stout in that as in so many other things.

Some descriptions have Archie's desk in front of one of the two windows on the east wall. Others have things hanging on the wall above his desk. Perhaps his desk sits between the two windows, providing both a view out of them and a place above it to hang things.

In the early years, Archie has a portrait of Sherlock Holmes above his desk. Other authors have tried to draw some implications from that. I won't speculate on their speculations but will refer you to their works in the bibliography and let you do your own speculating. Rex Stout once wrote a non-committal reply to the Holmesian society of The Baker Street Irregulars on that speculation although it seemed to me to be with tongue firmly in cheek. By the mid-1960's, the portrait had been replaced with a mirror so Archie could watch the office door and most of the office behind him when he was facing his desk. In 1967 it was four feet high and five feet wide. By 1969 it was six feet wide. At first, Archie would also use it for straightening his tie and combing his hair but a few snorts of derision from Wolfe at his vanity reduced him to using it to keep an eye on people.

In the southwest corner of the office, on the south wall is a tier of shelves containing odds and ends along with mementos of past cases. Among these souvenirs are a couple of pieces of shrapnel, black on one side and pink on the other, from an H14 hand grenade that killed an Army Military Intelligence colonel in 1943 and a letter to a U.S. Congressman.

Along the hall or west wall in that corner are filing cabinets. These contain case files, germination records for the orchids and a drawer with a wide selection of keys that Archie and the other operatives periodically use to get past locks to discover people's secrets. On top of the filing cabinets are two vases that contain pussy willows in the springtime.

On the south office wall towards the east side is the center of the center of the universe—Wolfe's desk. It is made of arcwood, a Brazilian hardwood. In 1933 it has only one drawer—a shallow wide lap drawer in which Wolfe keeps only his eighteen-carat gold beer opener and the bottle caps from keeping count of his beer intake. By 1957, his desk sits flat on the floor, there is no space under it and it has more drawers—a middle drawer, three on the left side and four on the right. The drawers contain the oilstone he uses to sharpen the penknife he always carries and rarely uses but he sharpens it once a week regardless. The drawers also contain a paper knife for slitting envelopes and a large magnifying glass.

The desk is covered with memorabilia. A paperweight of petrified wood that was once used to bust a guy's skull makes its debut in 1934. It remains a constant feature and in 1957 is joined by a second, similar paperweight, a chunk of jade used by a woman to crack her husband's skull. A vase with the daily orchids is at Wolfe's right on the desk. After 1954, he used a horn-handled knife that was thrown at him in Albania as a letter opener. Others items include a French telephone, a desk blotter, a scratch pad, pen and his desk lamp.

There are five chairs in the house that are specially built and rated up to 500 pounds (which Archie says is not utterly beyond the limits of possibility). They are in Wolfe's bedroom, the kitchen, the plant rooms, the dining room and the office. But the one in the office is special even among them. In the early years it is made of polished mahogany but by 1957 it is of Brazilian Mauro wood. This is the one that cost $650. It is a high-backed swivel chair with a headrest and is upholstered in brown leather. It is the only chair on earth that he's really comfortable in. In the southeast corner is a wastebasket and at that corner of the desk is a stand that contains his dictionary.

Insofar as possible, Wolfe has also turned the desk into a remote control center. The office contains a radio cabinet and, by 1955, a television. There are buttons on the desk that allow Wolfe to control both from his chair. He likes to push the button that cuts the radio off when the commentator says something that irritates him. In the early days his favorite radio program was the Joy Boys which Archie thought was vulgar. Archie likes to watch New York Giants baseball games on the television but Wolfe doesn't have a favorite program. He likes to watch it for a few minutes, condemn whatever's on (silently or verbally) and turn it off. He especially likes turning it off on Sunday evenings. There is also a buzzer on the desk that alerts Fritz in the kitchen to bring beer.

In the later years, they submitted to new technology to a degree. In 1961 there was a switch on the wall between Archie's desk and the wall. The switch activated a concealed microphone near the red leather chair that recorded the chair's occupants' words on a recorder kept in a cupboard in the kitchen. There was also a speaker in the office for playing the tape back. In 1969 there was a miniature camera in a fake jar of pencils on Archie's desk. They used it to uncover a client's fake identity.

They also used these new technologies outside of the office. One of the most elaborate instances was in John Piotti's restaurant on Fourteenth Street between Second and Third Avenues. A bowl of artificial flowers on a table was wired with a microphone while Stebbins and Archie listened to Zoltan Mahaney trying to blackmail suspects one at a time.

There are five yellow chairs in the office but the best and most comfortable chair (excluding Wolfe's) is the red leather one situated diagonally to the left front of his desk, four feet from the corner. It is deep enough that short people cannot scoot all the way back in it. In 1936 Archie nicknamed it The Dunce's Chair because that was where Westchester County District Attorney Anderson sat when Wolfe made a dunce of him.

Whoever is sitting in that chair is obviously in charge of the gathering, yielding only to Wolfe. It is usually reserved for paying clients but, left to his own devices, Archie has been known to decorate it with the most attractive woman of a group unless he chooses to seat her nearer to his desk. Wolfe has been known to displace people from it for Inspector Cramer, who favors it during his visits. Archie thinks the office furniture should be rearranged because on those occasions when Wolfe imperiously rises and stalks out on someone, he has to detour around the red leather chair and Archie thinks that ruins the drama of the exit.

A small table is situated to the right of the red leather chair. It is made of massandruba wood, a Brazilian hardwood also known as bullet wood because it is so hard that iron nails would bend when trying to hammer them into it. It is perfectly placed for people to write checks on, preferably checks with a lot of zeros.

The table also contains an ashtray. Archie finally quit smoking after about twenty years, Wolfe doesn't smoke and cannot abide a dirty ashtray. He has been known to walk all the way to the office bathroom to empty one personally. Nevertheless he allows smoking in the office, by certain people under certain circumstances. He hates pipes and screws up his face when someone lights a cigar, preparing for the assault on his nostrils. His forbearance occasionally has a business connection, however. In 1945, the way a client handled a cigar convinced Wolfe that the man was not what he said he was.

Predating the new technology for eavesdropping, Archie and Wolfe made do in simpler ways. As early as 1938, there was a triple-sectioned panel on the left hall wall, three paces toward the kitchen from the office door. Outwardly it was a wood carving but the two side sections were hinged. The right section swung out and there was a peephole into the office. Archie has to stoop slightly because it is drilled at the level of Wolfe's eyes. The peephole is camouflaged on the office side with two little apertures backed by gauze. By World War II, it is replaced with a peephole behind a picture to the right or hall side of Wolfe's desk. It may be four feet to the right, or eight feet or fifteen feet but it is to the right, from the perspective of someone facing the desk. The hole is approached through an alcove off of the hallway on the way to the kitchen. I realize this conflicts somewhat with the two windows that Rex Stout places behind Wolfe's desk at one point but—see the part about suspending belief in feet and inches. The hole is covered on the alcove side by a metal panel that slides open noiselessly. Someone sitting in the red leather chair is about ten feet from someone peering through the peephole.

On the office side, the peephole is covered by a 14x17-inch oil painting of a waterfall. It has been mistaken for an unsigned Van Gogh but was actually painted for Wolfe by a grateful former client named McIntyre. In 1943, it was apparently temporarily replaced by a more patriotic picture of the Washington Monument but after the war, the waterfall returned.

The peephole gets lots of use. Among many other occasions, Cramer used it in 1951, 1955 and 1957, Stebbins used it in 1953, and Wolfe used it in 1944, 1960 and 1961. Amy Denovo used it in 1967 to find out who her real father was and Wolfe used it to keep Archie from getting shot in the back. Archie once stood there for three hours recording Wolfe's conversation with an embezzler.

There are eight lights in the office—one in the ceiling above a big bowl of banded oriental alabaster, one on the wall behind Wolfe's chair, one on his desk, one on Archie's desk, one flooding the big globe and three for the book shelves. There is a clock on the east wall almost at a right angle to Wolfe's desk but he will rarely exert the effort to turn his head to look at it if he can ask Archie the time.

As late as 1941, the house was not air conditioned because of Wolfe's distrust of machinery. He later relented and, by 1967, he wants to know how long it will take it to get rid of the stench of a cigar.

Leaving the office, we may proceed up the stairs to the second floor. Only two rooms are on this floor. The front bedroom has its own bathroom and two windows that face out on Thirty-Fifth Street. For the first few adventures this was Archie's room but he later moves up to the front room on the third floor. This room is then unoccupied and used mostly for storage.

Six paces down the hallway from the stairwell is Wolfe's bedroom. It extends to the rear of the house and has windows on the south wall so he gets the sun in the winter. It also has some automated security features. There is a switch in the room that, when Wolfe activates it, sounds a gong under the head of Archie's bed on the third floor if anyone steps within a certain distance of Wolfe's door or touches any of his windows during the night. At one point, the crucial distance was five feet but increased to eight feet by 1936 and ten feet by 1944. Archie tells us that the gong was installed because Wolfe got a knife stuck in him once. Like Rex Stout, Wolfe likes to leave his windows open at night for fresh air year round but by 1948, he has a contraption installed that automatically closes them at 6:00 A.M. He wants a warm room for breakfast.

The central feature is undoubtedly the bed. Although not specified, we can probably assume it is king-size. It has a double mattress, a black headboard and a low footboard of streaky anselmo, yellowish with sweeping dark brown streaks. The linen, sheets and pillowcases are invariably yellow and it is covered with a black silk coverlet. The bed is enclosed on all three sides by a black canopy controlled by a cord on the right side of the bed.

There is a bedside table with a clock on it. At one time his yellow telephone was on a table by one of the windows because Wolfe refused to concede the possibility that he would ever be willing to talk on the phone while in bed but it seems to have later moved to his bedside table. Apparently he conceded. When Archie goes to bed, he flips a switch that allows the phone to ring only in his room. If Archie leaves during the night, he flips another switch that allows it to ring in both Wolfe's and Fritz's rooms.

Another clock is on one wall. One of his special chairs, this one covered in tapestry, is on one wall with a strong reading lamp next to it. Another table is in front of one of the windows. This is where Wolfe eats his breakfast promptly at 8:15 every morning while reading the newspaper. For his other reading, a set of bookshelves holds a few dozen of his favorites, among them a set of Casanova's *Memoirs*.

Up one more flight to the third floor, this floor also has two bedrooms. The front or north room is Archie's since his move after the early years and the guest bedroom, directly above Wolfe's room, is called the South Room. Leaving the stairwell, you turn left to the South Room and right to Archie's room, which presupposes that the stairs open from the east side of the hall on that floor.

Archie furnished his room himself and owns everything in it including the furniture and the pictures on the walls. It has a big bed and the gong alarm from Wolfe's security system is on the wall under the head of the bed. There are three roomy, comfortable chairs including one with a reading lamp and a tile-top table next to it. There is a radio on the table and the entire room is carpeted because Archie doesn't want rugs to slide on. Nevertheless, as long as they don't slide, Archie has apparently acquired some of Wolfe's appreciation for fine rugs because he has a Kirman there, eight feet four inches by three feet two inches. During a case, he admires a similar one twice as big in Otis Jarrell's home.

Other furnishings include a desk with plenty of drawer space and a personal typewriter, presumably the manual Underwood upon which he acts as Wolfe's Watson. The pictures on the walls include one of Mount Vernon, a colored one of a lion's head, another colored one of woods with grass and flowers, and a framed photograph of his parents. There are some bookshelves upon which Archie keeps a few books, one of which is *Here and Now* by Herbert Block. Wolfe asks him to retrieve that book from his room in 1957 but he doesn't really want the book, he just wants Archie to see what's lying on top of it. It isn't mentioned whether the book belongs to Archie or Wolfe although we have seen that Wolfe allows Archie to borrow from his library. Archie's room has a private bathroom and a copy of the French artist Paul Chabas's (1869–1937) painting of *September Morn* is on the wall. Rex Stout owned one once and, considering the amount of unmerited "anti-pornography" furor it stirred up in the early part of the century, it was probably symbolic of his opinions against artistic censorship in all its forms.

Nero Wolfe, like all free men and much more than most, believes his home is his castle and takes it very literally as that. On many occasions, it has been much like a castle, it has been a fortress and that has been a benefit to many of his clients. The old brownstone's façade has protected more than a few of them not only from the elements of weather but from elements of the law seeking them. It has even saved the lives of a few of them by shielding them from plots against them.

When a guest stays in Wolfe's home, for any reason, they stay in the South Room, the rear bedroom on the third floor, directly above Wolfe's room and directly behind Archie's. The first recorded incident like this occurred in the third book set in 1935. Clara Fox became the first woman in many years to spend the night under Wolfe's roof but she was far from the last.

Other guests have included Mrs. Floyd Whitten, Phoebe Landy, Rose Lasher, Amy Duncan, Selma Molloy, Madame Zorka, a woman who had poisoned three husbands and was making a fourth very sick, a Secretary of State, a petty thief, a woman who intended to shoot Archie in the back, reluctant witnesses, frightened clients, clients who weren't smart enough to be frightened and one who was murdered in that room. By 1952, at least four murderers have slept there.

It is a large room with its own private bathroom and twin beds. In the early years, there are two windows on the south wall but that becomes three windows by 1974. The two end windows are usually kept open about five inches with the center one shut, locked and draped. A fire escape traverses the rear of the building and is accessible through the left window in the South Room. The fire escape also goes by one of the windows in Wolfe's bedroom, an especially touchy situation after one reluctant witness uses it to abscond.

The room is carpeted and also has a fifteen by eleven foot Kashan rug. A bookshelf holds several books for the occupant's diversion when they don't decide to run away. An armchair, a dresser and a mirror complete the room. A telephone is on a table but it can be switched on or off from remote locations like all the other phones in the house. In keeping with Wolfe's hospitality, the room is supplied with fresh orchids when occupied.

By 1966, the South Room is also supplied with something more in Wolfe's interest than the occupant's. It is bugged with the same system that records in the office and uses the same machine hidden in a kitchen cupboard. Wolfe uses the new system to eavesdrop on Inspector Cramer and a witness.

Returning to the stairwell, a slightly steeper flight of stairs ascends to the roof. The series of plant rooms are entered through an aluminum door. In the first story, Fritz lives in a room across from the plant rooms but soon moves to the basement which undoubtedly has more room and is more convenient to his work area in the kitchen.

There are three main plant rooms kept at different conditions of temperature and humidity for the different types of orchids in their various stages. The order of the rooms changes periodically. In 1933 in the first story, the front plant room is the "sun room". By 1950, the rooms are, in order as you enter from the stairs or elevator, the warm, medium and cool rooms. In 1958, they are cool, tropical and intermediate. The next year, they're moderate, tropical and cool. By 1961, they're cool, medium and tropical. This last arrangement lasts through the end of the series fourteen years later.

The rooms have narrow aisles lined with silver-painted angle-iron staging and concrete benches that display Wolfe's ten thousand orchids. The rooms have a special spraying system invented by Theodore Horstmann. After the three main rooms is a potting room with a long potting bench, a spraying chamber and a sink. In this room is Wolfe's special chair and the house telephone. Theodore has a small desk here and keeps some pet parakeets but Wolfe forbids him to teach them to talk. The potting room can also be used as a fumigation room because it is supplied with a system using poisonous ciphogene gas, a function that is utilized in one of the cases although not as originally planned.

A storage room for supplies and Theodore's bedroom and bathroom in one corner complete the floor. The plant rooms are all glassed in except for the potting room and Theodore's living area. The inside of the glass has shade slats that can be rolled up or down to control the amount of sunlight allowed to enter. All this is not cheap. When the plant rooms are machine-gunned into splinters in 1950, the repairs cost $40,000.

Speaking of repairs, perhaps we should address who does the housekeeping in this imposing residence. Doubtlessly each of the individual residents is relatively neat in their personal habits (Wolfe wouldn't tolerate anything less) and Archie, in particular, says he was "born neat." Both of them are uniformly natty in their appearance and no doubt Fritz and Theodore dress presentably in accordance with their specific duties. Therefore each resident probably assumes responsibility for the general cleanliness of their individual living areas. The "clutter" of Fritz's magazines and cookbooks may be interpreted here as a certain lack of systemized organization or disorderliness (except in his mind) rather than a lack of cleanliness. Nevertheless, dust, grit and grime accumulates in the residence just from the act of being occupied. It is full of valuable possessions, intrinsically as well as sentimentally to their individual owners. In one of the later cases, Wolfe is sending the office rug out to be cleaned as he undoubtedly does with the others in the house. The yellow couch in the office is regularly cleaned every few months. One can't imagine Wolfe pulling a book from a shelf, regardless of how long it may have rested there between readings, and a film of dust staining his fingers as he caresses the cover.

Archie voluntarily assumes responsibility for the perfunctory cleaning of the office on a daily basis. This is almost certainly merely an extension of his personal idiosyncrasy of not being able to stand a "messy desk." Theodore doubtlessly assumes the same responsibility for the plant rooms as Fritz must for the kitchen and probably the dining room.

In 1946, Charley the cleaning man makes a brief, single appearance in the saga and is never mentioned again. Stout later told an inquisitive interviewer that Charley had stolen an orchid and been fired (with extreme prejudice, no doubt).

The only other specific mention in this regard is in 1969 when Wolfe has three janitors from the Midtown Home Service Corporation come in to clean the house on a weekly basis. Naturally he has specified that his janitors be male personnel only but, in that year, a black female is slipped in due to staffing problems. Remarkably, there is no eruption as a result.

The Literate Wolfe

Nero Wolfe is a heavy reader, no pun intended unless you insist. In this respect, he again follows his creator. Rex Stout was a prodigy by any standard. He came from a family of readers, was given complete access to his father's prodigious library and made the most of that advantage.

Stout began reading at the age of *eighteen months*. Before he even began formal education, he was reading Macaulay's *Essays* and had begun delving into the five volumes of his *History of England From The Ascension Of James The Second*. Eventually he read all 1,126 (he never forgot the number) of his father's books. While his classmates were reading Dick and Jane primers, Stout was reading Gibbons, Twain, Dickens, Kipling, Alcott, Bacon, Emerson, Plutarch, Scott, Cooper, Dumas, Stevenson, Hugo, Defoe and dozens of others. He read all of Shakespeare's plays, memorized all his sonnets and could recite them verbatim for the next eight decades.

William S. Baring-Gould hypothesizes that Wolfe is a primarily self-educated man and, considering his progenitor, that seems a quite logical conclusion. No diplomas are displayed and not once has he alluded to an academic achievement or mentioned a fond remembrance of a former teacher. From what we are told of his adventurous youth, his personality and his idiosyncrasies, he hardly seems the type to easily mold himself into a rigidly structured schedule of classes, prerequisites and major courses of study. Like another great detective from the other side of the Atlantic Ocean, if Wolfe is interested in something, he's interested but if he isn't, he's totally disinterested. To the average man, and even the above average, the only thing as profound as Wolfe's knowledge is the gaps in it. He is totally oblivious to the fact that a client's alias was made up from two of the stars of the World Champion 1969 New York Mets until Archie enlightens him. He lives in the largest city in the world but has to ask Archie if the U.S. Secret Service has a branch office there.

Archie also says it is debatable whether Wolfe loves food or words more. He even treats them similarly sometimes. When reading the reports of Archie and his operatives, letters from international orchid-hunters and other business-related paperwork, Wolfe is a relatively fast reader. But when he reads for pleasure, as is most often the case, he doesn't gorge. Then he reads much slower, slower than Archie in fact. But he remembers what he reads, in perpetuity it would seem.

Wolfe always has a book he is currently reading and frequently as many as three at the same time. He takes turns with them, reading 20-30 pages in each before switching to another. Archie thinks it's ostentatious but I submit that he may not have thought that one through all the way.

There is no denying Wolfe has formidable powers of concentration when he chooses to apply them and there is certainly no evidence that he suffers from an attention deficit disorder. Only once, in 1954, has he quit a satisfactory book without finishing it and it took the death of someone close to him to cause that disruption. Again only once, in 1959, has he been so perplexed by a problem that he couldn't concentrate on his current book. Nevertheless, I can see several alternate explanations for Wolfe's reading habits that would seem to make more sense than merely showing off for Archie. It may be that he is resting those powers of concentration by using them in short bursts. It may also be that he is lightly flexing them like a toning exercise for a muscle. Or it may be that he is merely humoring the attention span of a self-indulgent man, which he admits to being.

Be that as it may, Wolfe reads about 200 books every year. Therefore he probably finishes a book every other day. He doesn't, however, feel compelled to waste his time or energy by finishing every one. If he deems a book unworthy during the reading, he is not above casting it aside immediately regardless of whether he is one page or one hundred pages into the work.

Another study in individuality are Wolfe's bookmarks. He may dog-ear the pages of a book, he may use a piece of paper from a notepad on his desk or he may use a custom bookmark. In 1936 he uses a thin strip of ebony and no history behind it is given. In 1952 he uses a counterfeit ten-dollar bill autographed in red ink by a former Secretary of the Treasury "for services rendered." No history is given for it either but it is not from the *Counterfeit For Murder* case which occurs five years later. Predating the counterfeit bill, however, and long outlasting it is Wolfe's favorite bookmark. It is a thin strip of gold, an inch wide and five inches long. It was a gift from an unspecified but grateful client who couldn't afford it but gave it in spite of the size of his bill.

Wolfe's current book (or books) is always on the right edge of his desk pad in front of the vase of orchids. Always honing his powers of observation and deduction, Archie has developed a method for grading Wolfe's opinion of his books and, by extension, the authors. The method depends upon Wolfe's actions when he comes down from the plant rooms at 6 P.M. every evening (except Sundays). He is parched from his two hours of labor over the orchids and, if not being pestered to solve a murder, has two hours before dinner. Therefore he needs beer and without doubt, between 6 and 6:05 P.M., Fritz is poised in front of a refrigerator in the kitchen waiting for the buzzer to signal that the resident camel is ready for his break-thirst. If Wolfe doesn't start reading until the beer has arrived, he has poured it and has marked his place by dog-earing the page, the book is a "D". If he rings for beer but starts reading the book before the beer arrives and the page is dog-eared, it's a "C". If he starts reading before he rings for beer and his place is marked with a piece of paper, it's a "B". If he starts reading before he rings for beer and his place is marked by the gold bookmark, it's an "A". Of the 200 or so he reads every year, no more than half a dozen get an "A". "A" books usually get a permanent place on the office shelves and he will not dog-ear their pages.

Wolfe buys his books from Murger's, probably not only because of their comprehensive selection (without which they would certainly lose his patronage) but also because they deliver and maintain a charge account for him.

Below is a list of the books that Wolfe has been known to read over the years of the Wolfe saga. Naturally this only includes those books mentioned in the series which is only the tip of the iceberg. The list also tells us what Rex Stout was reading at the time. Since books occasionally become part of the plots of the stories, fictional authors and books are marked with an asterisk (*). Comments are provided where appropriate.

> 1933—A book on South American vipers (Wolfe doesn't have this book in his library and has to send Archie to the public library for it)
> 1934—A book from Czechoslovakia with pictures of snowflakes
> *Devil Take The Hindmost* by Paul Chapin*
> *Iron Heel* by Paul Chapin*
> Three other books by Paul Chapin*
> *The Native's Return* by Louis Adamic (This book gave Rex Stout the idea to make Wolfe a Montenegrin. Adamic, a personal friend, told him that Montenegrin men were notoriously lazy. Thus…)
> *Outline of Human Nature* by Alfred Rossiter
> *The Chasm of the Mind* by Andrew Hibbard*
> 1935—*Metropolitan Biographies* (all years available)
> 1936—*Seven Pillars of Wisdom* by T.E. Lawrence (Re-reading it for the third time)
> 1937—*Inside Europe* by John Gunther
> 1938—*United Yugoslavia* by Henderson
> 1943—*Under Cover* by John Roy Carlson

1946—*Modern Crime Detection* by a university psychologist named Gottlieb. (Probably a "D". Wolfe says every intelligent criminal should send a copy to every detective he knows)

1947—*The Sudden Guest* by Christopher La Farge

Love From London by Gilbert Gabriel

A Survey of Symbolic Logic by C.I. Lewis (dog-eared)

1948—A book of poetry by Mark Van Doren

1949—An unnamed book by Laura Z. Hobson

1951—A book of lyrics by Oscar Hammerstein

1952—*Pilgrims Progress* and *Essays of Ella* (Not currently reading these two books but both are present in his library)

1953—*Mathematics For The Millions* by Lancelot Hogben

1954—*But We Were Born Free* by Elmer Davis

1955—*Beauty For Ashes* by Christopher La Farge

Party of One by Clifton Fadiman

The Letters of Dorothy Osborne to Sir William Prince

Power and Policy by Thomas K. Finletter

1956—*The Fall* by Albert Camus

A Secret Understanding by Merle Miller

1957—*Here and Now* by Herbert Block

1958—*World Peace Through World Law* by Grenville Clark and Louis B. Sohn

1959—*Why The Gods Laugh* by Phillip Harvey*

1960—*An Outline of Man's Knowledge of the Modern World* edited by Lyman Bryson

Inside Russia Today by John Gunther

The Rise and Fall of the Third Reich by William Shirer

1961—*The Lotus and the Robot* by Arthur Koestler

My Life In Court by Louis Nizer

The Coming Fury by Bruce Catton

1962—*African Genesis* by Robert Ardrey

His Own Image by Richard Valdon* (An "A")

Never Dream Again by Richard Valdon* (Lower than a "D". Wolfe gave it to a library)

Travels with Charley by John Steinbeck

Silent Spring by Rachel Carson

1964—*The Minister and the Choir Singer* by William Kunstler

William Shakespeare by A.L. Rowse

The Group by Mary McCarthy (Wolfe read two chapters and ditched it)
Science: The Glorious Entertainment by Jacques Barzun
Wolfe also quotes the economist Thorstein Veblen during this year.
1965—*The FBI Nobody Knows* by Fred Cook
The Treasures of Our Tongue by Lincoln Barnett
1966—*Invitation to an Inquest* by Walter and Miriam Schneir
The Jungle Book by Rudyard Kipling (A re-read)
1967—*Incredible Victory* by Walter Lord
The Future of Germany by Karl Jaspers
1968—*Man's Rise To Civilization As Shown By The Indians Of North America From Primeval Times To The Coming Of The Industrial State* by Peter Farb
The First Circle by Alexander Solzhenitsyn
1969—*The History of Human Marriage* by Westernarck
Grant Takes Command by Bruce Catton
1974—*The Palace Guard* by Dan Rather and Gary Gates
Special Report by Herblock
The European Discovery Of America: The Southern Voyages A.D.1492–1616 by Samuel Eliot Morison

Since Nero Wolfe reads what Rex Stout reads and their literary opinions coincide, we now know more details about the extent of Wolfe's reading habits and the contents of his library.

In 1934, he has a volume of *The Shepheardes Calendar* by Edmund Spenser (1552–1599) on the office shelves to the right of the hall door. Printed in London, it was bound in dark blue, tooled leather in New York City "by a Swedish boy who will probably starve to death during the coming winter."

As a companion to his globe, Wolfe has a Gouchard Atlas (the finest to be had) and uses it frequently. Archie sits back and observes him with bemusement as Wolfe mentally scales the heights of Mount Everest or hacks his way through the jungles of Burma seeking orchids.

In 1946, a vital clue is hidden on one of the bottom shelves behind a dozen bound volumes of the *Lindenia*. If you are as ignorant of the implications of this as I was, here's help. The *Lindenia* is a multi-volume iconography of orchids published by J. Linden, L. Linden and R.A. Rolfe between 1885 and 1906. It contains hundreds of large color plates of orchids.

Wolfe never demeans anyone's religion or spiritual beliefs but he does not attend church and has not been known to pray during the adventures (although we are not privy to all that is going on behind those eyes when he has them closed). Like Rex Stout, he is an agnostic. Stout said in an interview that the only thing he had faith in was the idea of American democracy. Nevertheless, in 1961 Wolfe has five versions of the Bible in four languages on the second shelf from the top near the end of his bookshelves. By 1969, he has nine Bibles, four English versions and five in foreign languages. If he is like his creator, and we have seen that in many ways he is, Wolfe has read the Bible from cover to cover at least twice. Rex Stout admitted that, unlike Wolfe, he was limited to the English version.

Wolfe keeps a copy of Montaigne's *Essays* in his bedroom. He owns at least one volume by the French writer and philosopher Francois Voltaire (1694–1778). He owns four translations of Homer's *The Iliad* including one by Edward Fitzgerald (1809–1883). Complete sets of the works of William Shakespeare and the Encyclopedia Britannica are well worn. Also available are:

Histories by Polybius (205–125 B.C.)

Colloquies by Desiderius Erasmus (1466–1536)

The Works of Existentialism edited by Maurice Freedman (dog-eared)

My People by Abba Eban

History of England From The Ascension Of James The Second by Thomas Macauley (1800–1859)

Gilbert Murray's translation of Euripides

Your Mirror To My Times by Ford Madox Ford

Fable of Man by Mark Twain

Plain Speaking: An Oral Biography of Harry S. Truman by Merle Miller

All God's Dangers: The Life of Nate Shaw by Theodore Rosengarten (This book is listed in other works as "*All God's Dangers* by Nat Shaw". I can find no record of any such book but the listed book seems to fit the necessary parameters.)

Coleridge On Shakespeare

Emma by Jane Austen

A 1975 biography of Samuel Johnson

Some of the works of the Russian novelist Ivan Sergeyevich Turgenev (1818–1883). (He doesn't dog-ear them)

And he is re-reading some of the works of the French critic

Charles Augustin Sainte-Beuve (1804–1869).

Among the more mundane tools of his profession, the bottom shelves also contain telephone books for all five New York City boroughs, Westchester County, Washington, D.C. and seven others.

There are about 600,000 words in the English language. Researchers have estimated that the average American adult has an active vocabulary of 10,000-20,000 words that they normally use in speaking and writing. If words that are recognized and understood but not normally used are included, the number goes up to between 30,000-40,000. Seems like a terrible waste, doesn't it? If most of us use or understand less than ten per cent of those words, why do we have the extra half million-plus?

Nero Wolfe is one of those reasons. He uses many of those extra words. It would be an extraordinary Wolfe reader who hasn't been driven to consult a dictionary at least once during the process of reading the works. Speaking of dictionaries, Wolfe venerates them—at least Webster's New International Dictionary, Unabridged, Second Edition. He keeps a leather-bound edition on a stand at one corner of his desk where he can consult it by merely swiveling his chair on those rare occasions when he is confronted with a word that is unfamiliar. He has worn out three editions and is working on a fourth.

Wolfe's veneration is not reserved for dictionaries but extends to all books, at least in the sense of what their physical form represents for him. When he picks one up, he gently, lovingly caresses the cover with his palm before he opens it. As we have seen, once opened, the book's contents come under more critical scrutiny and its sanctity may even be threatened.

Wolfe is picky about words. Sometimes he takes action on his criticisms. He has been known to use Webster's Third Edition for kindling because it "threatened the integrity of the English language." He called it an *auto-da-fe'* which compelled me to learn that it is a Portuguese phrase meaning literally "act of faith" and was used during the Spanish Inquisition as a euphemism for the punishment of heretics. He once burned a cookbook because of its treatment of a recipe for ham and lima beans. In 1966, Wolfe expunged a copy of Sir Thomas More's *Utopia* from his shelves after concluding that More had framed Richard III for the murders of Edward V and his brother, the Duke of York, in the Fifteenth Century.

When Wolfe isn't working or reading, he does difficult crossword puzzles. He likes the Double-Crostic in the New York Times, the one by Ximenes in The London Observer and the one in The London Times. He consistently subscribes to The New York Times, the Gazette and occasionally the Star. They get three copies of each, one for Wolfe, one for Archie and one for Fritz. At one time, back copies of the papers were kept in the office for three days. By 1956, they keep a five-week file of them in a cupboard below the bookshelves. In 1974, Wolfe keeps a month's worth of the Times in his bedroom.

In 1935, he forbids Archie to use the words "louse" or "unquote" and upbraided him once for using "tantrum" as a verb. Wolfe has chastised him for saying "ad" instead of "advertisement", "newscast" as an abbreviated version of "news broadcast", "lulu" as a vulgarization of the word "allure" and strongly disapproves of him calling Doctor Vollmer "Doc". He refuses to allow the word "contact" to be used as a verb in his presence with impunity. Johnny Keems did it once and, when corrected, compounded his error by trying to get Wolfe to see it his way. He didn't. Helen Lugos did it in 1969 and suffered for it. On the other hand, he will always stretch a point for someone who uses words as he thinks they should. He once took a case because a woman said "We shall see" instead of "We will see" or making a contraction out of it.

Wolfe also makes use of his literacy in his work. In 1937, upon learning that an important witness in a case is a student of anthropology, Wolfe impressed him by quoting Paul Lawrence Dunbar (1872–1906) and told him that he owns autographed books from Franz Boas (1858–1942). In 1943, when Archie read a quixotic poem taken from a military intelligence officer's briefcase that could reasonably have been suspected of being a code, Wolfe immediately identified it as a poem by William Butler Yeats (1865–1939). The fact that a woman once called him "a big gob of fat" on the telephone in 1957 convinced him that he wasn't talking to the person he thought he was and provided an important clue to the solution of a murder. In 1960 he recognizes a quote from *The Duchess of Malfi* (1613) by John Webster (1575–1634) but admits he is unfamiliar with the works of the English writer Sir John Harington (1561–1612) and says the works of the English poet Robert Browning (1812–1889) repel him. From a man's conversation, Wolfe accurately deduces that he is a teacher of literature.

In 1934, Archie tells Wolfe that he reads books but he never got any real satisfaction from one. Wolfe tells him that he shouldn't bother because culture is like money, it comes easiest to those who need it least. Archie's opinions change in time. In the course of the adventures and his years with Wolfe, some things rub off. Eventually Archie is known to borrow, read and appreciate some of Wolfe's books. That he has that privilege speaks highly of Wolfe's opinion of and trust in him. Archie keeps some favorite books on a shelf in his room but we are not told what they are. In the course of a case, he is able to recognize a quote (even the volume and page!) from the Aventuros edition of Giovanni Casanova's *Memoirs*. This is one of the revered works that Wolfe keeps in his bedroom (as does Rex

Stout). From all those speeches, denouements and dining room conversations he is subjected to, Archie's vocabulary improves apace as well. He uses some of the words listed here, and in the proper context.

Not intending to reproduce the entire corpus, this is only a partial list of those words Wolfe uses that fall outside the average vocabulary. Also, not intending to reproduce the dictionary, I haven't included their definitions. If you want to broaden your horizons, look them up. I did (which is not to say they are now incorporated into my vocabulary):

abditory
acarpous
amphigoric
apodictal
arquebus
blatherskite
boniface
caracoles
cavil
chambrer
choler
chouse
churlish (Wolfe knows Archie thinks he is but he maintains he is not, merely
    self-indulgent)
cockatrice
concupiscence
contumacy
craichy
demesne
deshabille
dotard
dubiety
dysgenic
egregious
fatuous
feeze
flagitious
flummery
flummox

fructify
geegaws
helot
jocund
kale
lave
mendacity
metonymy
necromancer
obreptitious
parturition
persiflage
plerophory
pother
probity
propinquitous
puerile
quibble (One of Wolfe's pet words, When a client tosses it back at him in 1958, Archie is delighted.)
ramekin
recondite
rodomontade
sapient
sennight (Wolfe calls it a fine old word)
springe
subdolous
taboret
thaumaturgy
trylon
tyro
usufruct
weltschmerz (God help Wolfe when Archie learns a word unfamiliar to Wolfe. Archie bombards him.)
witling
yclept

In 1937, Archie did some homework and called Wolfe a "werowance", glee-fully noting that "a word he didn't know invariably got him." I feel certain that

Wolfe learned in short order that the word, or actually title, dates from the days of the first colonization of Virginia. Chief Powhatan was the chief of the Indians in the area and had about 30 separate tribes under his command. The chief of each tribe was called a "werowance" and was subservient and owed allegiance to Powhatan.

So Archie got him but he inevitably gets paid back for seeking out opportunities to use words Wolfe doesn't know (yet). To Archie's occasional consternation, Wolfe is multi-lingual and proves it. In 1969 he says he speaks six languages. In 1954 he said it was eight. It may even be more. To wit:

In 1935, he recites poetry in Hungarian.

In 1938 he speaks Serbo-Croat with Carla Lovchen and in 1954 he speaks it fluently with a number of natives in his homeland. In the latter year, he also demonstrates a fluency in Albanian.

He converses in Italian in 1954 and quotes adventurer Giacomo Casanova (1725–1798).

He speaks fluent Spanish with the Perez family in 1960.

He speaks French with Madame Mondor in 1937, Nathaniel Parker in 1955 and with Leon Ducos in 1974. He also quotes liberally from the works of essayist Michel de Montaigne (1533–1592), mathematician and philosopher Blaise Pascal (1623–1662), and writers Francois Voltaire (1694–1778) and Victor Hugo (1802–1885).

Wolfe quotes from the historian Leopold von Ranke (1795–1886) and philosopher Friedrich Nietzsche (1844–1900). We don't know if he read their works in the original form but one of his uncredited languages may be German.

Another is possibly Latin. He quotes passages from the ancient Roman emperors Servius Galba (3 B.C.-69 A.D.), Aulus Vitellius (15–69 A.D.) and the historian Cornelius Tacitus (55–120 A.D.). On several occasions when talking with lawyers, Wolfe glibly recites several Latin phrases dealing with legal principles.

An obvious complement to Latin is Greek (particularly for someone from the Balkans) and his knowledge of ancient Greek mythology is profound. He asks one person if they presume to "usurp the fatal dignity of Atropos." Atropos was the eldest of the three Fates. Her name means "unalterable" and she makes the decisions of her sisters irreversible. He asks another if they think they are one of the Erinyes and which one, naming them. The Erinyes were a trio of avenging gods: Alecto (unceasing in anger), Megaera (jealous) and Tisphone (avenger of murder). The latter one seems particularly apropo in Wolfe's case. In another story, he tells someone he is "neither an Astraeas nor a sadist." Astraea was a daughter of Zeus and had the job of distributing blessings among men, a function Wolfe was obviously unwilling to perform.

And, of course, in his adopted primary language of English, Wolfe was very conversant with the works of John Bunyan (1628–1688), Cornwall (1787–1874), Paul Laurence Dunbar (1872–1906), Benjamin Franklin (1706–1790), Edward Gibbon (1737–1794), Robert Greene (1558–1592), Charles Lamb (1737–1834), Dorothy Osborne (1627–1695, William Shakespeare (1564–1616), John Webster (1575–1634), William Butler Yeats (1865–1939) and many others.

The Epicurean Wolfe

Everyone eats but Nero Wolfe dines. Whether it's at his own table, in a Yugoslavian hovel making tagliarini (anchovies, tomato, garlic, olive oil, sweet basil, parsley, Romano cheese, salt and pepper) in primitive circumstances, collecting herbs and vegetables while Archie sleeps in haystacks or seated on a hard, narrow bench in a police station with a ham sandwich and a beer, Nero Wolfe always dines.

The reason for his gargantuan profile is simple. In his youth, he roamed the world, partaking equally of its adventures and its culinary treats along the way, expanding his tastes, knowledge, abilities and cosmopolitan nature. With all this activity, he burned off the residual calories. When he eventually moved to New York and settled into the routines he would maintain for the rest of his life, the physical activity of the past was absent and the calories collected. Thus the tonnage increased to its notable level. Thus also his association with the master chef, Fritz Brenner. It is no accident of timing that this collusion occurred before his association with Archie. The arrangements for the food comes before the continuing means for paying for it. Speaking of the routine;

Fritz delivers Wolfe's breakfast to him on a tray in his bedroom at 8 A.M. or, in later years, 8:15 A.M. He has usually fasted since the previous evening's dinner, almost twelve hours earlier. He rarely eats between dinner and breakfast except under unusual stress. On those occasions, he eats in the kitchen and not in the dining room. While they are rare, they are usually memorable. He once disposed of a ten-pound goose, completely and single-handedly, between 8 P.M. and midnight.

Therefore he usually eats hearty breakfasts. The fare is usually some combination of the following; peaches and cream, fresh figs and cream, five slices of bacon, two slices of broiled Georgia ham, sausage, eggs (frequently *ouefs au beurre noir*, eggs prepared in a black butter sauce, a favorite), ramekins of shirred eggs and sausage, hash browns, hot blueberry muffins, toast and green tomato jam. He usually drinks orange juice and steaming hot cocoa with his breakfast. It is imprudent to approach him before he's had his orange juice and he refuses to gulp it. Archie once checked with Fritz to make sure Wolfe had a good breakfast (of melon, eggs a' la Suisse, oatmeal cakes and croissants w/blackberry jam) before goading him into a case. On gray, rainy or overcast mornings, Wolfe will eat sitting up in bed but when it's clear and sunny, he prefers to eat at a table by a window in his bedroom. In either case, he's reading his morning papers simultaneously. Since he reads everything about every murder reported in the press, he probably thinks he's working during the meal.

Archie eats his breakfast about 8:10 A.M. in the kitchen while Fritz works. His morning meals are usually less exotic and more traditional than Wolfe's. Archie says he's a swallower and Wolfe's a taster, a distinction that probably eternally separates them at their respective tables. Wolfe is primarily interested in the love affair the food has with his taste buds while Archie is merely interested in making sure it gets to his stomach on time and in sufficient quantity.

Oatmeal, grapefruit, bacon or Canadian bacon, eggs, blackberry jam, griddle cakes with wild thyme honey and coffee are Archie's usual fare. About the most exotic thing Archie might have for breakfast is an anchovy omelet. Wolfe says there was a man in Marseilles who made a better omelet than Fritz but Archie doesn't believe it.

Since Fritz refuses to fry eggs, potatoes or chicken in his kitchen, if Archie ever desires those delicacies, he has to go to Al's Diner around the corner. If he wants baked beans or rye bread for lunch, he has to go to Sam's Diner on Tenth Avenue because those are two more things that never appear on Wolfe's table.

Rex Stout's favorite breakfast (his appreciation for *ouefs au beurre noir* aside) was always oatmeal with plenty of sugar and cream.

Wolfe is very picky about his food and doesn't get it (or Fritz his ingredients) down at any corner market. He goes to a great deal of trouble and expense for it. He uses wild thyme honey imported from Greece (or perhaps Syria or both). The fresh figs for his breakfast are flown in from Chile every March. In the early years, his sausage comes from a Swiss farmer near Chappaqua who prepares it himself from specially raised pigs and ten kinds of herbs. In 1950, he orders Bill Darst's sausage specially from Mummiani's on Fulton Street.

In mid-May of every year, a farmer near Brewster in Putnam County, New York, shoots 18 to 20 starlings and delivers them to Wolfe within two hours. Fritz prepares them with melted butter, salt and sage leaves, then serves them on a platter of hot polenta, a thick porridge of cornmeal with butter, cheese, salt and pepper. In 1953, Wolfe refuses to eat the meal because Fritz foregoes the sage for saffron and tarragon without consulting him.

He gets his ham from pigs in Georgia that are fed on a special diet of peanuts, acorns and cured to his exact specifications. In 1950, while a murder in his office is being investigated, Wolfe and Archie dine on ham sandwiches from those pigs.

Wolfe provides the sandwiches to his guests and the witnesses but not to the cops, a petty retribution because they have sealed his office off as a crime scene.

Between 5:30 and 6:30 every Tuesday afternoon between July 20 and October 5, a Putnam County farmer named Duncan McLeod delivers 16 freshly picked ears of corn to Wolfe's door. Wolfe says that sweet corn is edible if boiled in water but if roasted in the hottest possible oven for forty minutes and basted with butter and salt, it is ambrosia. The usual corn delivery is divided as eight ears for Wolfe and four each for Archie and Fritz. In 1961, the delivery is late and when it does arrive, it's delivered by Inspector Cramer! The ears aren't ripe enough and Wolfe begs the question "Who picked it?" That later leads to the solution of a murder. Ever resourceful, Fritz replaces the corn with stuffed eggplant and later makes corn fritters, bacon and homemade blackberry jam.

Wolfe is so finicky about his food that Archie occasionally uses it as a weapon against him. While in the Army during World War II, Archie is trying to wangle an overseas assignment and is concerned that Wolfe might use his influence in Washington, D.C., to try to block it. Archie threatens that if he does, he'll put gristle in his crabmeat and sugar in his beer. Wolfe is horrified at the prospect of sugar in his beer. Occasionally Wolfe retaliates by ordering less tarragon in his dishes because he knows Archie loves tarragon.

As previously noted, Wolfe loves beer. In fact, at the very beginning of his first published case, Fritz is fetching him beer on June 7, 1933. Wolfe has been surviving Prohibition by buying bootleg beer in barrels, storing them in a basement cooler and has it served at his desk in pitchers. Now that beer is legal again, he is trying all the available brands to select the most worthy. Fritz brings him 49 different brands along with a supply of salty crackers, to clear the palate, no doubt. Wolfe settles on Remmers. Wolfe is also planning to cut down from his customary six quarts a day to five quarts (twelve bottles-a bottle doesn't hold a pint, Wolfe rationalizes). Archie is skeptical of the attempt, much less its success.

Wolfe has it served at his desk two bottles at a time with a chilled glass. In later years, the allotment is increased to three bottles at a time. The code from the buzzer on his desk to Fritz in the kitchen changes occasionally. Two short buzzes in 1936 and 1947 changes to one short and one long in 1955. Keeps Fritz on his toes, I suppose. Archie will substitute for Fritz occasionally when Fritz is occupied elsewhere and Archie is feeling merciful towards Wolfe.

When the beer arrives, Wolfe enters into his drinking ritual. After opening the bottle with one of his gold openers and placing the cap in his middle desk drawer, he pours it so it develops a head of foam, allows the foam to rise to within a specific distance of the rim and then drinks it. He obviously enjoys it since he gulps it down (five gulps per glass is average) in one long pull. He smacks his lips lustily and then wipes the foam off of his upper lip. Starting afresh every Sunday morning, he keeps a weekly count of his beer intake by the bottle caps in his middle drawer. When he's ahead of his quota, he will occasionally surreptitiously drop an empty bottle in his wastebasket to conceal it from Archie but he never cheats on the bottle caps count. In 1949, he gets in an argument with Archie because Wolfe has had five beers since dinner and wants a sixth before going to bed. Fritz is on Wolfe's side but Archie dissuades them both by threatening to resort to the gun in his pocket.

Wolfe has trepidation about drinking beer outside of his own home since 1936 when he is unhappily served Schreirer's beer too cold at Boyden McNair's offices. However sometimes emergency circumstances call for risks. While Wolfe was hiding from the law at Saul Panzer's apartment in 1954, Saul fed him seven beers in three hours. In 1968, we have the very special treat of Wolfe drinking beer out of cans chilled in Montana mountain streams and being called to dinner with "Come and get it before the grease sets!"

Wolfe seldom drinks beer for one hour before dinner. At his afternoon and evening meals, Wolfe drinks almost nothing except an occasional sip of Schweppes tonic water and, afterwards, coffee. He never drinks wine with meals, saying it interferes with the taste of the food.

Lunch is usually at 1 and later moves up to 1:15. A typical lunch might be chicken livers, tomato halves fried in oil and trimmed with chopped peppers and parsley, rice cakes and honey, shad roe mousse Pocahontas or corned beef hash prepared with mushrooms, white wine and grated cheese.

Wolfe doesn't always look at his relationship with Fritz as employer/employee. Occasionally they are collaborators and sometimes even with Wolfe as the teacher. In 1936 he instructs Fritz in the preparation of shish kabob, saying he had it in Turkey in earlier years. When Wolfe takes it upon himself to instruct Fritz, sometimes he is and sometimes he's just trying to impose his standards upon his chef. When that happens, occasionally the artisans disagree. One of their disputes occurs in 1947 when Wolfe disagrees with Fritz over using sweet basil in clam chowder.

When they are collaborating, things get better. During World War II, he and Fritz accomplish wonders in spite of war rationing but all with their legitimate ration of coupons. In the midst of the New York black market, Wolfe's kitchen was as pure as cottage cheese. Their wartime fare included Creole tripe without the salt pork, pigs feet, clams, frog legs, roast duck Mr. Richards, roasted corn on the cob, green salad, blackberry pie and cheese. Lunch usually lasts until at least

2:30. Stainless steel implements are not allowed in dining room or kitchen and Fritz always sharpens his own knives.

Wolfe dislikes eating with strangers but violates that principle fairly regularly, usually for clients and witnesses in his current case. As a general rule, only two kinds of people eat at Wolfe's table; people he has personal feelings for and people in his current case. Of the former group, Archie says there are only eight and only two of those are in New York. I think he has understated the case somewhat. We know Marko Vukcic dined with him at least once a month until 1954, the editor of the Gazette dines with him monthly and others welcome at his table with some regularity include Lewis Hewitt, Doctor Vollmer, Nathaniel Parker and Lon Cohen. Of course Orrie Cather is welcome during a case and Saul Panzer could probably wangle an invitation anytime he wanted. Fred Durkin would have to continue to eat in the kitchen with his vinegar. Johnny Keems and Bill Gore could probably get a bite if they were starving to death but probably not otherwise.

When it comes to sustenance, Wolfe's hospitality knows no bounds. In 1935, too many guests (five) show up for dinner. Wolfe tells Fritz that they cannot dine but they can eat. They split up filets of beef with sauce Abano, add fresh stock to the soup and include Hungarian petits poissions and fruit. When Fritz suggests giving the guests something else, Wolfe declines, saying that he must share their hardships.

Wolfe will dig in his heels and stop the world if any guest has not eaten. When told by a group of clients that they didn't need to eat, he came as close as he gets to throwing a tantrum, exclaiming "Great hounds and Cerberus!" He once stopped a line of questioning to see a client got some of Fritz's homemade pate and a drink before continuing. In 1941, he feeds Daniel Goldwyn soup, crackers, cottage cheese and hot tea. In the same year, he shares his precious *saucisse minuit* (read *Too Many Cooks*) with a reluctant witness. In 1948 he tempts Dr. Michaels to dine with him on fresh pork tenderloin with all the fiber removed done in a casserole with a moderately spiced sharp brown sauce. The lure also includes Remisier brandy. There were only 19 bottles of it in the entire United States, all of them in Wolfe's cellar. In 1951, several female guests are served Mondor patties, duckling and almond parfait, albeit without Wolfe's presence. In 1960, he ordered tea with honey, toast, pot cheese and Bar-le-Duc for a hungry client. In 1962, the fare is bowls of Madrilene with beet juice, lemon sherry pudding with brown sugar sauce, cheese, watercress and hot tea for another client. In 1964, Paul Whipple and Harold Oster (yet another lawyer) dine with him on wild duck with Vatel sauce prepared from wine vinegar, egg yolk, tomato paste, shallots, tarragon, chervil, peppercorns, cream, salt and pepper. In 1965 Lon Cohen is treated to clam cakes with chili sauce, beef braised in red wine, squash with sour cream and chopped dill, avocado with watercress and black walnut kernels, and Liederkrantz. In 1969, Doctor Vollmer shares shad roe Creole, baked bluefish stuffed with ground shrimp and endive salad with watercress. When he has guests, at the end of a meal Wolfe always introduces Fritz to them, giving the master his due recognition. Wolfe's most lavish praise for a meal is "Most satisfactory!" It was bestowed for Danish pork pancakes in 1953 among other occasions.

NOTES: To save you the trouble of looking them up as I had to; Cerberus is the three-headed dog in Greek mythology that guards the gates of Hell. Madridlene is a consommé flavored with tomatoes created in Madrid, Spain, hence the name. Liederkrantz is a semi-soft cow's milk cheese created by New York cheese maker Emil Frey in 1882 that is especially good with beer, dark bread and onions.

Wolfe thinks more than six at a table spoils a meal. He sat at a table with nine others in 1955 but it wasn't his table. He did violate the rule at his own table in 1956 when he invited five private detectives (including Dol Bonner—Fritz was probably in a tizzy) to dinner after a case's conclusion. He did it again in 1958.

The reason Wolfe doesn't like more than six at a table is because he thinks that is the maximum number that can sustain and share an interesting conversation. The topic might be women's shoes, the importance of the New Moon in Babylonian astrology, Yugoslavian politics, dogs (occasioned by Archie bringing home a black Labrador retriever from a murder scene which, unbeknownst to him at the time, belonged to a murder victim), why sustained chess-playing would ruin any good field general (during World War II), Egypt, tiles, the use of a camel's double lip, the theory that England's colonizing genius was due to her repulsive climate, T.E. Lawrence's success in keeping Arabs together for the great revolt or almost anything else he's learned in those thousands of books. To avoid business conversation, Wolfe has also resorted to such desperate measures as reciting Hungarian poetry to a female client and humming folk dance tunes.

As with everything else, Wolfe has rules for meals, especially dinner. As with the other rules, they all get violated sooner or later. One is no business talk at the table or during meals. Although considered the most inviolate of rules, it is violated by Inspector Cramer in June of 1947. Wolfe cut the meal short by two rice cakes and a cup of coffee. He then stalked across the hall to the office, attempting to freeze Cramer with an icy silence until it suited him to break it only to have Cramer call him a goddam liar, for which Cramer paid the price for his effrontery for the remainder of the case. Wolfe allowed a slight departure from the rule during the *Christmas Party* case on the excuse that it wasn't business, it was personal for Archie. In a bizarre, situation in 1959, Wolfe actually refused to eat dinner. He survived.

Although conversation about business is not allowed at his table, Wolfe is not above using the gustatory temptations of his kitchen to obtain information related to business. He did it with illegal Russian immigrants in the first recorded case and later with a Green Meadow Club golf pro (sorry, professional).

Other rules are no interruptions during meals and no rushing the meal. He usually forbids Archie to interrupt a meal by answering the phone. Since he eats at different times, Fritz gets it on the kitchen extension. An exception is a female client. When notified of a murder at 7:22 one evening, Wolfe says he's barely started his dinner and will require a minimum of one hour and ten minutes before seeing guests. However, again both rules are plundered.

In 1952, Wolfe skipped dinner salad, cheese and coffee to rescue Archie from a predicament. In 1953 he had to devour his dinner in one-quarter of the usual time because of a case. He also ate with Inspector Cramer and broke one of his strictest rules by reading documents while eating. The next year he postpones lunch for a case. In 1960, Wolfe advances the lunch hour by 15 minutes and then had to hurry through corn fritters, sausage cakes, wild thyme honey from Greece, cheese and blackberry pie without allowing sufficient time to enjoy it.

One of the truly rare occasions is when Wolfe allows someone else into his (and, make no mistake, Fritz's) kitchen to prepare food. Probably the most radical departure in this manner occurred in 1941. Wolfe allows Maryella Timms, a good old-fashioned southern girl, to suggest pig chitlins fried shallow in olive oil with onion juice as the remedy for his dry corned beef hash. He later allows her in the kitchen again and she even gets to hang on his arm. Fritz must have been absolutely beside himself. A lesser departure, this time with Fritz's blessing, occurred in October of 1952 when the world-renowned chef Pierre Mondor was a houseguest and prepared *quenelles bonne femme*. Archie had three helpings. Wolfe's intake was unrecorded but almost certainly superior to Archie's effort.

A true carnivore, Wolfe considers a meal without meat as an insult. As far as we know from the canon, Wolfe has never been confronted with a vegetarian or a vegan but his reaction would have been interesting if he had ever unknowingly invited one to his table. Undoubtedly it wouldn't have strained Fritz's talents but Wolfe's sufferance may have been quite another matter.

Wolfe is very fond of roast Waterdown goose but had banned it from his table because it had been served to a female husband-poisoner at his table once. His intemperate lust for meat during the Great Meat Shortage of 1946 got them involved in a melee between New York City gangsters that ended with a four-way shootout, literally in front of his desk. One of the meals they made do with during the meat shortage was broiled chicken and grilled sweet potatoes.

Other typical fare in the Wolfe household over the years include;

—Corn cakes with breaded fresh pork tenderloin, hot sauce of tomatoes and cheese, and honey.
—Squirrel stew with black sauce in a casserole with butter, eggs, lambert sausages and seasonings.
—Rognons aux Montagnes, lamb kidneys cooked in broth, red wine and spices.
—Sauerkraut and spareribs.
—Veal and mushrooms, pumpkin puffs, cottage chess with pineapple soaked in white wine.
—Fried shrimp, cape cod clam cakes, sour sauce thick with mushrooms, braised boned ducklings, potatoes baked with mushrooms and cheese, salad, baked pears and cheese.
—Balalhau, a dish of salt cod, an adaptation of a Portuguese recipe, served with veal and walnut pudding.
—Poached and truffled broilers, broccoli, stuffed potatoes with herbs, salad and cheese.
—Broiled pork loin wafers, melon, salad with Wolfe's own dressing and blueberry pie.
—Peruvian melon, kidney pie, endive with Martinique dressing.
—Chicken livers and mushrooms in white wine with rice cakes.
—Celery and mushroom omelet, ham and sweetbreads mousse.
—Braised pork filets with spiced wine.
—Couronne de Canard au Riz a la Normande.
—Red snapper filets baked with butter, lemon juice and almonds.
—Apricot omelet, Creole fritters with cheese sauce.
—Shrimp Bordelaise without onions but with garlic.
—Lobsters simmered in white wine with tarragon.
—Partridges in marinade en escabeche (breaded with flour and a mixture of onions, peppers, garlic, olive oil, oregano, vinegar and lime).
—Rice-and-mushroom fritters.
—Braised duckling stuffed with crabmeat.
—Shad roe with a sauce of chives and chervil in a casserole with anchovy butter, sheets of larding rubbed with five herbs, cream sauce with onion and three herbs.

(If possible, Wolfe would have it three times a day during roe season which is short.)

—Guinea chicken Braziliera and diced watermelon sprinkled with granulated sugar and refrigerated in a cup of sherry for one hour.

—Rice fritters with black currant jam, endive with tarragon fricandeau, endive salad, chilled '28 Marcobrunner.

—Artichokes barigoule (a stew of artichoke hearts with seasonings).

—Corn fritters with autumn honey and sausages.

—Fried chicken, cream gravy and mushrooms.

—Shad roe casserole with parsley, shervil, shallots, marjoram, bay leaf, cream, chestnut soup.

—Brazilian lobster salad consisting of eight baby lobsters, eight avocados, young leaf lettuce, chives, onion, parsley, tomato paste, mayonnaise, salt, pepper, paprika, pimentos and dry white wine, deep dish blueberry pie smothered in whipped cream.

—Brook trout Montbarr baked with parsley, onions, chives, chervil, tarragon, fresh mushrooms, brandy, bread crumbs, fresh eggs, paprika, tomatoes and cheese.

—Wolfe's own recipe for salmon mousse and a peck of summer salad (a peck not meaning a snippet, rather the volumetric measurement meaning about a quarter of a bushel).

Wolfe seldom drinks beer one hour before a meal. He makes no effort to join his fingers at the high point of his middle mound sooner than a full hour after a meal. Following the meal, Wolfe adjourns to the office, gets settled in his favorite chair and Fritz serves coffee. Wolfe's is always black, no cream or sugar.

When he has guests, they are invited to partake from the sideboard table next to the Gouchard globe. Common fare includes several brands of scotch, rye and bourbon including 12-year-old Big Sandy and Old Woody, two brands of gin including Follansbee's, two brands of cognac, vermouth, Meyer's rum, eight brands of whiskey including B&B, Old Corcoran and Mangam's Irish whiskies, Korbeloff vodka, Armagnac and 1890 Guarnier brandies, Coca-Cola, ginger ale, Alymer's soda, White Rock spring water, cream sherry, dry sherry, four fruit brandies, a variety of cordials and liqueurs (including Pernod which killed a guest when laced with cyanide in 1955), a decanter of port wine, a chilled white wine, Madeira, Solera, Dublin Stout, a Hungarian vin du pays and Tokaji Essencia. A vacuum bucket of ice, canapés, snacks, cherries, tree-ripened olives, onions, lemon peel, nuts, Tom Collins mix, napkins and other accessories are also supplied. Dom Perignon champagne is available but is usually reserved for celebrations among the operatives at the successful end of a difficult case.

MORE NOTES: Like most of his cars and guns, I suspect most of Stout's brand names here may be fictional but I know B&B Whiskey and White Rock Spring Water are actual brands. Armagnac is a very fine brandy made from white grapes from southwestern France. Madeira is a red Portuguese wine like a full-bodied sherry, named for the Portuguese island where it is produced. Solera might be a rum or a single malt scotch but is most probably a Venezuelan beer. Dublin Stout is an Irish beer, very dark brown and with a rich, smoky malt flavor. "Vin du pays" means "wine of the country." Tokaji Essencia is the ultimate and rarest in Tokay wines from the Tokaj region of Hungary. It is the nectar referred to in the Hungarian national anthem. Made from aszu grapes, it has a very high sugar content, is aged at least 20 years and has very little fermentation.

Wolfe almost never eats between dinner and breakfast but in 1953, he took a late night break from interviewing suspects for cheese, provender and il pesto (canestrato cheese, anchovies, pig liver, black walnuts, chives, sweet basil, garlic and olive oil). When offered some and being told what was in it, Inspector Cramer exclaimed "Good God!" but later asked for seconds. The general ban on late night snacks doesn't apply on Sundays when the rest of the schedule is altered. A typical Sunday evening snack is in the kitchen with Fritz eating endive cores and Wolfe and Archie eating buttermilk biscuits, Wolfe using honey on them and Archie using molasses.

Probably one of the primary reasons Wolfe doesn't like to leave his home is because one must eat under all circumstances and the quality of the food in the outside world is, at best, capricious and at worst, inedible.

The harrowing journey to West Virginia was almost certainly salved somewhat by the knowledge that the 1937 meeting of *Les Quinze Maitres* would not leave his palate wanting. Similarly, his 1958 foray to the banquet of the Ten For Aristology (the science of dining) held much promise although it was spoiled by a man seated next to him dropping dead from poison (in food prepared by Fritz!). Speaking of which, poison crops up as a method of murder much more frequently in the Nero Wolfe series than it proportionately does in real life. It takes no great leap of the imagination to surmise how poisoning would be viewed by someone with Wolfe's appreciation for food.

His many substandard experiences of that nature are doubtlessly one source of his hesitancy to leave the brownstone but there are enough pleasant, or at least adequate, experiences to continue to make the journeys worth the risk.

In 1948, he is forced to eat at The Covered Porch restaurant near Scarsdale. The meal consisted of two dozen oysters, a few spoonfuls of an evidently substandard clam chowder, a slice of rare roast beef, a pile of zwieback cheese and grape jelly. He had no complaints about the food but the meal was an unhappy one simply because he was away from home and consumed with a purpose as yet unfulfilled.

In 1956 at the Latham Hotel in Albany, he survived on oysters, consommé, roast beef, creamed potatoes, broccoli, salad, apple pie with cheese and coffee. Again the meal was edible but gloomy because Wolfe refused to talk, furious at having been arrested as a material witness and being out on bond.

At the other end of the spectrum, a trip to Westchester County in 1954 yielded cheese he pronounced inedible, crackers and beer. On the other hand, hiding from the law in Saul Panzer's apartment and faced with the prospect of sleeping in a strange bed (probably too small) he was treated to liver pate, herring, sturgeon, pickled mushrooms, Tunisian melon and three kinds of cheese. Saul was absolutely prancing with pride. On another foray near home base, he discovered chili (three orders) from a little dump on 170th Street run by a guy named Dixie who knew how to make it.

On rare occasions, Wolfe is not above finagling an invitation away from home solely for the promise of a unique dining experience. He wangled such an invitation to Lily Rowan's penthouse (yet another example of his unusual esteem for her) in the summer of 1960. The lure was two dozen young blue grouse from her ranch in Montana. It seems that in August, the blue grouse chicks are about ten weeks old and have a main diet of mountain huckleberries. Predictably, the excursion developed into a murder case.

The only outside interest that Wolfe allows to interfere with his single-minded pursuits of luxury and comfort is also food-related, namely Rusterman's Restaurant. Marko Vukcic, his oldest and closest friend, was the founder and sole owner. When Marko died, he left it to members of its staff and made Wolfe his executor. Marko left a letter for Wolfe, asking him to see that the standards and reputation of the restaurant were maintained. Wolfe makes one or two unannounced visits very week and dines there to check on the quality. Considering the arbiter, we can probably depend upon that.

The Horticultural Wolfe

Many people would consider Nero Wolfe a man without passion but they couldn't be more wrong. He has a triumvirate of great passions. The third of Nero Wolfe's great loves is orchids. The food nourishes the body and the books nourish the intellect but the orchids nourish the soul although, agnostic that he is, he would doubtlessly have a different word for it.

Before I started this book, my knowledge of orchids stopped in high school. They are pretty, it's nice to buy one for the girl you're taking to the prom and that's about it. Let me tell you a few of the things I've learned since.

Did you know that the flavoring agent vanilla comes from the dried and fermented pods of an orchid? I didn't. In fact, *vanilla* is a genus of orchids, the same ones that provide the extract and its name.

The orchid family is related to the lily family. There are over 35,000 species, it is the largest plant family in nature and one of the most diverse. Some of them are the size of a small coin and some grow twenty feet tall. Some have blossoms that are barely visible and others are a foot across. They grow wild in every country on the planet and on every continent except Antarctica. Each one has three small sepals or leaves and three larger leaves called petals. One of the petals is modified into a smaller labellum or lip that is usually highly colored.

The names they are given look intimidating but are actually scientifically descriptive. The first name, always capitalized, is the genus. The second name, usually not capitalized, is the species or hybrid name. They can also have third and fourth names for the variety and a specialized name which may reflect its color (or lack of it), the country it was discovered in or the name of the person who hybridized it.

To partially explain all of the trouble Wolfe goes to, here are some brief facts about some of the more prevalent orchids in his collection;

Brassovola—About 15 species range from Central and South America through the Caribbean. They are a fairly easy species to cultivate.
Brassacattleya—A hybrid of *Brassavola* and *Cattleya*, they range through Mexico and Central America.

Cattleya—One of the most common types of orchids, they are gaudily colorful and like bright sunlight but not at mid-day. There are about 65 species indigenous to Central and South America. Temperatures of 55-60 degrees at night and 10 or 20 degrees higher during the day are best. Relative humidity should be 50-80 per cent.

Coelogyne—About 150 species range from China through the Pacific Islands, usually in colors of green, yellow or brown.

Cymbidium—Ranging from China to Australia, they grow 1 ½ to 4 feet tall. There are more than 44 species and they are relatively difficult to grow indoors. Strong sunlight is preferred with temperatures ranging from 65-85 during the day and 45-60 at night.

Endrobium—The second largest genus of orchids with over 1,000 species. They range from the Himalayas to Australia. They like bright light, 50-70 per cent humidity and temperatures no lower than 55 at night.

Miltonia—Brilliantly colored flowers that resemble giant pansies. They grow in low to medium light, over 50 per cent humidity, temperatures of 45-55 at night and not above 85 during the day.

Odontoglossum—Over 300 species range from Mexico through South America.

Oncidium—Over 750 species range from Florida through South America. Usually very showy flowers in yellow or brown colors.

Phalaenopsis—Also known as moth orchids, supposedly because Charles Darwin thought that's what they resembled when he saw them in the Philippines. Over 50 species range from India to Australia and like low light. Temperatures not below 60 at night and between 70-85 during the day are best.

Vanda—Over 70 species range from the Himalayas to Australia. They usually have large blossoms.

As an introduction to Nero Wolfe and his orchids, I can think of no better words than those of his own creator. I can also think of no better way to answer some of the questions I have been asking myself for years and which many other readers must have echoed; Why does he grow orchids?; How did he get started?; What in God's name can he find to do up there for four hours every day and with a full-time gardener at that?; What is so voluminous about the germination and propagation records that requires Archie's typing several hours every day and several filing cabinets to hold them? Questions that only Wolfe (or Stout) could answer. An added benefit is that, as you read the article, you can hear all three of them; Stout, Wolfe and even lapses into Archie.

The following article is reprinted from the April 19, 1963, issue of Life Magazine:

"WHY NERO WOLFE LIKES ORCHIDS
By
Rex Stout

When people ask me why Nero Wolfe grows orchids I ask them which they are interested in, orchids or him. If they ask what difference that makes, I say it makes all the difference. If they are curious about orchids, the best and simplest answer is to take them up to the plant rooms, but if they're curious about Nero Wolfe, there are a dozen different answers and they are all complicated.

Wolfe's flowers go all the way from the showiest to the shyest. He has a *Cattleya* hybrid, bred by him, which threw its first flower last year, that is twice a gaudy as anything you ever saw in a florist shop, and he has a *Cymbidium* hybrid, *ensifolium x Sanderae*, bred by him in 1953, so coy that it makes one little flower each year—off-white, the size of a dime, hidden down in the foliage. Once I saw him scowling at it and muttering, "Confound you, are you too timid or too proud?"

If he ever talks to himself he keeps it strictly private, but I have often heard him talk to orchids. He'll cock his head at a bench of *Miltonias* in full bloom and say distinctly, "Much too loud. Why don't you learn to whisper?" Not that he ever whispers.

Wolfe started on orchids many years ago with a specimen plant of *vanda suavis*, given to him by the wife of a man he had cleared on a murder rap. He kept it in the office and it petered out. He got mad, built a little shed on the roof and bought 20 plants. Now the plant rooms are 34x86, the size of the house. He hasn't bought a plant from a commercial grower for 10 years, but he sells some—a hundred or more a year.

Of the four hours a day he spends up in the plant rooms—9 to 11 in the morning and 4 to 6 in the afternoon—not more than 20 minutes is spent looking at flowers. First he makes a tour through the aisles, which are 30 inches wide instead of the usual two feet—the tropical room, the intermediate and the cool—and then on to the potting room. He nods to Theodore, the gardener, and says, "Well?" Theodore says either, "Well enough," or something like, "A pod of *Coelogyne* will be ready in two days.

Then work. It may be real work, like bringing a dozen old plants from one of the rooms for dividing and repotting, or opening a bale of osmunda fiber and inspecting it; or it may be merely getting a tape and going to the cool room to measure the panicles of *Odontoglossums*. It can be any of the thousand chores that orchids take—mixing fertilizer, labeling, presoaking new pots, checking ventilation and humidity, adjusting shade screens, stripping bulb sheaths, chipping charcoal, and so forth, forever and ever with no amen. Except spraying. Wolfe hates it, and Theodore does it when he's not there.

Of course, most of the chores are for breeding, not growing. Buying a dozen or so orchid plants and keeping them going and blooming in a house or apartment is no trick at all, but hybridizing is a career. Usually an orchid flower is both male and female, so deciding on father and mother is up to Nero Wolfe. Having cross-pollinated, he waits seven months to a year for the seed pod to mature and ripen. A large pod will have a million or more seeds. They are among the smallest of plant seeds.

The preparations in a hospital operating room for an appendectomy are nothing compared to the fuss of planting a batch of orchid seed. If one microscopic fungus cell gets in a bottle with the seed, it goes to work on the nutrient jelly in which the infant flower is planted, and goodbye seed. If he does it right and is lucky, in nine or 10 months he scoops the tiny half-inch seedlings out of the bottle and plants them in community pots. A year later he transplants them to individual three-inch pots and in another two years to 4½-inch pots, and crosses his fingers. Then five or six or seven years since he put pollen to stigma, he sees an orchid no one ever saw before. It is different from any orchid that has ever bloomed, including those in the Garden of Eden. The differences may be very slight, or there may be flaws, but about once in every five times his orchid will be worthy of dad and mom, and there is one chance in ten thousand that it will be an absolute stunner. Since he has seen only a fraction of the many thousands of named and listed hybrids, he can't be sure until the day some grower takes a long hard look at his baby and says casually, "Interesting little plant. I'll give you $400 for it." Then he'll know that in a few years orchid catalogues will list one more named for him, or at least by him.

In the past 20 years Nero Wolfe has had that happen 14 times, and he has on his benches a total of 112 unnamed varieties bred by him and good enough to keep. Okay, that's very satisfactory, and it's one of the reasons he grows orchids; but it's not the main one. He grows orchids chiefly for the same reason that he wears bright yellow shirts: for the color.

I said he spends only 20 minutes of the four hours looking at flowers, but that's a lot. Anyway he gets some special kind of kick from the color. He says you don't look at color, you feel it, and apparently he thinks that really means something.

It doesn't to me but maybe it does to you and you know exactly how he feels as he opens the door to the plant rooms and walks in on the big show. I have never known a day when less than a hundred plants were in bloom, and sometimes there are a thousand, from the pure white of dainty little *Dendrobium nobile virginalis* to the yellow-tan-bronze-mahogany-purple of big and gaudy *Laelia tenenrosa*. It is unquestionably worth a look—or, if you react the same way Wolfe does, a feel.

One question I don't know the answer to and can only guess at is why he cuts the ones he brings down to the office every morning for the vase on his desk. Why not bring the plant, since then the flowers would be good for another week or more? Because he would have to take it back up again? No; he could just add that to my daily chores. Because he thinks that particular spike or raceme has been around long enough? No; sometimes it will be a very special item, like the dwarf Vanda with green dots that a commercial grower offered him $1,200 for. Because he hates to carry things? That could be, but he carries plenty of them from the growing rooms to the potting rooms and back again. The best guess is that he doesn't want to give a plant a shadow of an excuse not to go on blossoming at peak efficiency. If a *Zygopetalum* has a cluster of eight flowers this year, and next year only six, it could blame it on the day in the office—not enough light and the temperature and humidity wrong; and although you can say pfui to an orchid plant, and Wolfe often does, there's no real satisfaction in it.

How does he decide each morning which one he will cut for his desk vase that day? I have had various theories, but none of them has stood up. One was that it depended on the bank balance. If the balance was high, say 50 grand, he would pick something extra flashy; if it was low, down to four figures, it would be something subdued like a brown speckled *Dendrobium*. That theory lasted three days. When I told him about it he grunted and said, "The flower a woman chooses depends on the woman. The flower a man chooses depends on the flower." ©YEAR 1963 Inc., reprinted by permission.

I have some comments after reading the above. I realize Wolfe says on more than one occasion that he doesn't sell orchids but Stout says differently. Evidently changing his mind, like many other things in his life, is not only a female prerogative. It also occurs to me that Wolfe's antipathy for being around when the plants are sprayed might have something to do with cases he had in 1941 and 1948.

In 1944, four years before he recruited Andy Krasicki to temporarily replace Theodore, Wolfe had a ciphogene tank installed in the plant rooms to replace systems he called Cyanogas and Nico-Fume. The last two were probably based upon, respectively, cyanide and nicotine, both very deadly poisons in concentrated forms.

Incidentally, there is no chemical named Ciphogene. Rex made it up. However, it seems reasonable that we may assume it is meant to be an insecticide or pesticide since on at least one occasion Wolfe is raging about "Thrips!" (tiny woodworms that suck plant juices). We may also assume it is safer and less lethal than the previous systems.

The prefix Cipho is a derivative of the word cipher, from old French, Latin and Arabic, meaning "zero", "empty" or "nothing." The suffix "gene" comes from ancient Greek and means "something generated or produced." Therefore it could be translated as "generated from nothing" or "generating nothing."

To anyone familiar with general chemistry, the name Ciphogene brings to mind Phosgene. Why they named it that is beyond me because it has nothing to do with phosphorus except its' toxicity. Phosgene (chemical name Carbonyl Chloride) is produced by combining chlorine and carbon monoxide. It is also produced by the degeneration of chloroform which should tell you something about its effects. It is a colorless gas and was used by the Germans in World War I. It is heavier than air, will collect at ground level and is very corrosive to lungs, eyes and skin. The effects are burning, coughing, short breath and lung damage. It is related to phospho-organic nerve agents like Sarin but less deadly. Class dismissed.

Now on to Wolfe and his plant rooms. They cover the entire fourth floor of the residence which was originally the roof. They are 34x86, the same dimensions as the house. They are reached by either the elevator (for Wolfe) or the stairs (for mere mortals). At the top of the stairs, one goes through an aluminum door into a small vestibule and then through another door into the plant rooms proper.

The area commonly called the plant rooms consist of four rooms. They are identified by the different temperature and humidity conditions maintained in them. The number of plants and the order and terminology of the rooms from the entrance inwards changes periodically, and occasionally their order has to be determined by a process of elimination.

In 1935 we don't know the order of the rooms but they contain 10,000 plants. In 1940, they are the warm room, the cool room, the tropical room and the potting room, but down to 3,000 plants. Propagation redefined, in 1941 there are 20,000 plants. The room order is still the same in 1951. In 1953 they are the warm, medium and cool rooms. In 1955, they are the cool, tropical and warm rooms. In 1956, they're the cool, medium and tropical. In 1957 they are described as the tropical, intermediate and cool rooms. In 1958, they are in the order of warm, moderate and cool rooms. In 1967 they are the cool, moderate and warm rooms.

If you want to raise orchids, I suggest you consult some other publication because it can get confusing which flowers belong in which room. The rooms can apparently change as the flowers do also. Apparently *Odontoglossums, Oncidiums* and *Miltonia* hybrids belong in the cool room. The *Odontoglossums* are the ones that got thrips in 1953. Some *Coelogynes* coexist in here at times. In 1947, Wolfe had a dispute with Theodore because his gardener had allotted some space in the cool room to three begonia plants named Thimbleberry. Begonias! Pfui!

The medium, warm or intermediate room seems to be the same. By whichever name, it seems to contain some *Miltonias* (at least the *M. roezli's*—they particularly impressed Archie one winter day) and *Phalaenopsis* when they are blooming. The latter seem to be grown in the tropical room but I guess they shift them when they sprout blossoms. They are also allegedly the hardest ones to grow well, closely followed by the *Miltonias*. This room also contains *Cattleyas, Laelias, Cymbidiums*, some hybrids and miscellaneous plants. The room has adjustable muslin shades.

The tropical room also contains *Renanthera inschootiana* and *Laelia gouldiana*. There was also a pink *Vanda* there that someone once offered to buy for $6,000. Germinating flasks are also kept in this room and the glass is painted over above that area. The tropical room has lath screens that can control the amount of sunlight and has 14 varieties of mossiae.

The whole area is lined with angle-iron staging painted silver, concrete benches and shelving, and covered with 10,000 square feet of glass in aluminum frames. It is also covered by a spraying system invented by Theodore to maintain the proper humidity in each room.

Archie has said that the *Miltonia* hybrids are his favorites although he also likes the *Odontoglossums* and the *reineckiana* (white, yellow, lilac and violet) in the tropical room.

After the three plant rooms is the warm, humid potting room. At a big bench is a stool made-to-order for Wolfe and another one for Theodore (at half his weight). Archie likes to wax poetic about Wolfe's yellow smock containing half an acre of cloth, in typical Archie hyperbole. There is an unheated, unglazed storage room alongside the elevator shaft for supplies like pots, crocks, sand, sphagnum, leaf mold, loam, osmundine and charcoal. Behind the potting room is the fumigating room where Wolfe employed a unique strategy to solve a murder in 1941. There is also a room in one corner they use for propagation and the bedroom where Theodore sleeps, the only area not glazed.

The adventures are replete with Wolfe's orchidae. In most of the cases they are embroidery but they are actually the catalysts for some of them. In the second case, Wolfe got a shipment from Richardt in Caracas that was a dozen bulbs short. In spite of his pique, he placed *Brassocattaelia truffautiana's* in the South Room for a guest. Two years later, he entered the case of Molly Lauck's murder because of an entreaty from half a dozen of the most imminent orchid growers in America. His primary motivation was the name of Winold Glueckner who had just received four bulbs of a pink *Coelogyne pandurata*, never seen before, and had scorned Wolfe's offer of $3,000 for two of them. Wolfe solved the murder and two subsequent ones but we aren't told if Glueckner was sufficiently grateful to grant his request later.

In 1941, it's all about three black orchid plants owned by his client, fellow orchid fancier Lewis Hewitt. Well, not actually black—"cannel coal colored with a thin coat of open kettle molasses, large labellum, not as large as aurea, cepals lanceolate, throat tinged with orange." Hewitt gave him two *C. nanssellis* plants and Wolfe only took them as a way of ingratiating himself with Hewitt. Wolfe eventually abandoned the plants since he had nicer ones in his own nursery. After solving the case, Wolfe virtually extorted all three black orchid plants from Hewitt as his fee. Nevertheless they formed a continuing friendship and Hewitt appeared in 14 more cases over the next 26 years.

Wolfe sent eight of the blossoms to a lady's funeral in that case, probably from some sense of guilt that he might have prevented her murder. After Wolfe called his new black orchids "matchless, incomparable, absolutely unique", Inspector Cramer didn't endear himself to him by damning them with faint praise. He called them "pretty [but] drab...not much color." Then came the final insult, that he liked geraniums better. It is a wonder he was allowed to continue appearing in the series after that.

In 1948, Wolfe is seeking out Andy Krasicki because he has successfully crossed an *Odontoglossum cirrhosum* with an *O. Nobile veitchianum*. During Wolfe's quest, his looking for a *Tibouchina semi-decandra* led him to a dead body.

In 1957, Wolfe covets Millard Bynoe's flamingo-pink *Vanda* (both petals and sepals true pink with no tints, spots or edgings). He solicited petty thievery for a spray of it ($200) and eventually made it a portion of his fee. Earlier in the case, he lamented "I wish I had never heard of orchids." Extraordinary.

Wolfe's daily hours (except Sunday) with the plants are 9 to 11 in the morning and 4 to 6 in the afternoon. They are supposed to be inviolable and so is business in the plant rooms. To Wolfe's occasional consternation, neither are.

During World War II, Wolfe initially cancelled all his plant room sessions when he was training to join the Army and exercised during the modified hours. Eventually disabused of that notion, he apparently resumed some sessions but frequently cancelled them whenever they interfered with the work he was doing free gratis for the Army.

Exclusive of this, however, the schedule is adhered to fairly well. In 1951, he sneaked down from the morning session to check out the Dazzle Dan comic strips but, after all, his license was in jeopardy. In 1956, Archie tells us that there have been only five occasions when he cut his afternoon session short, that being the fifth.

In 1961, he cut the afternoon session short by half an hour to intercept a box of corn that was dynamite. The next year he delayed the afternoon session to arrest a murderer.

The orchids are expensive concubines. Wolfe routinely corresponds with orchid hunters the world over including Ecuador, Honduras, Guatemala, Peru, Panama, New Guinea and Venezuela. In 1958 he bought a single *Coelogyne* from one in Burma for $800. Justifiably proud of them, Wolfe will yield to requests to show them to people on occasion but it depends. He won't tolerate children. He can stand gushers and jostlers but he can't stand those who say they can tell one from another but can't. The rule that no one but house staff goes there except to look at orchids hasn't been broken more than half a dozen times over the years.

Wolfe appreciates his orchids but is not totally enamored with them. During a tour of the plant rooms for Sarah Barstow, she remarks that they present "too much beauty." Wolfe agrees that they are "at first but long intimacy frees you from that illusion and acquaints you with their scantiness of character."

Wolfe will go to some extraordinary lengths for his orchids. In 1938, he took a road trip to show his albinos gotten by three new crosses with *Paphiopedilum lawrenceanum Hyeanum* just to show up Charles Shanks who had refused to trade albinos with him. This led him into a case fraught with precedent-breaking behavior on his part. He rode with two strange drivers (both females!), walked in crowds, called on a public official and obeyed a summons from a prospective client albeit primarily motivated by a search for a chair large enough to hold him comfortably.

In the *Christmas Party* case, Wolfe is prepared to take a road trip in a strange limousine with a strange driver to meet Mr. Thompson, the best hybridizer in England. If Wolfe will go to extraordinary lengths for his flowers, he will also do it for those personal associations he values. He cancels the trip to forestall what he thought was Archie's impending marriage.

The orchids also find a place in Wolfe's professional life. In 1946, Cramer got Wolfe a handsome *Brassocattleya thorntoni* as a gift when Wolfe had him reinstated to his old command. Archie offered to throw it out and Wolfe accused him of having no sentiment which I consider unjust.

In 1951, Archie sends 48 orchids to 16 girls as an inducement to submit to mass interrogation. Wolfe agrees but with qualifications—"no *Cypripedium Lord Fisher*, no *Dendrobium Cybele*." Archie is instructed to stick to *Cattleyas*, *Brassos* and *laelios*. He chooses *Cattleyas Dionysius, Katadin* and *petersi*, *Brassocattleya Calypso, tournierae* and *Nestor, Laeliocattleya barbarossa, Carmencita* and *St. Gothard*. When Archie offers to bill the client for three dollars each for them, Wolfe refuses, saying "I do not sell orchids." In a tour of the plant rooms during the conclave, one of the women wrecked two *Oncidium varicosum*. Two years later, a visitor offers to buy a *Vanda caerulea* and Wolfe repeats that they don't sell flowers. By 1974 he admits to selling some.

He provided a *Phalaenopsis Aphrodite*, one of his most treasured plants, for the 1958 dinner of the Ten for Aristolgy. In 1961, Archie sacrificed a *Dendrobium nobile* when he doused Sue McLeod with the two quarts of water in the orchid vase on Wolfe's desk. In the same case, Wolfe had a notary come up to the plant rooms during the morning session, breaking another rule.

He offers a pure white *Miltonia roezli alba* for a client's funeral. In 1961 he sends a *Dendrobium chrysotoxum* to Helen Gillard and *Laelia purpurata* to Doctor Vollmer for hiding he and Archie overnight. The next year Archie wears a green and white *Cypripedium lawrenceanum hyeanum* in his buttonhole so a witness can recognize him in a meeting. He notes that it is no great sacrifice since Wolfe has 200 varieties of the flower. In 1967, Wolfe sends a *Phalaenopsis Aphrodite sanderiana* to Dorothy Sebor.

Some of the other varieties in Wolfe's collection are:

Acampe pachyglossa
Broughtonia sanguinea
Dendrobium chrysotoxum
Cattleya trianae
A cross of *Cochlioda* with *Odontoglossum armainvillierense*
Cymbidium holfordiamum
Cymbidium pauwelsi
Cypripedium Minos
Dendrobium chrysotoxum
Dendrobium nobilius

Laeliocattleya Jaquetta (Archie calls this genus "big showoffs)
Laeliocattleya luminosa aurea
Laeliocattleya Lustre
Lycaste delicatissima
Miltonia charlesworthi
Miltonia vexillaria
Oncidium marshallianum
Oncidium varicosum
Odontoglossum harryanum
Odontoglossum hellmense
Odontoglossum pyramus
Peristeria elata
Phalaenopsis Aphrodite

The Cost Of Doing
Business—The Fiscal Wolfe

Nero Wolfe likes money, needs money and uses a lot of it. He values his services highly and, luckily, his particular talents attract many clients who are able to afford him—and allow him to afford to pay for his chosen lifestyle.

So, money is important to Wolfe but it is not his God. As is the only reasonable way to handle any necessary manmade addiction, he handles it and doesn't allow it to handle him, for the most part, at least. Of the 74 cases being considered for this work, Wolfe either receives no fee for the case, refuses a fee or returns the proffered fee in at least 15 of them. That is over 20 per cent of the total. Of course, the cases Archie has written and published are only a fraction of the whole. Many others are alluded to in the saga, many of which were profitable because Archie announces their successful conclusion after having just returned from the bank.

One of the office rules is that Wolfe sees all incoming checks before Archie stamps the endorsement on them and takes them to the bank. In the first adventure, Wolfe banks at the Metropolitan Trust Company Bank on Thirty-Fourth Street. The next year he has changed to the Continental Bank and Trust Company on Lexington Avenue.

In some of the cases, the precise fee is not mentioned. Archie ends these cases with statements like "a very attractive check", "a really nice hunk" or that Wolfe's bill was "pretty stiff." Adding up the amounts mentioned over the 42 years of recorded cases, Wolfe's total income adds up to $756,810.96 not including 10,000 British pounds back in the days when the pound sterling was worth about five American dollars. This gives an approximate total of $806,810.96. Without taking the cases without fees or retainers into consideration, this works out to a little over $19,200 a year, obviously unsatisfactory. The bulk of Wolfe's earnings obviously reside in the cases Archie never reported.

Also a factor are the number of cases that occurred within the year that Archie reported. These reached a high of five cases in 1959 with 1963 being the first year in which no case was reported. This was, of course, the year in which the case occurred and not the year in which it was published.

No cases—1963, 1970, 1971, 1972, 1973, 1975.
One case per year—1933, 1934, 1935, 1936, 1937, 1939, 1940, 1942, 1943, 1944, 1945, 1961, 1964, 1965, 1966, 1967, 1968, 1969, 1974.
Two cases per year—1938, 1941, 1946, 1950, 1952.
Three cases per year—1947, 1948, 1949, 1953, 1954, 1955, 1958, 1960.
Four cases per year—1951, 1956, 1957, 1962.
Five cases per year—1959.

This amounts to 74 cases including the two cases that were rewritten but set in the same year as the original. As counted, these would make the fourth case in 1957 and the fifth in 1959.

Below is a list of Wolfe's earnings in the reported cases along with some hopefully instructive comments in those areas where the inexactness overwhelms us.

1933— The first recorded case and a $60,000 fee. Obviously enough to last the entire year, especially at Depression prices. We also get a look at Wolfe's sense of frugality. Archie buys information from one witness for a dollar and, later, Wolfe carps at him for giving a woman $1000. In an unrecorded case mentioned a decade later, a man named Hallowell unsuccessfully tried to bribe Wolfe with $150,000 to avert a death sentence Wolfe was weaving around him.

1934— Wolfe billed the members of The League of Atonement $56,915, each in different amounts according to his ability to pay, from $5 to $9,000. The final fee may have been lower by $7,000 because the person scheduled to pay that amount was unable to but his next of kin may have.

1935— Wolfe took the case for a $1 retainer and eventually obtained $50,000 for his client. We aren't told how much he dunned him for, if any.

1936— One case for $10,000.

1937— Wolfe turned down several potential clients as well as a $50,000 bribe. The eventual fee was what he had been pursuing from the outset, a sausage recipe.

1938— No retainer and an unknown fee for the first case although the client was very wealthy so we may assume his services were not *pro bono*. He refused a $10,000 fee in the second case but this case had an unusual personal connection. Without that feature, he would have no doubt followed his inclination to ignore business when the bank balance is in five figures.

1939— God only knows what the fee was but some of the clients were multi-millionaires.

1940— No mention of a fee for this year's single case but Wolfe isn't living on Spam since he paid $11,412.83 in income tax this year.

1941— The fee for the first case was three black orchids. In the second, there was a $2,000 retainer and if there was any fee, it was unspecified. Then he spent part of the first fee on the second case, to boot.

1942— In high patriotic dudgeon over Pearl Harbor and Nazi efforts at world conquest, Wolfe has given up his detective business (at least the remunerative aspects of it) for the duration of the war. The entire cast of operatives is overseas fighting Germans and Japs except for Bill Gore, who is neither mentioned nor utilized. Archie is drawing a Major's pay from U.S. Army Intelligence without a subsistence allowance since he is still living with Wolfe.He mentions that his Major's pay (about $2,400 annually) was about one-third of the salary he had been drawing from Wolfe, placing him in about the $7,200 range. In another financial conundrum, Archie is faced with how he is going to write off $100 he gave a murderer to get out of town.

1943— Archie is still making Major's pay and evidently feels it is enough because he turns down a $10,000 bribe but not before playfully getting the man to up the ante to a million. Archie also dryly remarks that a million dollars would have bought Wolfe four million bottles of the best beer available then.

1944— No fee for the single recorded case this year.

1945— For this year's case, Wolfe receives $5,000.

1946— The privations of the war have apparently not reduced Wolfe too far and the bank balance is doubtlessly sufficient. Wolfe turns down a $300,000 bribe and Archie mentions that he has more *Cattleyas* than he has room for and could easily sell 500 of them for $12,000 if that were necessary to stay out of the soup line. It doesn't come to that because he receives a $100,000 fee for one case followed by a $5,000 retainer and a $50,000 fee for the second.

1947— A productive year. The first case involved some considerable expenses but they were peanuts compared to the fee. It is unspecified but the client was worth $20 million so let your imagination run wild. In the second case, Wolfe receives a $2,000 retainer and an unnamed fee but it was from a millionairess. More than adequate to manage Archie's salary of $200 a week ($10,400 a year). We aren't told the exact amount of the third but you can be damned sure they paid every cent of it because Wolfe added ninety-five cents to the expense list for a client's sandwiches.

1948— A first case that netted a $20,000 fee and two more that netted nothing but a refused $50,000 bribe offer.

1949— In this year's pair of cases, Wolfe receives fees of $5,000 for the first and $55,000 for the second. This is hardly balanced by the $40,000 damage sustained by his machine-gunned plant rooms in the second. Although his tormentor sends him $50,000 to cover the damages, most of it is placed in escrow to fund the coming battle against him.

1950— It is at this point in the saga that Archie reveals that Wolfe needs a minimum of $10,000 a month to pay the salaries and run the house (i.e. pay for the food, books, orchids, etc.). When Wolfe takes the $10,000 retainer for the case that eventually forces him out of his home, Archie says that half of Mrs. Barry Rackham's four-million dollar fortune would pay his salary for 167 years, putting him in the $12,000-a-year range. Wolfe suggests that Marko Vukcic pay Fritz twice the $1,000 monthly salary he does and suggests Lewis Hewitt pay Theodore $200 weekly ($10,400 yearly). That is probably what Wolfe pays Theodore and certainly not double like the recommendation he made to Vukcic on Fritz's behalf. On that note, we may simply assume the obvious, that his food is closer to his heart than his orchids. He obviously differentiates between material and emotional sustenance. Take away his orchids and he mourns. Take away his food and he dies.

1951— They have just finished the unrecorded Pendexter infringement case and received an indeterminate five-figure check. Wolfe receives no fee for one of this year's cases and an undetermined fee for another but since one of them was from an oil millionaire who was part-owner of the New York Giants, it probably wasn't too tawdry. For the other two, he receives $5,000 for one and a $3,000 retainer with a $20,000 fee for the other.

1952— Wolfe gets an undetermined fee for one of this year's cases. In the other, the President of Softdown Inc. makes $65,000 annually and Wolfe seems peeved that a mere towel merchant makes half as much as he does. He ends up with Archie as his client and, in the end, tears up Archie's check for $1,624.37. It's a symbolic gesture because Archie has to bear about $200 in expenses out of his own pocket. To teach him a lesson, Wolfe won't allow him to write it off on his expense account. To account for Wolfe's intransigence in one of the cases, Archie mentions that Wolfe had previously returned a $40,000 retainer to a man named Zimmerman who proposed to tell Wolfe how to run his case.

1953— Not a profitable year for Wolfe. In the first case, the client is rendered unable to pay the $500 fee before he has the opportunity. The second yields $5,000 and the third is taken for a record low retainer—$4.30 from a 12-year-old client. This later evolves into a $10,000 fee but even so—

1954— Perhaps as a result of the previous year's paucity, the cupboard is getting bare this year. The bank balance is down to $26,000, there is $3,800 in emergency reserve and $194 in petty cash. One case is taken with no client and no promise of a fee but, after refusing a $10,000 bribe, Wolfe got "a really handsome check" from a man he prevented from being falsely convicted of murder. The other two are feeless and one of them is expensive because it requires international travel. For Wolfe, it was even more expensive emotionally.

1955— This year the books played catch-up. One case brought a fee of $50,000 plus expenses. Another began more modestly with a $1,000 retainer but ended with "a really nice hunk" from a uranium millionaire. The last case produced an emerald ring the size of a hazel nut but Wolfe returned it because it was an attempted bribe from a murderer.

1956— To make up for the case he was trapped into by circumstances, Wolfe got $2,000 for one and $50,000 for another. In the latter one, however, he split the fee three ways with the relatives of two murder victims. Wolfe took the smallest third of $16,666.66. Two others were feeless.

1957— One of the cases was feeless and two others were less than remunerative but, luckily, it apparently didn't matter much. One was for a proffered $100 retainer but Wolfe returned it because his tax bracket would have reduced it to $16 anyway, analogous to only four days worth of beer. The other was for a $300 retainer which equaled three weeks of beer or two days of Archie's salary. Archie also reveals that he and Fritz are paid about the same salary and that running the kitchen costs only slightly less than the orchids. The former may or may not include Wolfe's $100-a-week beer bill. Doing the grade school math, we can see that Archie and Fritz make about $39,000 annually (if figured on a five day week) or $54,750 (if figured on an everyday basis). One case that helped take up the slack produced a $10,000 retainer and "a very attractive check" for a fee. The case that probably meant the most to Wolfe was one that yielded an unnamed fee and a very special orchid.

1958— One case was on the cheap but in the second one, there was a $20,000 retainer and the final bill was "pretty stiff". Archie had to refuse another $5,000 in bribes. The last case gleaned $50—$25 for Wolfe and $25 for Archie.

1959— One case evolves because someone offended Wolfe. Another brings $5,000 in, they have just finished the unrecorded Brigham forgery case and deposited a check for $7,417.65 which leave Wolfe in a position to refuse Hattie Annis's offer of $42,000 and even dodges her second offer of $5,621.65. The rewritten version brings the same fee schedule. Lily Rowan then retained Wolfe with $1,000 and produced an unspecified fee. The last case is feeless.

1960— The fees followed the bell curve this year. The first started with an offer of $100 for a half hour of Wolfe's time. The next produced $50,000 but Archie had to solicit the case because the bank balance was only $14,000 five weeks before tax day. The last was accepted for one dollar of an offered $500.

1961— The single case this year yielded $100,000 minus Archie's $75 for Archie's bail in Westchester County.

1962— An ambiguous year. In the summer of 1962, Archie is concerned because the fiscal harvest for the first seven months of 1962 is $9,000 behind 1961. The $22,000 from the first case helped offset the $47.50 dictionary Wolfe incinerated. The next two cases started with $1,000 retainers and unnamed fees. The second one was apparently was apparently substantial because Archie remarked that the client paid his bill promptly. The fourth case started because someone screwed up Wolfe's scheduled delivery of special corn. Archie ended up the subject of two arrest warrants in the same week (although the second one wasn't actually served) and Wolfe had to cough up $20,000 bail.

1964— One case, a refused fee and a 27-year-old debt repaid.

1965— A banner year even with only one recorded case—$100,000, the largest retainer in his experience. Plus some lasting perks for one-upmanship.

1966— Another internal case with no retainer and no fee, bailing Orrie Cather out of a false murder charge.

1967— The year's single recorded case started with a $22,000 retainer which Wolfe refunded but it eventually produced a $50,000 fee.

1968— Wolfe has to travel clear across the country to get Archie out of a jam in a case with no promise of a fee. Maybe he feels guilty because Archie's salary is now stated at $400 a week, nearly half of his 1957 wages. Inflation or too much *pro bono* work?

1969— The year's single recorded case started with a $20,000 retainer and circumstances later blossomed it into another $100,000.

1974— A Family Affair. Enough said.

When he gets paid for his services, Wolfe's fees are always exclusive of expenses but the client must bear these also. These can include everything from train and plane tickets to dinner at Rusterman's with a client or witness (accompanied by Archie, of course, not him), bribes and a myriad of other things as mundane as cabfare (Archie again, naturally). The primary expense, however, is usually the fees of his other operatives. These are generally skimped over in the early adventures but treated more thoroughly in later years. The prices reflect the economy of the times and, when given in fuller and more comparative detail, clearly reveal the pecking order of the operatives. Not unexpectedly, this also reveals the pattern of their individual value to Wolfe and his personal esteem for them. Below are listed the rates for the operatives and the respective years in which they are mentioned.

	SAUL PANZER	FRED DURKIN	ORRIE CATHER	JOHNNY KEEMS	BILL GORE
1934		$1/hr.			
1935				$1.50/hr.	
1939			$1/hr.		
1945	$20/day				
1946	$30/day				
1955	$50/day				
1957	$60/day				
1958	$70/day	$35/day			
1960	$10/hr.	$7.50/hr.			
1968	$500/wk.	$8/hr.			
1969	$15/hr.	$8/hr.	$8/hr.		
1974	$20/hr.				

In 1951, Saul, Fred and Orrie together cost $15 an hour or $200 a day. In 1962, the trio costs $25 an hour. In 1956, Saul, Fred, Orrie and Johnny Keems together cost $160 a day. These figures will show why Wolfe charges high fees since a little simple math will show how fast the bills can pile up depending upon the number of operatives he employs and for how long. It can also show the limits of his dedication to a case when he has no client, is getting no fee and is absorbing these costs personally. On a few cases when Saul has failed to deliver, he always offers to forego his fee but Wolfe never takes advantage of that.

Admittedly there are a lot of blanks in the above table but a general formula may be discerned from Archie's comments at various times. Saul is always the highest paid operative, always receiving at least twice what the others do which is also what he's able to charge on the open market when he's not working for Wolfe. Fred and Orrie usually make half what Saul does because, as Archie bluntly states, that's what they're worth, at least monetarily. Although all five are not compared at one time, Johnny Keems and Bill Gore are probably paid a slight increment less than Fred and Orrie at any given point in time. From their abilities, professional shortcomings and Archie's relative respect for them, they too seem to get paid what they're worth. He also mentions that, in his opinion, Orrie is worth somewhat less than Fred (as an investigator) even though they receive the same rate of pay.

The Not—So—Immobile Wolfe

Nero Wolfe doesn't like to leave his house, we are told. That is why he has gone to such great trouble and expense to make it so amenable to all his wants and needs. He once described Archie as "intrepid" for venturing out in a rainstorm to go to the bank. Even so, Wolfe does leave his home with remarkable frequency, sometimes voluntarily, sometimes not.

An unabashed believer in American democracy, exercising his rights and responsibilities as a voter is one of the things that will always get Wolfe out of the house. He never fails to vote. It is one of the few personal errands that will get him out in any weather.

In the second adventure in 1934, Wolfe reacted to Archie's suggestion that he go out on the front stoop of the brownstone as "a frantic sortie." Nevertheless, he yields to this kind of expedition in cases set in 1952 and 1960. In the same case in 1934, he leaves his home twice; once voluntarily for the honor of dining at the same table as Albert Einstein and once, not so voluntarily, when he is temporarily but productively kidnapped by a cab driver. He also might or might not have taken a trip to the New York City Jail (attractively called The Tombs) to visit Paul Chapin. Archie has varying opinions on the subject but no concrete evidence.

In fact, in the 74 stories we consider in this volume, Wolfe leaves his house in almost half of them, 35 of the 74 if you count the two trips out to the front stoop.

As a necessity of life in New York, Wolfe always owns one or two cars although he doesn't drive himself. He gets a new one every year (probably to salve his brain into believing it minimizes the chances of catastrophic mechanical failure while he's riding in it), he pays for the cars and Archie selects them, within reason, no doubt. The cars are always kept immaculately. Wolfe hates and fears moving vehicles of all kinds and subjects himself to their whimsy only in dire circumstances. He thinks all machinery that have moving parts are out to get him. Archie says he is the only one in the house who drives although in the first case, Fritz is returning from beer shopping in Wolfe's big shiny black roadster with a rumble seat. Archie used this car to chase a young man named Lon Graves in a

Pierce coupe with a satchel of emeralds between his knees from New Milford all over Pike County in a driving rainstorm. Following Fritz's trip for beer, none of the others drive as far as we're told.

Wolfe's first car is kept in a garage two blocks from the house on Thirty-Sixth Street near Tenth Avenue. In 1939, the garage is on Eleventh Avenue but is back to Tenth the following year. Thereafter the location vacillates between Tenth and Eleventh Avenues but in 1961 he settles on Curran's Garage on Tenth Avenue between Thirty-Fifth and Thirty-Sixth Streets.

When he does venture out, Wolfe never rides in the front seat of a vehicle. He thinks the glass will carve him up in the inevitable crash. His normal posture in a moving vehicle is rigidly erect with an iron grip on a safety strap and his lips compressed into a thin, colorless line. He refuses to talk when he's in a moving vehicle and although he breaks that rule occasionally, it is always under great pressure. He dislikes motion or bumps and believes Archie deliberately seeks out potholes to jostle him. Occasionally Archie will tease him by driving with one hand or passing a slower car. On those occasions, Wolfe compresses his lips to a line so thin no lips show at all. When he's irritated, Archie has a tendency to speed up unconsciously, another reason for Wolfe not to goad him when they're moving.

By the time of the second case in 1934, Wolfe owns a roadster and a sedan. Surely the roadster is for Archie's sense of adventure. I can never picture Wolfe riding in one and the last mention of the roadster is in 1941. In October of 1945 he has a brown Wethersill sedan, the first mention of a car by make (albeit fictional). Of the more than 6,000 makes of cars that have been produced, none has ever been a Wethersill. By the next year, he has a convertible and a dark blue Wethersill sedan. The latter car is the one in which Archie took him to Police Headquarters where he was placed under arrest from 3:15 until 6:00. Wolfe missed his afternoon session with the orchids and slapped a police inspector. Altogether a memorable afternoon.

By June of 1947, Wolfe has decided to switch (at least temporarily) to traditional American makes and had just bought a new Cadillac sedan. By this time, Archie is undeniably the only driver in the household. Wolfe is obviously out, Theodore insists on walking because it's healthy, and Fritz has allowed his license to expire and now pretends that he doesn't know how to drive. In 1949, along with the omnipresent sedan another convertible is mentioned although, like the roadsters, why Wolfe owns one is unknown. God knows he'd never ride in it, one hand holding his hat on against the unfettered gales or, even with the top up, nothing but mere fabric between him and the pavement when it inevitably turns over. So the ragtop may be another sop to Archie's sporty vanity.

In 1958, he has switched to a gray Heron sedan. Another fictional marque, no car has ever been named after the heron, a long-legged, long-necked wading bird resembling a small flamingo. It is simply described as "big" but is apparently satisfactory because he remains loyal to Herons through the remainder of the cases. His 1961 Heron sedan has a push-button automatic transmission, a new feature on Chrysler products that year indicating that Stout may have had that brand in mind. However, the hood ornaments of Cadillacs in the early 1930s featured a heron so, as Archie would say, it's a tossup.

Returning to the mobility of an allegedly immobile Wolfe, in 1935 he takes a trip to Boyden McNair's offices at the entreaty of half a dozen of the most eminent orchid growers in America. On this excursion, he is resplendent in an overcoat, scarf, gloves, walking stick, gaiters and what Archie describes as a black felt pirate's hat (size eight).

In 1937 he endures a fourteen-hour ride on a train (!) to West Virginia, humbling himself for a sausage recipe. In 1938, he leaves to show orchids at a show in upstate New York before he is sidetracked. In the same year, he faked a trip outside to get rid of a Nazi agent. In 1941 he went out to see some black orchids because he just had to see them for himself.

Wolfe scraps his entire schedule in early 1942 for the war effort. Archie enlists in the Army and goes to Georgia to work for Military Intelligence, at least temporarily. Wolfe closes the office, mail and dust piles up, and the kitchen is denuded except for salads and fruits. Wolfe and Fritz walk during the modified plant room hours (7-9 A.M. and 4-6 P.M.), Wolfe stops drinking beer, goes on a diet, loses weight and goes to bed at 9:00 P.M., saying that he's training to kill Germans because he didn't kill enough in 1918.

This situation doesn't last too long and Archie returns home to help Wolfe with the war effort from home. In 1943, Wolfe's mobility increases even more. Completely suspending his rule on outdoor travel, the only wartime concession he demands and receives is enough gas for his car under war rationing. Even with Archie at the wheel, he's flitting all over Manhattan, even making two trips to Military Intelligence Headquarters in a single day and making other substantial sacrifices. During one trip, Wolfe even lost his head to the point where he asks Archie to *Speed Up!*

After the war is won, Wolfe's travel declines but is still substantial. In 1946, Archie takes him to Police Headquarters for the memorable incident in which he slapped Inspector Ash. In 1947, he has to testify in court. In 1949, Archie drives him to the Sperling country place near Chappaqua when Mr. X destroys his plant rooms and Wolfe goes without sleep for thirty hours. In more amenable trips over the years, he goes to Rusterman's to dine with Marko Vukcic.

The year of 1951 was a bad one. He has to go to a New York Giants baseball game at the Polo Grounds to humor a world-famous chef (imagine him perched on the edge of one of those seats!). The next year, he has to get Archie out of jail again.

He gets to stay home in 1953 but he needs the rest. The next year he travels halfway around the world to solve Marko Vukcic's murder and then, not long after he returns, he's subpoenaed to testify in court. He ducks out of court and hides out at Saul's to solve the case. In 1955, he travels to River Bend in upstate New York's Adirondacks at the request of the State Department to cook brook trout for an ambassador. Archie is pretty gentle with him on this trip. He takes seven hours to cover the 328 miles.

The next year is also trying for Wolfe. He intends to take a limousine to Long Island without Archie to meet Mister Thompson, the best orchid hybridizer in England but the trip has to be cancelled. Instead, Wolfe ends up tramping over a mile through a snowstorm with the law on his tail. Then he has to go all the way to Albany to testify before a committee about wire-tapping. That was another gentle trip for Archie, taking four hours for the 160 miles. Finally, he agrees to deliver a speech to the United Restaurant Workers of America to end union pressures on Fritz. Naturally each excursion causes him to have to work.

By 1957, Archie estimates that Wolfe has asked him to drive him somewhere between 18 and 20 times, which he says is positively peripatetic for him.

In 1958 he attends the Ten For Aristology dinner because Fritz is cooking it and what begins as a personal favor turns into a professional one. The next year he goes to a committee meeting for the National Association of Authors and Dramatists when faced with three murders and the matter complicated by a self-imposed beer and meat strike. In 1960 he goes to Lily Rowan's apartment to dine on blue grouse. In both 1961 and 1962, he and Archie have to sneak out of the house and hide from the cops. In the first case, to Doctor Vollmer's house and in the second, to a client's.

Wolfe's friend and fellow orchid grower Lewis Hewitt figures in several of the last trips. In 1965 Wolfe goes to his Long Island estate to create a scheme to fool the FBI and in 1967 he's there just to enjoy the orchids.

And in the final adventure in 1974, Wolfe goes both to Rusterman's and to meet Pierre Duco's father.

One reason Archie didn't believe Wolfe's story about taking a trip to visit Paul Chapin in The Tombs was because Wolfe said he had asked for a driver from the garage because Archie was busy elsewhere. Wolfe once told Archie that for him (Wolfe) to ride in a strange vehicle with a stranger driving was foolhardy but with Archie driving a car of his choice, it was merely imprudent.

In spite of those beliefs, Wolfe has been that foolhardy on occasion. In 1939 he took a taxi to the Hawthorne residence on Sixty-Seventh Street on an investigation. In 1942 and 1952 he has to go to the Tenth Precinct to get Archie out of jail. On the first occasion in March of 1942, Wolfe haughtily threatened to have the NYPD abolished. In 1948, he travels to Westchester County to try to get a temporary replacement for Theodore. Try to picture the desperation that has Wolfe, Archie and Saul infiltrating the Pitcairn mansion grounds on foot, in the dark, in a snowstorm, even wading streams, falling twice and rolling down a cliff. Remarkable!

In 1949, Wolfe has to go to the Goldenrod Barber Shop to meet Archie, get a haircut and solve a cop's murder. By the way, he refuses to allow the use of clippers, he's strictly a comb and scissors man. In 1950 he has to abandon the house for most of the year for his final battle with Arnold Zeck.

In 1952, Wolfe is lured to the Lewent home on Sixty-Ninth Street between Fifth and Madison Avenues by a ruse. Archie concocts a phone call that he's in trouble at the scene of a murder. It's one of only four times that Archie has seen Wolfe speechless. Even so, Wolfe solves the case in a barely adequate chair.

In 1955, he again takes a taxi to the offices of Lippert, Buff and Assa but he was motivated by personal affront. A murderer had poisoned a man in his office with his pernod.

In 1968, he has spent three days on Hewitt's estate before he has to dash (perhaps too strong a word?) across the country to rescue Archie in Montana.

But the ultimate example of Wolfe's mobility and willingness to break precedents has to be 1954's *The Black Mountain*. He not only allowed business to intrude upon a meal but suffered it in the form of a death notification from Archie. He went to the morgue for the first time and later *walked* to Rusterman's Restaurant (where he dined nine times in the next three weeks) when other transportation was available. He spent over $3,000 of his own money on an investigation with no client and made at least 14 expensive international telephone calls, one of which cost $40. He personally interviewed 31 people in his home, actually went out to meet five others, went to two conferences in the District Attorney's office and talked in moving vehicles. Finally he got a passport, flew to Europe, walked all over Yugoslavia, climbed rocks and got shot in the leg.

Immobile? By choice, perhaps, but not by necessity.

Moriarty

Without wishing to insult anyone's intelligence or experience, I feel it necessary to add another Archie-like disclaimer here. Because of this, I realize I should have probably put this chapter at the very front of the book but I hope you'll understand that it just didn't belong there.

If the title of this chapter has no meaning for you, if you are wondering why in the hell a chapter about a man named Zeck should be titled "Moriarty", you should return this book and get your money back immediately. Now, on with the show.

Whether in front of Archie, his operatives or an audience of suspects, Nero Wolfe enjoys reconstructing the crimes he is investigating in minute detail. To keep his audience (and readers) off balance and temporarily in the dark as to where his logic is leading, he often presents these reconstructions as hypothetical situations. During these articulations, he has an affinity for calling a suspect or a witness he wants to keep temporarily anonymous by the traditional mathematical symbol for an unknown—X.

Of course, the X of the moment is not truly an unknown. X is known to Wolfe, perhaps to Archie if he has figured it out for himself or if Wolfe has enlightened him, one or more of the operatives if they came up with the nugget of information that identified X and possibly to one of the witnesses if they are trying to conceal X's identity. Of course, X knows who he or she is but they don't know that Wolfe knows. So they too sit through the denouement.

So there have been dozens, perhaps hundreds of X's in Wolfe's career, recorded and unrecorded. But for the faithful of the Canon, there is only one true X. Arnold Zeck. He merits his own chapter in this volume simply because of his unique status in the Wolfe saga.

Rex Stout created only one continuing villain who appeared as a protagonist in more than one of the stories. Arnold Zeck, the master criminal, appeared first in *And Be A Villain*, set in March and April of 1948. He returned in *The Second Confession*, set in June of 1949. His final appearance at the Reichenbach Falls (see the disclaimer above) took place in the story entitled *In The Best Families*, set in the Spring and Summer of 1950.

Oddly enough, Stout's biography tells us that this was unintended, at least on the level of conscious planning. Stout said "When I wrote *And Be A Villain* I didn't plan, or even consciously contemplate, subsequent appearance or appearances of Zeck, but I suspect my subconscious thought he would show up again. When I wrote *The Second Confession* I must have felt he would appear again, but I had no idea how or when."

Arnold Zeck is a master criminal, not on a firsthand basis but as a manipulator, somewhat analogous to the boss of an organized crime family. He is fabulously wealthy and, in Wolfe's words, his income stems from "narcotics, smuggling, industrial and commercial rackets, gambling, waterfront blackguardism, professional larceny, blackmail, political malfeasance—that by no means exhausts his curriculum, but it sufficiently indicates his character".

Wolfe's first independent knowledge of Zeck came to him in 1938, roughly the same time period in which Wolfe was being menaced by a bull named Caesar in a pasture in upstate New York. An unnamed policeman consulted Wolfe about a murder case the officer was investigating and Wolfe detected the presence of an ominous guiding hand behind the crime. He passed on what information he had developed and dropped it.

Their first contact came on Wednesday, June 9, 1943, when Zeck called Wolfe using the alias of Mr. Duncan. He gave Wolfe "some advice" about a job Wolfe was doing for Lieutenant General Carpenter in the Pentagon. During World War II, Wolfe had essentially placed his entire private detective business, resources and talents at the beck and call of the government for the duration. Most of those cases were highly secret and unrecorded. We are given no further information about the case or the "advice" although it may be instructive that only two months later, Wolfe was investigating a case of war profiteering at the highest levels of the U.S. government.

The next contact was on Wednesday, January 16, 1946, when Zeck "advised" Wolfe to limit his efforts on behalf of a Mrs. Tremont. Although Zeck compliments Wolfe on limiting his efforts in both cases, Wolfe coldly assures him that the efforts were limited only to the point of accomplishing what he was hired for and no more.

Even on the telephone, Zeck's voice is memorable—"hard, slow, precise and cold as last week's corpse." Not long after the second phone call, Wolfe hires some of Del Bascom's operatives to learn more about his anonymous caller. He does so deliberately without informing or using Archie or any of his usual operatives.

He learned that the man's name was Arnold Zeck, he was fabulously wealthy and lived in a large mansion named Eastcrest. The mansion is on a hill in Westchester County, five miles from Mount Kisco, New York. Lon Cohen has heard rumors that Zeck owns twenty assemblymen, six district leaders and if you print something about him he doesn't like, your body washes up on Montauk Point, mangled by sharks. Zeck also is blackmailing a NYPD Inspector named Drake but that is known only to Wolfe. About the only concrete information he has about Zeck is that a few years before 1948, he gave his yacht to the U.S. Navy, presumably during the war. Perhaps it was a gesture of appreciation for the profits he was making out of the war effort but from what we know of the man, it was more likely an attempt to appear as a munificent patriot.

Wolfe and Zeck finally came into direct conflict in March of 1948. On March 13, Wolfe became involved in the investigation of the murder of Cyril Orchard. Seventeen days later, on Tuesday, March 30, Zeck called Wolfe for the third time. This time they had a lengthy and rather snippy conversation, obviously placing them at odds.

The case reached a satisfactory conclusion for all concerned (except the murderer) four days later. Slightly over six weeks passed until the murderer was sentenced. The next day, Wednesday, May 18, 1948, Wolfe received his fourth phone call from Zeck. This time he was again congratulated on keeping his investigation within the limits Zeck had prescribed and Wolfe again assured him that was not the case. Zeck hung up abruptly and once more their affairs were not entangled. This was not to last.

Fifteen months after the conclusion of the Orchard case, Wolfe was hired by James Sperling to find out if Louis Rony was a communist. Two days later, on Saturday, June 18, 1949, Zeck calls for the fifth time. Archie is at the Sperling estate near Chappaqua and is unaware of the call until Wolfe informs him later. Zeck demands that Wolfe end his investigation of Rony. Wolfe, as he puts it, "demurred" and hangs up. Thirty-two hours and twenty-four minutes later, at 2:24 A.M. on June 20, some unidentified marksmen pump 192 machinegun slugs into his plant rooms, rending them to shreds. Zeck sends Wolfe $50,000 to cover the damages and, possibly, soften the blow of the warning. If that was his intent, he didn't know his adversary very well. Some of the special hybrids were irreplaceable. Wolfe spent $40,000 on new glass and plants but it wasn't Zeck's money. That was placed in escrow in a bank in New Jersey for later eventualities.

Another mysterious figure appears at this point. Archie is banished from the office and is forbidden to snoop. A "Mr. Jones" has an appointment with Wolfe. Mr. Jones comes and goes, unseen and unheard by anyone but Wolfe. Archie later finds that Mr. Jones has been given $15,000 by Wolfe for unknown duties. Archie never finds out and neither do we. But, a few weeks later, Zeck calls again in the summer of 1949. He again congratulates Wolfe that his investigation has not intruded too far into his affairs and Wolfe again assures him that was only happenstance. The next day, Zeck sent Wolfe another $15,000, the exact amount paid to Mr. Jones for his mysterious duties. That too goes into the New Jersey bank account.

At the time of the third phone call from Zeck on March 30, 1948, Wolfe had ordered Archie to forget Zeck's name. At that time, the eternally temerarious (as his boss would have described him) Archie started calling him "X" or "Whosis", more to irritate Wolfe than as a means of identification. On the same occasion, Wolfe told Archie that if he ever had to go to battle with Zeck, "I shall leave this house, find a place where I can work—and sleep and eat if there is time for it—and stay there until I have finished." After an uneasy ten-month truce, that time came and it happened very nearly as Wolfe had predicted.

On Thursday, April 6, 1950, Mrs. Barry Rackham made an appointment with Wolfe for the next day. He accepted her commission to discover the source of her husband's secret income. On Saturday, a tear gas bomb disguised as a package of sausage was delivered to Wolfe's house and went off in his office. Within minutes, Zeck made his sixth phone call to him. Zeck had only just begun making his strident demands when Wolfe crisply hung up on him. The Rubicon had been crossed.

On Sunday, April 9, Archie returned home to find the front door standing open, mutely signaling the abandonment of much more than just a house. Wolfe's public notice of his retirement appeared in the papers the next day. The orchids and Theodore went to Lewis Hewitt's estate on Long Island. Fritz went to work for Marko Vukcic in Rusterman's Restaurant. Archie was left, without instructions, to fend for himself, obviously because Wolfe knew he could.

Nero Wolfe's longest case, it wends on for more than five months. Zeck is a pale shadow of the original Moriarty but he stretches the other characters to new limits.

Nero In Hollywood

Motion Pictures

Nero Wolfe was only one novel old when the bright lights of Hollywood came calling. Columbia Pictures bought the film rights to *Fer-de-Lance* for $7,500 (remember this was the mid-1930's) and the wrangling began. Since Stout had created such a unique lead character, casting for the movie version of *Fer-de-Lance* naturally became an artistic morass of opinions and counter-opinions.

John McAleer tells us that the negotiations were initially in the hands of John Farrar of Stout's publisher, Farrar & Rinehart. It is just as well that Farrar was able at the publishing business because he may have starved had he chosen the profession of casting agent. His personal favorite for the role of Wolfe was an actor named Nigel Bruce, soon afterwards to become famous as the rather buffoonish Watson to Basil Rathbone's definitive (until Jeremy Brett half a century later) characterization of Sherlock Holmes. Thankfully, it didn't come to pass.

Film producer Walter Wanger preferred journalist, author and drama critic Alexander Woollcott (1887–1943) for the role. Although Woollcott was not an actor, what may have influenced Wanger's preference was Woollcott's personal opinion that Rex Stout modeled the character of Wolfe after him. Woollcott's deserved reputation as a fat, acerbic, opinionated, egocentric genius was apparently conclusive as far as he was concerned although Rex Stout said he was wrong and that's good enough for me. Wanger's choice also went by the wayside.

As the person who conjured the first mental image of Nero Wolfe, Rex Stout had his own opinions. His personal favorite for the role was Charles Laughton. Naturally every Wolfe aficionado has his or her own mental image of the characters. While I have great respect for Mr. Laughton's professional abilities and while Wolfe is physically huge, I always pictured his countenance as not unattractive, certainly not on a par with the actor who made the role of Quasimodo his own. That said, in my mind's eye I can see Laughton's intellectual, arrogant, superior sneer from other roles and I can understand Rex Stout's attraction. Years later, Laughton's wife, actress Elsa Lanchester, told McAleer that she had wanted to play Dora Chapin in the film version of *The League of Frightened Men*. But that was not to happen, either. The studio wanted Laughton to agree to a series of Wolfe films but other obligations prevented that.

Edward Arnold finally got the role of Wolfe in the film adaptation of *Fer-de-Lance*, titled *Meet Nero Wolfe*. Arnold played the fat detective as sternly unlikable. As a sop to the soon-after-Prohibition times, Wolfe's fondness for beer was changed to hot chocolate which Rex Stout must have thought a ludicrous condescension. Film critics generally rate the film above average but the second one, *The League of Frightened Men*, although generally considered to be a better story, rated lower in their estimation. In that one, the Wolfe role went to Walter Connolly and although he played Wolfe as more genial, critics generally considered him badly miscast.

The same criticism has been made for Lionel Stander's casting as Archie, a criticism shared by Rex Stout. As an insight into Stout's mental image of Archie, years later he said he thought actor George Sanders would have made a good Archie. For those interested in making the comparison, Sanders later made three films as Michael Arlen's amateur detective The Falcon, a sardonic, witty, dapper, light-hearted sleuth with a tough core under an urbane exterior. Sound like anyone familiar? In later years, Stout even said that he thought that a young Humphrey Bogart would have made a good Archie. He was not, however, receptive to a suggestion of Paul Newman in the role.

Meet Nero Wolfe—1936, Columbia Pictures, 73 minutes.
Starring Edward Arnold as Nero Wolfe
Lionel Stander as Archie Goodwin
Also starring Joan Perry, Victor Jory, Nana Bryant, Dennie Moore and Rita Cansino (later more famous as Rita Hayworth)
Directed by Herbert Biberman
The League of Frightened Men—1937, Columbia Pictures, 65 minutes.
Starring Walter Connolly as Nero Wolfe
Lionel Stander as Archie Goodwin
Also starring Eduardo Ciannelli, Irene Hervey, Victor Kilian, and Walter Kingsford.
Directed by Alfred E. Green

Radio

During the spring of 1943, radio producer Himan Brown managed to get Stout to agree to allow Nero Wolfe to be portrayed on a radio series. In spite of the fact that it was intermittent since the networks vacillated between winter and summer programming, it was more successful than the movies, at least with the public. The first attempt was from April 7 to June 30, 1943. They were half-hour shows on the ABC Radio network on Wednesdays and starred J.B. Williams. Louis Vittes' scripts were not based on Stout's books and Stout did not collaborate on them.

Between July 5 and September 27, the programs moved to Mondays at 8:30 P.M. (Eastern time) and were sponsored by Williams Shaving Cream. Santos Ortega took over the role of Wolfe and John Gibson played Archie. Both were prolific radio veterans with several dozen series between them. Between January 21 and July 14, 1944, the show moved to Fridays at 7 P.M. During this period, Santos Ortega was replaced by Luis van Rooten.

In late 1945, it returned as *The Amazing Nero Wolfe* on the Mutual Network on Sunday evenings sponsored by Jergens Lotion. Former silent movie star Francis X. Bushman played Wolfe and Elliott Lewis played Archie. It lasted through December of that year. As before, the scripts were not Stout's but the network's. I have only heard the final broadcast but John McAleer provides the following analysis—"The humor verged on slapstick. As Wolfe, Bushman seemed pontifical. Ortega's Wolfe had been sardonic—a greater disparity separated the Archies. John Gibson's Archie was both forthright and poised. Too much roughneck showed in Elliot Lewis's version of the role." The last episode broadcast with Bushman on December 15, 1946, was entitled "The Shakespeare Folio" and dealt with the theft of an original play by the Bard.

The series became dormant after that until it was resurrected by NBC four years later in a series of 25 half-hour radio programs created by Edwin Fadiman (an old friend of Stout's), produced and directed by J. Donald Wilson, and narrated by announcer Don Stanley. As *The New Adventures of Nero Wolfe*, it was sponsored by Plymouth automobiles and ran between October 20, 1950, and April 27, 1951, at 8 P.M., moving from Fridays to Sundays in mid-season.

Managing to even *sound* corpulent (which shouldn't have been too much of a stretch for the hefty actor), Sydney Greenstreet of *The Maltese Falcon* fame played Wolfe. Some critics have accused Greenstreet of grossly overacting the part. Although I have not heard any of the first series and only one of the Bushman series, John McAleer writes that the scripts for the Greenstreet series were better although not based upon the Wolfe books and still written without Stout's collaboration.

I have found most of the programs in this last series fairly entertaining. The plots are as adequate as half an hour of dialogue (minus commercials) would allow but obviously no work of Rex Stout. Greenstreet made a creditable Wolfe although I felt that a bit too much of his British accent spilled over (he was English by birth) and he was usually a little too condescending to Archie without justification. The ratings were not good and Greenstreet, unable or unwilling to accept the fault as his own, blamed the other primary character. Over the course of a mere six months, Archie was played by a succession of half a dozen actors. The best known was the character actor Gerald Mohr. He was joined by "an angry Herb Ellis, a needling Larry Dobson, an earnest Wally Maher, an assured Everett Sloane—".

For the Wolfe purist who may have tuned in, the series had enough flaws without faulting the multiple Archies. The airy theme music would have done as well for *Ozzie and Harriet* as for a detective program and was certainly no match for their competition like *Dragnet*, *Gangbusters* or *The Whistler*. Some episodes identified the brownstone as being at "601 West Thirty-Fifth." In one, Wolfe called Fritz "my cook." Wolfe seemed to answer his own telephone with alarming regularity and Archie called him "Boss" without retribution. Overdoing one of Stout's artifices, the household always seemed to be a heartbeat away from the poorhouse and Archie was constantly delivering rather patronizing lectures on economics to Wolfe. The rotating Archies didn't help the ratings and the series was cancelled after six months. Of this last series, the following episodes were broadcast on the indicated original air dates (with full casts listed where known):

Stamped For Murder—10/20/50—Wally Maher as Archie with Jeanne Bates, Howard McNear, Jay Novello, Larry Dobkin, Bill Johnstone and Herb Vigran.

The Case of the Dear Dead Lady—11/3/50—Herb Ellis as Archie with Lee Morah, Monica Neely, Larry Dobkin, Bonnie Phillips and Jerry Hausner.

The Case of the Headless Hunter—11/10/50

The Case of the Careless Cleaner—11/17/50—Larry Dobkin as Archie with Betty Lou Gerson, Howard McNear, Dan O'Herlihy, Vic Perrin and Bill Johnstone.

The Case of the Beautiful Archer—11/24/50

The Case of the Friendly Rabbit—12/1/50—Larry Dobkin as Archie with Marva Shaw, Hal Gerard, Herb Butterfield, Howard McNear and Bill Johnstone.

The Case of the Impolite Corpse—12/8/50—Larry Dobkin as Archie with Donald Morrison, Betty Lou Gerson, Bill Johnstone, Howard McNear, Mary lansing and Barney Phillips.

The Case of the Girl Who Cried Wolfe—12/15/50—Larry Dobkin as Archie with Charlotte Lauren, Howard McNear, Monica Nealy, Lamont Johnson and Herb Butterfield.

The Case of the Slaughtered Santas—12/22/50

The Case of the Bashful Body—12/29/50

The Case of the Deadly Sell-Out—1/5/51

The Case of the Killer Cards—1/12/51

The Case of the Calculated Risk—1/19/51—Gerald Mohr as Archie with Lorraine Carter, Bill Johnstone, Howard McNear, Herb Butterfield and Victor Rodman.

The Case of the Phantom Fingers—1/26/51—Gerald Mohr as Archie with GeGe Pearson, Howard McNear, Tim Graham and Eddie Fields.

The Case of the Vanishing Shells—2/2/51—Gerald Mohr as Archie with Jean Bates, Betty Lou Gerson, Bill Johnstone, Peter Leeds and Vic Perrin.

The Case of the Party For Death—2/16/51—Harry Bartell as Archie with GeGe Pearson, Herb Butterfield, Peter Leeds, Evelyn Eaton and Bill Johnstone.

The Case of the Malevolent Medic (sometimes mislisted as The Benevolent Medic)—2/23/51—Harry Bartell as Archie with Jeanne Bates, Vic Perrin, Bruce Payne, Bill Johnstone and Mary Lansing.

The Case of the Hasty Will—3/2/51—Harry Bartell as Archie with Victor Rodman, Louise Arthur, Hal Gerard and Bill Johnstone.

The Case of the Disappearing Diamonds—3/9/51—Harry Bartell as Archie with GeGe Pearson, Bud Heaston, Gray Stafford, Dick Ryan and Bill Johnstone.

The Case of the Midnight Ride—3/16/51—Harry Bartell as Archie with Jeanne Bates, Peter Leeds, Bill Johnstone, Grace Lanar and Jay Novello.

The Case of the Final Page—3/23/51

The Case of the Tell-Tale Ribbon—3/30/51

The Case of A Slight Case of Perjury—4/6/51

The Case of the Lost Heir—4/20/51

The Case Of Room 304—4/27/51—Harry Bartell as Archie with Lucille Alex, Val Brown, Bill Johnstone, Hal Gerard, Betty Lou Gerson, Victor Rodman and Ed Bailey.

After Stout's death, another radio series played on Canadian Broadcasting in 1982. It was created by the following:

Mayver Moore as Nero Wolfe
Don Francs as Archie Goodwin
Frank Perry as Fritz Brenner
Alfie Scott as Saul Panzer
Cec Linder as Inspector Cramer
Guest appearances by Jackie Burroughs, Layly Cado, Jane Eastwood, Brian George, Martha Gibson, Lynn Griffin, Barbra Hamilton, Patricia Hamilton, Helen Hughs, Chamin King, Bud Knapp, Jack Krely, Maria Loma, Arch MacDonald, Meana E. Meana, Neil Monroe, Mary Peery, Eric Peterson, Fiona Reed, Aileen Seaton, August Shellenberg, Terry Tweed and Sandy Webster.
Adapted and Produced by Ron Hartman
Music By Don Gillis

Apparently it was quite successful and Francs in particular has been praised for a good characterization of Archie. The following thirteen episodes were produced, all based on Stout books, and broadcast on the following dates:

Disguise For Murder—1/16/82
Before I Die—1/23/82
Counterfeit For Murder—1/30/82
The Cop Killer—2/6/82
Christmas Party—2/13/82
Cordially Invited to Meet Death—2/20/82
Man Alive—2/27/82
Instead of Evidence—3/6/82
Eeny Meeny Murder Mo—3/13/82
The Squirt and the Monkey—3/20/82
The Next Witness—3/27/82
Death of a Demon—4/3/82
Murder Is No Joke—4/10/82

This was the end (so far) of Nero Wolfe on the radio but, on November 26, 1956, the Nero Wolfe comic strip—yes, comic strip—began. It was written by John Broome and drawn by Mike Roy. McAleer says it ran for several years and "made less of an effort than radio had to catch the spirit of Rex's stories." He also says that one of Wolfe's adversaries in the strip is a mechanical man. Good God. What next, Wolfe versus Godzilla? Changing into a caped yellow costume in the elevator and emerging as Calorie Man, able to reduce his enemies to fats, carbohydrates and proteins with a glance? Pah!

Television

And now, the final insult, as Rex Stout would probably express it. That vast wasteland, television. In fact, why should I put words in his mouth? I'll let him express it the way he did to his biographer—"I despise television. It exhausts and debilitates creative writing talent. For years I have refused all offers from movie and television producers, and shall go on refusing. I wouldn't trust either of those media with Jack and the Beanstalk if I had written it. In the contracts for two Nero Wolfe movies forty years ago, I insisted on excluding radio and television use."

I'll include another Archie-like disclaimer here. Since I haven't seen the movies, heard some of the radio shows or seen the comic strip, I've given you other peoples judgements of them. But I'm a television baby so I've seen these efforts with my own eyes, after reading the books. Bear in mind, I'm no critic, just another media consumer so, by all means, don't take my word for it. Catch them yourselves and judge for yourself. They'll be on cable in perpetuity. Enough digression.

His biographer says that during the last ten years of his life, Stout refused more than fifty offers from movie and television producers who were interpreting the nine-year run of the Perry Mason TV series as a mandate and salivating over the idea of following it up with a Nero Wolfe series. One of the reasons for his jaundiced view might have been similar to what befell the early movie efforts, the producers' suggestions for casting. Orson Welles as Wolfe and Darren McGavin as Archie? Welles with Bill Cosby as Archie? What would they have done with the dramatizations of *Too Many Cooks* and *A Right To Die*? Forgive the inside-joke inference here but read those two books, if you haven't yet, with that it mind. Lorne Greene as Wolfe? Zero Mostel as Wolfe and Dick Cavett as Archie? Burlesque? They even yielded to the obvious and suggested Raymond Burr (the TV Perry Mason) as Wolfe.

Wolfe did make it to television in Stout's lifetime but not in America. German TV stole a Wolfe story in 1964 and Stout successfully sued them. A few years later, he let Italian TV produce a dozen Wolfe stories for $80,000 but "only because he would never see them."

After Stout's death in 1975, Wolfe finally made it to American TV. The first effort was a made-for-TV movie in 1977. Entitled simply "Nero Wolfe", it was based on the novel *The Doorbell Rang*. I remember seeing it but must have found it unremarkable because I have very fragmented memories of it, none positive. The primary ones are that (1) it didn't do the book justice; (2) Thayer David's characterization of Wolfe brings to mind the words "phlegmatic" and dyspeptic"; and (3) Biff McGuire would have made (and did) a much better Mike Hammer than an Inspector Cramer. The movie was intended as the pilot for a Wolfe series but Thayer David's premature death stalled the project for several years.

The second effort, and the first successful attempt at a series, came from NBC-TV in January of 1981. It lasted for fourteen one-hour episodes, most based upon the Stout stories although only six carried the titles of the books. The series was cancelled after less than six months although some episodes were rerun throughout the summer. My primary impression of the show was that the Wolfe stories didn't translate well into an hour. At any rate, the novels didn't. They seemed rushed. Therefore the half-hour radio shows I have never heard must have been terribly abbreviated and doubtlessly suffered from it. The ones I have heard did. Again, I watched the series, saw all the episodes and my primary memories are of the characterizations, again mostly negative.

William Conrad was cast as Wolfe and I thought he had the perfect Wolfean voice which had served him so well as a widely-used radio actor years before. It also occurred to me that he represented the perfect dichotomy between the aural and visual mediums. Conrad had created the role of Marshal Matt Dillon on the radio series *Gunsmoke* in 1949. When the series moved to television in 1955, Conrad allegedly wanted the TV role badly but he was short, fat and balding, hardly the image TV producers wanted for the heroic, stalwart U.S. Marshal. Six-foot-seven-inch tall James Arness got the role on the recommendation of western icon John Wayne. Conrad's stentorian basso profundo voice continued as the radio personification of Matt Dillon until 1960. At least he *sounded* tall.

In his early sixties when he began the Wolfe role, Conrad had the demeanor down much better than Thayer David's effort but reviewers apparently agreed with me overall. One said that Conrad's characterization of Wolfe seemed to be an extension of his previous TV role as *Cannon* (1971–1976), a fat, analytical gourmet detective with expensive tastes. They also said that Conrad's Wolfe "looked like Cannon in retirement." But it got worse. As Archie, Lee Horsley was too pretty and too cute without the talent for sarcasm and hyperbole. In the books, Archie is a 180-pound six-footer and Wolfe is only an inch shorter but Horsley's six-foot-three-inch height only accentuated Conrad's lacking stature when they had scenes standing together. Allan Miller was a pathetic shadow of Inspector Cramer and although his rantings at Wolfe were well-acted, they portrayed neither the frustrated menace nor the innate intelligence of the print Cramer. I don't remember anything about the actor who played Saul Panzer (George Wyner) except that he came nowhere near portraying Saul's innocuous cunning and competence. I'm certainly no actor but I can see a treasure trove of possibilities wasted for such a richly drawn character. On the positive side, I thought George Voskovek and Robert Coote, respectively, were outstanding as Fritz and Theodore and made the most of their roles although my mental image of Theodore is a lot wimpier than Coote played him.

The most recent effort was, in my opinion, by far the best. Considering the inherent differences in the print and film mediums, it came as close to actually duplicating the experience of reading the books as Hollywood has come thus far.

In March of 2000, the Arts and Entertainment (A&E) Cable TV Network produced a dramatization of the Stout novel *The Golden Spiders*. At two hours in length and with more modern editing, it was better able to do justice to the original story. The characterizations of Wolfe and Archie were the best I've seen so far with Timothy Hutton doing an exceptional job of nailing Archie. Maury Chaykin as Wolfe displays the proper degrees of imperious arrogance, impatience and petulance. Even better, he fits the best physical impression I've always had of Wolfe, not so much fat as just *big all over*. Wolfe himself once responds to the word "fat" as applied to himself by saying he prefers "gargantuan".

There were some minor lapses or instances of dramatic license taken but only an avid fan of the books would notice. Purley Stebbins is identified as a detective in *The Golden Spiders* which, of course, he was in the beginning of the tales but he had long since been elevated to Sergeant by that time. Also, as a detective, he shows up at Wolfe's house in uniform. The routine meal times are a little skewed, Wolfe's leather chair is yellow instead of brown and Lon Cohen works for the New York Mirror instead of the Gazette. There were a few other minor *faux pas* but overall it seemed a very worthy effort.

Apparently the majority of viewers agreed with me because the ratings for the movie were a success and A&E ordered a dozen new episodes, turning it into a weekly series in April of 2001. Timothy Hutton, the driving force behind this incarnation, was one of the executive producers and also directed some episodes.

Between the initial offering of *The Golden Spiders* and the onset of the series, two cast changes were made in the main characters, both for the better. While Saul Rubinek made a creditable Saul Panzer in the TV movie, he made a much better Lon Cohen when the series debuted and Conrad Dunn made an even better Saul Panzer. The series also used a recurring ensemble of actors who played different roles in each episode.

Another of the executive producers, Michael Jaffe, said that the series was "the first and only series in the history of dramatic programming that has had no non-author written material." *Huzzah!* They were relying solely on Rex Stout's words as published in the original works. Someone in Hollywood finally refrained from tossing Stout's books in front of a screenwriter and trying to "adapt" them or "punch them up".

Another problem with the 1981 Conrad/Horsley series for purists was that it was modernized into the 1980's. The Chaykin/Hutton series did not make that error. It was a period piece set firmly in the years when Wolfe was at the peak of his career. Of the nine novels and twelve novellas eventually filmed, one was set in the Thirties (and that one probably solely for the purpose of humanizing Wolfe by introducing his daughter), five in the Forties, eleven in the Fifties and four in the Sixties. After viewing the first installments, I was extremely impressed, not only with the actors but the screenwriters, costume designers and set decorators. The brownstone, the cars, the character's clothing, the price of a phone call from a pay phone. In general, most details, large and small, were accorded the same attention.

In an apparent attempt not to shortcut the stories, the novels were allotted two hours and the novellas a single hour. The character's names and most if not all of the rapid-fire dialogue was verbatim from the Wolfe books, even including Archie's voice-overs. Although impossible to prove, I would be willing to bet their episode of *The Doorbell Rang* marks the first and only time the word "thaumaturge" has ever been used on film. The plots are unsullied by Hollywood "punch-ups"—i.e. no superfluous gunfights, explosions or car chases. For the most part, if Stout wrote it in the story, it's there; if not, it hasn't been added.

The opening graphics gave a hint of the up-scale *film noir* and art deco to come, punctuated by the aforementioned peppy big band beat. The sets were impeccable, steeped in the Wolfean trappings; the omnipresence of yellow in Wolfe's shirts, breast pocket handkerchiefs, pajamas, the hallway's walls, the brocaded dining room chairs, the office chairs and couch, even Wolfe's chair in spite of the fact that it's brown in the books. But the massive red leather chair, the orchids, the plant rooms, the elevator, the picture of the waterfall with the peephole, the huge globe, the basement's billiard table, they were all there and in a credible approximation of where Rex Stout had said they were. The costumes were equal to the occasion as well; enough 1950's-vintage cars to stock a major car show (the Heron's stand-in is a Rolls Royce), the ladies hair styles, hats, pump shoes and dresses with peplums, Archie's snap-brim fedoras and two-toned saddle shoes, the men's wide-lapeled suits and wide ties, even the black-and-white Fifties-vintage shows on the television back when they were made as a piece of furniture.

The cast was uniformly steeped in their roles and had done their homework well. The subtle nuances in their interactions were all familiar, as much portrayed by their facial expressions and body language as their words: Wolfe's innate superiority, Archie's insouciance, Lon's symbiotic relationship with them based upon information but still tinged with mutual respect and friendship, Fritz's elegance and artistic temperament, Saul's cunning, Fred's stout character but mental limitations, Orrie's undeserved arrogance and the eternal frustrations of Cramer, Stebbins and Rowcliff. Purley's initial appearance in uniform was rectified when he reverts to an honest plainclothes cop's off-the-rack wardrobe in the series.

If I *had* to make some criticisms, they would be that (1) sometimes the big band background music moves too far into the foreground, overshadowing the precious dialogue and (2) while Conrad Dunn was an excellent Saul Panzer, they dressed him much too well. Saul's patented rumpled, anonymous look was totally absent.

Thank God they made no effort to drag Wolfe and Archie, doubtlessly kicking and screaming, into the Twenty-First century. Wolfe does not need a fax machine and a computer with Internet access sitting next to his desk. He needs his globe, dictionary, books, orchids and his brain. That's it. Archie doesn't need a Glock nine-millimeter with a 14-round clip and a cellular phone to do his job. A snub-nosed Marley .38, a nickel or dime for the nearest pay phone (not a dime *and* a quarter) and his "intelligence guided by experience" will do nicely, thank you very much.

THE EPISODES:

Nero Wolfe—1977, Paramount Pictures
Based on the novel The Doorbell Rang
Starring Thayer David as Nero Wolfe
Tom Mason as Archie Goodwin
David Hurst as Fritz Brenner
John O'Leary as Theodore Horstmann
Lewis Charles as Saul Panzer
Biff McGuire as Inspector Cramer
Periodic guest stars included Anne Baxter, Frank Campanella, John Randolph, John Gerstad, John Hoyt and Brooke Adams.
Written and directed by Frank D. Gilroy
Music by Leonard Rosenman

Nero Wolfe, NBC, 1981
Debut 1/16/81
Last telecast 8/25/81
January-April 1981 on NBC, Friday at 9 P.M. (Eastern time)
April-August on NBC, Tuesday at 10 P.M. (Eastern time)
Starring William Conrad as Nero Wolfe
Lee Horsley as Archie Goodwin
Allan Miller as Inspector Cramer
George Voskovec as Fritz Brenner
George Wyner as Saul Panzer
Robert Coote as Theodore Horstmann
Executive Producers Ben Roberts and Ivan Goff

Air Date	Episode
1/16/81	The Golden Spiders
1/23/82	Death on the Doorstep
1/30/81	Before I Die
2/6/81	Wolfe at the Door
2/13/81	Might As Well Be Dead
2/20/81	To Catch A Dead Man
3/6/81	In The Best of Families
3/13/81	Murder By The Book
3/20/81	What Happened To April?
4/3/81	Gambit
4/10/81	Death and the Dolls
4/17/81	The Murder In Question
5/5/81	Blue Ribbon Hostage
6/2/81	Sweet Revenge

Nero Wolfe—The Golden Spiders
Two-hour made-for-TV movie on the A&E Cable Network
First telecast: March 5, 2000
Starring Maury Chaykin as Nero Wolfe
Timothy Hutton as Archie Goodwin
Bill Smitrovich as Inspector Cramer
Colin Fox as Fritz Brenner
Saul Rubinek as Saul Panzer
Fulvio Cecere as Fred Durkin
Trent McMullen as Orrie Cather

R.D. Reid as Sgt. Stebbins
Gerry Quigley as Lon Cohen
Also starring Hrant Alianak, Nancy Beatty, Robert Bockstael, Elizabeth Brown,
Robert Clark, Norma Clarke, Phillip Craig, Nicky Guadagni, Mimi Kuzyk,
Larissa Laskin, Dwayne McLean, Peter Mensah, Brian Miranda, Jack Newman,
James Purcell, Gary Reineke, Rothaford and Beau Starr.
Directed by Bill Duke

Nero Wolfe Mysteries—The Series
Leading Characters:
Starring Maury Chaykin as Nero Wolfe
Timothy Hutton as Archie Goodwin
Bill Smitrovich as Inspector Cramer
Saul Rubinek as Lon Cohen
Colin Fox as Fritz Brenner
Conrad Dunn as Saul Panzer
Fulvio Cecere as Fred Durkin
Trent McMullen as Orrie Cather
R.D. Reid as Sgt. Stebbins
Bill MacDonald as Lt. Rowcliff
Ensemble Cast: Hrant Alianak, Boyd Banks, Wayne Best, Robert Bockstael,
Steve Cumyn, Nicky Guadagni, David Hemblen, Ken Kramer, Ted Ludzik, Kari
Matchett, Marty Moreau, David Schurmann, Aron Tager and James Tolkan.
Executive Producers: Michael Jaffe, Timothy Hutton and Howard Braunstein
Producer: Susan Murdoch
Music: Michael Small

The below listed episodes assume the participation of the leading characters as
required by the individual story and the ensemble cast. The "ALSO STAR-
RING" section contains those supporting actors who do not fit into one of those
categories except where noted.

Episodes:

The Doorbell Rang
Two-hour series premier on the A&E Cable Network
First telecast: April 22, 2001
8:00 P.M on Sundays (Eastern time)
Ken Kramer as Doctor Vollmer

David Hembler as Lewis Hewitt
Also Starring Peter Cox, Gretchan Egolf, Michelle Holden, Howard Hoover, Billy Linders, Peter Mensan, B.J. McQueen, Debra Monk, Mathew Sharp and Francie Swift.
Directed by Timothy Hutton

Champagne For One
First telecast: Part I-April 29, 2001
             Part II-May 6, 2001
Also Starring Bruce Beaton, Nancy Beatty, Christine Brubaker, Kimwun Perennec, Alex Poch-Goldin, Michael Rhoades, Marian Seldes, Janne Therault, Kathryn Zenna and Patricia Zentilli.
Directed by Timothy Hutton

Prisoner's Base
First Telecast: Part I: May 13, 2001
             Part II: May 20, 2001
Also Starring Dina Barrington, Shauna Black, Jody Racicot, Gary Reineke and Ron Rifkin.
Directed by Neill Fearnley

Eeny Meeny Murder Moe
First Telecast: June 3, 2001
Also Starring Christine Brubaker, George Plimpton and Janne Therault.
Directed by John L'Ecuver

Disguise For Murder
First Telecast: June 17, 2001
Also Starring Nancy Beatty, Elizabeth Brown, Tramara Burford, Nicholas Campbell, Phillip Craig, Debra Monk, Beau Starr, Richard Waugh and Kathryn Zenna.
Directed by John L'Ecuver

Door To Death
First Telecast: June 4, 2001
Also Starring Nancy Beatty, Kristin Booth, Christine Brubaker, Nicholas Campbell, Marian Seldes, Beau Starr and Michael Rhoades.
Directed by Holly Dale

Christmas Party
First Telecast: July 1, 2001
Also Starring M.J. Kang, Jody Racicot, Francie Swift and Richard Waugh.
Directed by Holly Dale

Over My Dead Body
First Telecast: Part I-July 8, 2001
                Part II-July 15, 2001
Also Starring Dina Barington, Peter Mensah, Brad McGinnis, Debra Monk, George Plimpton, Ron Rifkin, Francie Swift and Richard Waugh.
Directed by Timothy Hutton

Renewed for a second season, the series continued with no changes in the major characters. As in the first season, Theodore Horstmann was ignored except for an occasional mention. The ensemble cast of Banks, Bockstael, Guadagni, Matchett, Tolkan, et al, returned.

Season Two Episodes:

Death Of A Doxy (Two-hour premiere)
First Telecast: April 14, 2002
Also Starring Kari Matchett (in a double role as Julie Jaquette and Lily Rowan), George Plimpton (as Nathaniel Parker), Araxi Aklanian, Carolyn Balogh, Gillian Banyard, Christine Brubaker, Rachel Cerekwicki, Heather Corby, Anna Freake, Christine Haverkate, Laria Moore, Danielle Ortman, Lisa Phillips, Julian Richings, Carlo Rota, Janine Therault, Hayley Verlyn and Nicole Vilano.
Directed by Timothy Hutton

The Next Witness
First Telecast: April 21, 2002
Also Starring Brittney Banks, Christine Brubaker, Sean Wayne Dovie, Rebecca Jenkins, Beau Starr, Francie Swift, Carolyn Taylor, Richard Waugh and Kathryn Zenna.
Directed by James Tolkan

Die Like A Dog
First Telecast: April 28, 2002
Also Starring Bill MacDonald, Alex Poch-Goldin, Kari Matchett, Julian Richings, Romie Rox and Angelo Tsarouchas.
Directed by James Tolkan

Murder Is Corny
First Telecast: May 5, 2002
Also Starring Robert Bockstael, David Calderisi, Marvin Hinz, Kari Matchett, Bruce McFee, George Plimpton (as Nathaniel Parker), Julian Richings, Troy Skog and Angelo Tsarouchas.
Directed by George Bloomfield

The Mother Hunt
First Telecast: Part I: May 12, 2002
                Part II: May 19, 2002
Also Starring Erinn Bartlett, Brooke Burns, Jim Davis, Griffin Dunne, Carrie Fisher, Manon Von Gerkan, Shannon Joye, Penelope Ann Miller, Richard Waugh and Kathryn Zenna.
Directed by Alan Smithee
NOTE: "Alan Smithee" is a common Hollywood pseudonym for any director who refuses to use his real name on a film project. The television commercials advertising this episode stated it was directed by Timothy Hutton.

Poison A La Carte
First Telecast: May 26, 2002
Also Starring Malin Averman, Dina Barrington, Lindy Booth, Sarah Boylan, Domenic Cuzzocrea, Judith Deboer, Emily Hampshire, Julia Hazelton, Michelle Holden, Shannon Joye, Lorca Moore, Alda Neves, Jack Newman, Gary Reineke, Carlo Rota and Hayley Verlyn.
Directed By George Bloomfield

Too Many Clients
First Telecast: Part I: June 2, 2002
                Part II: June 9, 2002
Also Starring Dina Barrington, Christine Brubaker, Lucy Flippone, Shannon Joye, Bill MacDonald, Debra Monk, Lorca Moore, Alec Poch-Goldin, Jeannette Sousa, Hayley Verlyn and Richard Waugh.
Directed by John L'ecuyer

Before I Die
First Telecast: June 16,2002

Also Starring Lindy Booth, Christine Brubaker, Seymour Cassel, Matthew Edison, Tom Farr, Doug Lennox, Bill MacDonald (as Lt. Rowcliff), Angela Maiorano, Joe Pingue, Bryan Renfro and Beau Starr.
Directed by John L'ecuyer

At this point, the network began interspersing reruns of old episodes with new episodes, presumably as they became available. It should also be noted that not all of the actors in the following episodes are listed because A&E began compressing the end credits to an unreadable mishmash so they could gain an extra ten seconds to advertise the program coming up on their schedule in the next couple of minutes. And one wonders why Stout had disdain for Hollywood?

Help Wanted Male
First Telecast: June 30, 2002
Also Starring Randy Butcher, Larry Drake, George Plimpton (as General Carpenter) and Richard Waugh.
Directed by John L'ecuyer

The Silent Speaker
First Telecast: Part I-July 14, 2002
              Part II-July 21, 2002
Also Starring Joe Flaherty, Bill MacDonald, Debra Monk, George Plimpton, Gary Reineke, Manon Von Gerkan, Cynthia Watros and Richard Waugh.
Directed by Michael Jaffe

Cop Killer
First Telecast: August 11, 2002
Also Starring Hrant Alianak, Nicky Guadagni, Kari Matchett, R.D. Reid and James Tolkan.
Directed by John R. Pepper

Immune To Murder
First Telecast: August 18, 2002
Also Starring Robert Bockstael, Seymour Cassel, Giancario Espositio, Susannah Hoffmann, Manon Von Gerkan, George Plimpton, David Schurmann and Richard Waugh.

Even though the producers presumably saved all that money on dialogue that Rex Stout had already written for them, evidently all that authenticity in costumes, set decoration and other ephemera was very expensive. After dramatizing nine of the novels and a dozen of the novellas, after its second season in 2002, A&E cancelled the series as "not cost effective." But hope springs eternal. Given the always-eventually-fickle attention spans of the average viewer for the mind-numbing sitcoms, gun-blazing cops, idealistic doctors and crusading lawyers, there is still plenty of original Wolfe material available for the next idealist to take up the quest.

As Archie would put it, it's better than even money that Stout's experiences with the entertainment industry's adaptations of his work showed up in Wolfe's future attitudes in the saga. For both, all of Hollywood's forms suffered in comparison to the written word.

There is no indication in the books that Wolfe has ever attended a movie and I doubt if his reluctance to leave the brownstone is the sole reason. Enough said.

Although Rex Stout never listened to the Wolfe radio broadcasts, he did attend one in person. Although he considered the actors "creditable", the plots made him cringe. In the later incarnations, he felt that "the wryness of Wolfe, for which Archie's drollness is a whetstone, was not felt in the Ortega or Bushman interpretations [but] Greenstreet caught it." In spite of Stout's general approval of Greenstreet as Wolfe, the overall aftertaste of the radio experience was not agreeable. Stout once listened to one of Greenstreet's episode's on tape but stopped it after five minutes, saying he "could take no more." Wolfe was always portrayed as so close to the budgetary basement that he was always being forced to work to fend off starvation. Pfui.

By 1953, Wolfe owns a television set which is in the office. Archie sarcastically informs us that it gives Wolfe much pleasure—he turns it on (and off) as many as eight times a night, glares at it for a few minutes to make sure it gets the point and goes back to his book.

Stout benignly allowed the Nero Wolfe comic strip to exist "to help a friend" but he contributed nothing to it, gained nothing from it and pointedly ignored it.

I like to believe that, despite his agnosticism, somewhere in the universe, there is a spark of electricity that used to be in Rex Stout's brain that can appreciate Hollywood's latest effort on behalf of his characters. I hope he would agree that they're trying harder and doing better.

Rex Stout once said that he hoped Nero Wolfe "lived forever." Old radio shows are being resurrected on tape and compact discs. Film restoration techniques, video tape, Digital Video Discs and satellite dishes are helping to ensure the immortality of almost everything ever filmed. The exponential multiplication of cable television networks is providing a medium for eternal reruns. So Stout may well get his wish but Wolfe will probably always be best represented in the form in which Stout originally created him—the books.

Unrecorded Cases

June 16, 1929—This is date when Wolfe returned little Tommie Williamson to his parents. They dine at Wolfe's house on every anniversary of this date. In *Fer-de-Lance*, 1933 is the fourth such anniversary.

1931—The Moschenden Case.

1931–1932—The two other cases Wolfe handled for Anthony D. Perry, one of which was an investigation of his competitor's trade practices. Perry objected to Wolfe's bill for the latter investigation but gained a high enough opinion of him to recommend his services to Clara Fox a few years later. Perry had much to object to in that case also.

1932—The Banister-Schurman case. Assistant District Attorney Dick Morley would have lost his job and maybe more if Wolfe hadn't pulled him out of a hole.

1933—The Hallowell case. Hallowell tried a $150,000 bribe on Wolfe to get out of a death sentence, unsuccessfully.

—The Hay Fever case.

—The Fairmont National Bank case.

1933–1934—The Whittemore Bonds case.

—The Case of the Hardest Guy to Deal With.

—The Case of the Highly Unremunerative Mission.

February 1935—the errand Wolfe sent Archie on that convinced him he should always carry a gun when leaving the office on business involving a murder.

Before 1936—The Diplomacy Club business with Nyura Promm.

November 1938—The Crampton-Gore case.

1938–1939—The Wetzler case.

July 1941—The Nauheim case.

December 9, 1941—Cora Leeds murdered.

Early 1942—Captain Goodwin straightens out the mess down in Georgia.

Early March 1942—Captain Goodwin promoted to Major.

June 9, 1943—The job Wolfe was doing for Lieutenant General Carpenter and the first case in which Arnold Zeck tried to interfere.

August 1943—Captain Albert Cross murdered at the Bascombe Hotel.

March 1944—The Captain Peter Root case.

January 16, 1946—The case involving Mrs. Tremont, the second Wolfe case involving Arnold Zeck's attempted interference.

Before March 1946—The Chesterton-Best case.

—The Boedikker case.

Before April 1946—The Fashalt case.

Spring-Summer 1950—The Poison Pen case

The Hot Insurance case

(handled by a self-employed Archie while Wolfe was working his way up the ladder of crime.)

July or August 1950—A complicated infringement case for a big client that netted five figures.

January-Early February 1951—The little mix-up with a gang of Hijackers.

Summer 1951—The Pendexter case.

1955—The Lamb—McCullough Insurance case.

October 1957—The Stolen Bottweil Tapestries case.

Before April 1958—John Piotti's former case.

The Body Count
Clients, Victims And Suspects

It is difficult to accurately count the number of Wolfe's clients during the saga because of several factors. He is often hired by large companies, corporations, organizations or more than one person. Since he is appreciative of his remuneration but not a slave to it, he also has an occasional habit of accepting a client's retainer but later repudiating the client and returning the retainer. He has also taken cases that promise little or no return and later been hired to serve someone else's interests who is more able to pay his prices (as long as the second commitment doesn't conflict with the first one). Nevertheless, an effort will be made.

As nearly as can be determined, in the 74 Nero Wolfe tales considered here, Wolfe has been hired by at least 46 males, 35 females and six business organizations or groups. Among his more recognizable clients who make more than one appearance in the adventures are fellow orchid fancier Lewis Hewitt, Lily Rowan, his adopted daughter Carla Lovchen, the United States Government and operative Orrie Cather. The first two have unseemly murders committed on their property, Lovchen and Cather are falsely accused of murders and the government has its officials killed in proximity to Wolfe and/or Archie.

Speaking of whom, Archie Goodwin also becomes Wolfe's client. Yes, *the* Archie Goodwin. One of Archie's primary functions has always been to goad Wolfe into working when he doesn't want to (which is always) to secure future books, orchids, beer, shallots and paychecks for their family unit. Occasionally Archie approaches this from the perspective of taking a case on himself that Wolfe is then obligated to either assist him with or bail him out of, depending upon which of their viewpoints you believe. Wolfe also has to periodically get involved in order to preserve, protect or defend Archie's personal freedom, professional ethics, sense of humor and good samaritanism. As previously mentioned, Archie even tried to pay him a fee once but Wolfe tore up the check.

Sometimes the client did it. On occasion, someone has the audacity and poor judgement to hire Wolfe to solve a murder they themselves have committed. This has happened on at least eight occasions but not all of these people really had that much shameless effrontery. On at least five of the occasions, the murderer was caught up in a group of people with aligned interests and inescapably trapped into helping to hire Wolfe, if only to prevent bringing suspicion upon themselves. Ultimately, it never worked out for them. Wolfe, incidentally, would disagree with these numbers because he has been known to repudiate someone as his client just before denouncing them as a murderer, thereby no doubt salvaging a fine point within his own psyche. He usually predicates his acceptance of someone as his client upon their being truthful with him although almost all lie to him at some point, even the innocent ones.

But what of the casualties? In the 74 Nero Wolfe tales, a grand total of 447 people met their deaths by misadventure. The vast majority died in a mass murder of 302 individuals in a bombing and fire in *The Zero Clue*. This would seem to make an average of over six murders per story. However, exclusive of the mass murder, 145 people were murdered or died in the course of the 74 stories, making a much more realistic score of less than two deaths per story. In addition, ten of the 145 who died were suspects who committed suicide which will be explained further later. Therefore 135 were actual murders.

Although it is legally impossible to murder an animal other than a human being, we might also include here a poignant honorable mention to a Doberman pinscher that was stabbed to death. We can include in the poor beast's eulogy that at least it provided a clue that led to justice for its killer. Another honorable mention should go to a prize bull who died from anthrax, albeit not accidentally.

Since men in our society are at least twice as likely as women to become murder victims, 97 of the 145 were males and 48 were females. The suspects follow the same pattern with the murderers in 50 of the tales being men and women in 25. These numbers add up to 75 for the 74 tales because in one story, one is included under both the male and female categories. In that story, a murderer is himself murdered by his wife who makes it look like a suicide.

Discounting the extraordinary number of deaths in *The Zero Clue*, the adventures with the most murders were *The Black Mountain* and *And Be A Villain* with five each. For the least, thirty of the tales have a single murder each.

As private detectives, Wolfe and Archie were usually much more interested in solving the crime than obtaining evidence to insure a successful legal prosecution of the suspect than their official counterparts in law enforcement agencies. Nevertheless, when practicable, efforts were usually made to obtain such evidence. Unfettered by *Miranda v, Arizona, Mapp v. Ohio* and other impediments placed upon their official colleagues, Wolfe and his operatives tended to operate on the principle that forgiveness is easier to obtain than permission. Thus, they were not above committing burglaries, thefts, extortion and occasionally robberies in order to obtain such evidence. However, in some of the cases, legally admissible evidence was not to be had by either official or unofficial means. In those cases, Wolfe was able to use the adroitness of a chessmaster to maneuver the suspect into a corner and what psychologists would call the ultimate approach-avoidance conflict.

When confronted with these dilemmas, thirteen suspects in the Wolfe Saga committed suicide—sort of. Ten were genuine suicides and three were self-destructive acts fueled by desperation and stupidity. One unintentionally killed himself with ciphogene gas while trying to kill a room full of his adversaries, one was shot in a gunfight in Wolfe's office and one apparently shot himself to death (complete with suicide note) but Archie believes, with much justification, the suspect was murdered by his wife who staged it to look like a suicide. In either case, Wolfe let it slide. Of the ten genuine suicides, three blew themselves up with bombs, two shot themselves, two drank cyanide poison, one hung themselves, one jumped out of a tall building and one gave himself an anthrax injection (which is not good for people and other living things).

CAUSE OF DEATH	MALES	FEMALES	UNKNOWN	TOTAL
Gunshot	38	4		42
Stabbed	12	4		16
Poison*	10	9		19
Auto Hit & Run	7	8		15
Bombs	7	1	302	310
Beatings	6	6		12
Falls	5	1		6
Strangled	4	12		16
Induced pneumonia	2**			2
Ciphogene gas	1	1		2
Drowned	1			1
Plane crash	1			1
Hanging	1			1
Smothered		1		1

CAUSE OF DEATH	MALES	FEMALES	UNKNOWN	TOTAL
Throat cut	1			1
Tortured to death		1		1
-------------	-------	-------	-------	-------
	97	48	302	447

*In the poison category, cyanide was the much preferred method, being used on five of the men and six of the women. The killers of the others were more inventive, on the men moreso than the women. Two men died by arsenic, one by snake venom, one by nitroglycerine and one by nitrobenzene. One woman died by strychnine, one of ptomaine poisoning and one by the tetanus virus.

**It occurs to me that the "induced pneumonia" category might require some explanation although it's much simpler than it might appear. When you expose a bedridden sick person to the winter cold, take away their sources of warmth and prevent them from receiving adequate and timely medical treatment, they will eventually progress to the point where medical science cannot save them. The official cause of death will be pneumonia but it is murder, nevertheless.

Speaking of casualties, this is probably an appropriate place to mention the walking wounded among the good guys as well. For a man who insulates himself from the outside world (and thus the inherent dangers of his profession) as much as humanly possible, Wolfe seems to spend an inordinate amount of time in harm's way. Granted, this occurs more frequently in the early adventures but perhaps, over time, he and Archie have honed their survival skills sufficiently to minimize the exposure.

At a minimum, Wolfe has been personally attacked on the following occasions:

—by a poisonous snake in 1933.

—shot in the left arm in 1935.

—received a grazing shot to the face during another assassination attempt in 1937.

—attacked by a murderer in his office and forced to defend himself with beer bottles in 1938.

—prior to 1939, a Cuban girl tried to stab him until Archie "smacked her."

—prior to 1944, Wolfe was stabbed in his bedroom during an unrecorded case which precipitated the installation of the security system on the second floor and the warning gong under Archie's bed.

—sat through another gunfight when a murderer tried to shoot him in 1946.

—survived a stabbing attempt only to get shot in the leg in 1954.

Acronyms

ABAV	And Be A Villain
AFA	A Family Affair
AOAB	Assault On A Brownstone
ARTD	A Right To Die
BE	Bitter End
BFO	Bullet For One
BID	Before I Die
BKM	Black Mountain
BM	Before Midnight
BO	Black Orchids
BT	Booby Trap
BWT	Blood Will Tell
CFO	Champagne For One
CITMD	Cordially Invited To Meet Death
CK	The Cop Killer
CM	Counterfeit For Murder
CP	Christmas Party
DD	Death Of A Doxy
DFM	Disguise For Murder
DLAD	Die Like A Dog
DOAD	Death Of A Demon
DOD	Death Of A Dude
DTD	Door To Death
EMMM	Eeny Meeny Murder Mo
EP	Easter Parade
FD	The Final Deduction

FDL	Fer-de-lance
FH	The Father Hunt
FJP	Fourth Of July Picnic
FUFM	Frame-Up For Murder
G	Gambit
GS	The Golden Spiders
GWW	The Gun With Wings
HWM	Help Wanted Male
HTR	Home To Roost
IDES	If Death Ever Slept
IMTM	Immune To Murder
IOE	Instead Of Evidence
ITBF	In The Best Families
ITM	Invitation To Murder
KNPL	Kill Now-Pay Later
LFM	The League Of Frightened Men
MA	Man Alive
MAWBD	Might As Well Be Dead
MBTB	Murder By The Book
MC	Murder Is Corny
MH	The Mother Hunt
MNJ	Murder Is No Joke
MTFM	Method Three For Murder
NQDE	Not Quite Dead Enough
NW	The Next Witness
OF	Omit Flowers
OMDB	Over My Dead Body
PA	Poison A La Carte

PB	Prisoner's Base
PIY	Plot It Yourself
PPTG	Please Pass The Guilt
RDBX	The Red Box
RB	Rubber Band
RM	The Rodeo Murder
SAM	The Squirt And The Monkey
SBC	Some Buried Caesar
SC	The Second Confession
SS	The Silent Speaker
TDB	The Doorbell Rang
TMC	Too Many Cooks
TMCL	Too Many Clients
TMD	Too Many Detectives
TMW	Too Many Women
TWKY	This Won't Kill You
WAMM	When A Man Murders
WFD	Window For Death
WTAW	Where There's A Will
ZC	The Zero Clue

Cast Of Characters

The following is a comprehensive list of all of the nearly 1,400 fictional characters mentioned by name (some just barely) in the Nero Wolfe series and a short synopsis of their roles in their respective cases. In parentheses following each entry is the acronym for the cases(s) in which they are mentioned.

The central characters (Nero Wolfe, Archie Goodwin, Fritz Brenner and Theodore Horstmann) are not included here. Wolfe and Archie, naturally, are the nucleus of every story. Fritz and Theodore, even in those rare adventures where they are not actively included or mentioned, may be considered to be omnipresent because you just know they're at their posts (Fritz in the kitchen and Theodore in the plant rooms) doing their duty. Otherwise all would be chaos.

The other series regulars and irregulars (Saul, Fred, Orrie, Cramer, et al) are not covered here either since their stories have been included in the beginning with the central characters. Authors are mentioned in the section on Wolfe's literate tastes along with their works. Widely known non-fictional characters (Willie Mays, Douglas MacArthur, et al) mentioned in the stories are not included here although some lesser known ones are.

Wolfe and Archie both admit that while trust and truth between them are basic necessities of their relationship, verbal dodges are occasionally permissible and, at times, equally necessary. I have used the same reasoning here. None of the information included here should ruin any of the stories for you and none of the suspects are identified so hopefully you won't be able to read this list and find out "who done it".

Characters

Aaron, Bertha—Private secretary to attorney Lamont Otis and murder victim. Bludgeoned with Wolfe's jade paperweight and strangled with his necktie. (EMMM)

Abbey, Agatha—Executive Editor of the Magazine *Mode*. One of the people waiting to see Leo Heller when he was murdered. (ZC)

Abbott, Cass R.—President of Continental Air Network. (PPTG)

Abe—Friend of Archie's at the Perlman Paper Company who helps him shake a tail. (CFO)

Abernathy, Mr.—President of Coninental Bank and Trust Company who got a free book that made him nervous. (TDB)

Abramowitz, Paul—Business associate of Otis Jarrell. (IDES)

Abrams, Deborah—Rachel Abrams' younger sister. (MBTB)

Abrams, Miss—Receptionist at Naylor-Kerr, Inc. (TMW)

Abrams, Mrs.—Rachel Abrams' mother. (MBTB)

Abrams, Nancy—Rachel Abrams' other sister. (MBTB)

Abrams, Rachel—Stenographer and typist who should have rented an office on the first floor. (MBTB)

Ackerman, Francis—Lawyer present at the meeting at Rusterman's Restaurant after which Harvey Bassett was murdered. (AFA)

Adams, Bob—New York Gazette reporter. (AFA)

Adams, Charlotte—Secretary of James A. Corrigan. (MBTB)

Adams, Lieutenant Colonel—One of General Carpenter's assistants in the Washington, D.C. office of U.S. Army Military Intelligence in 1943. (BT)

Adams, Lucille—Glenn Prescott's private secretary until her death from tuberculosis in May of 1939. (WTAW)

Adamson, Mr.—Lawyer for the National Industrial Association. (SS)

Adler, Julius—Lawyer and member of the League of Atonement. (LFM)

Aiken, Benedict—President of Continental Plastic Products. (TMCL)

Aiken, Mr.—Hireling of Guthrie Judd. (BE)

Aland, Jerome—Night-club performer and resident of 29 Arbor Street. (DLAD)

Albert—The doorman at Lily Rowan's building on East Sixty-third Street. (FH)

Alice—A friend of Mrs. Loring Burton. (LFM)

Allen, Mike—Peter Barstow's caddy on the day he died. (FDL)

Allenby, Mr.—Wealthy Philadelphian who contemplates hiring Augustus Farrell to design a library in Missouri. (LFM)

Alloway, Mr.—Deputy Police Commissioner in 1936. (RDBX)

Althaus, David—Women's clothier and Morris Althaus's father. (TDB)

Althaus, Ivana—Mrs. David Althaus and Mother of Morris Althaus. (TDB)

Althaus, Morris—Free-lance writer murdered while preparing a less than complimentary article on the FBI for Tick-Tock Magazine. (TDB)

Alving, Julie—Toy buyer for Meadow's Department Store and former paramour of Floyd Whitten before his marriage to Mrs. H.R. Landy. (OF)

Ames, Titus—Employee at the Dunn's country home in Rockland County, New York. (WTAW)

Amory, Ann—Friend of Lily Rowan employed by the National Bird League. Pigeons got her murdered. (NQDE)

Amory, Beatrice—Mrs. Robert C. Amory. (DOD)

Amory, Robert C.—Seattle physician. He and his wife are guests at Bill Farnham's dude ranch in Montana. (DOD)

Amsel, Steve—Private detective in New York City. Runs a one-man operation since he got fired from Larry Bascom's agency. (TMD)

Anderson, Fletcher M.—Independently wealthy District Attorney for Westchester County, New York. He took credit for the Goldsmith case in 1928 on information Wolfe gave him and not only didn't share the credit, he even turned it around so Wolfe got a black eye out of it. Wolfe calls him a shyster, a disease and forbids mentioning his name in the house. He lost a $10,000 bet to Wolfe in the first published case. (FDL)

Anderson, Mr.—Shoe salesman who, while serving as a juror, took a bribe from Con O'Malley. (MBTB)

Anderson, Mr.—A man who made an appointment with Archie in September 1960 only to have it summarily canceled by Wolfe. This led to another of Archie's resignations and another of Wolfe's cases. (MTFM)

Anderson, Walter M.—President of the Starlite Company. (ABAV)

Andy—Janitor for the Midtown Home Service Corporation. (PPTG)

Annis, Carol—One of the so-called Hebes, a dozen young women hired to serve at the annual dinner of the Ten for Aristology in 1958. (PA)

Annis, Hattie—Frowsy former actress who maintains a rooming house at 628 W. 47th Street for aspiring actors and actresses. She fainted on Wolfe's stoop, compared his girth to Falstaff and his ethics to that of a "bootlicker." Later finding a dead body in her parlor prompts her to label Archie as "no good." (CM)(AOAB)

Anstrey, Mr.—New York City FBI Agent who refused to give any information to the Rackells as to whether their nephew Arthur was an FBI undercover agent or not. (HTR)

Anthony, Harold—Broker on Nassau Street and estranged husband of Rosa Bendini. He and Archie go at it pretty good in 1947. (TMW)

Appleton, Mr.—Man at Naylor-Kerr, Inc. who got a promotion when a murderer died. (TMW)

Arango, Peter—Employee of Updegraff Nurseries. (BO)

Arbuthnot, Mr.—A Vice-President of the Seaboard Products Corporation. (RB)

Archer, Baird—Pseudonym on Leonard Dykes' list. (MBTB)

Archer, Cleveland—District Attorney of Westchester County who had good reason to remember the Fashalt case. He also had the good fortune (or misfortune, depending upon your point of view) to have Wolfe involved in three of his cases in successive years. (DTD)(SC)(ITBF)

Archie—No, not THE Archie. This one has a face that looks like it has already been embalmed and he serves as a bodyguard/hitman for gangster Dazy Perrit. (BID)

Arden, Phoebe—Murder victim and dupe in one of the most sinister ploys Wolfe ever encounters. (MTFM)

Arkoff, Jerome—Television producer and one of Michael Molloy's theater companions. (MAWBD)

Arkoff, Rita—Mrs. Jerome Arkoff. She invited Mr. and Mrs. Molloy to attend the theater with her and her husband. (MAWBD)

Armstrong, Mr.—Member of the Board of Directors of Naylor-Kerr, Inc. (TMW)

Arnold, Judge Henry—Gifford James's lawyer. (GWW)

Arnold, Thomas—American consul in Bari, Italy. (BKM)

Aronson, Herb—Taxi driver who helps Archie tail a suspect in 1946. By 1951, his rate as standby transportation is $5 an hour. (SS)(HTR)(MA)

Arrow, Johnny—Uranium prospector and partner with Bertram Fyfe in the Fyfe-Arrow Mining Corporation. Handy with his fists as he proved to Paul Fyfe. (WFD)

Arthur—Colored porter at the Miltan studio. (OMDB)

Ash, Inspector—See under the Homicide/Antagonists section. (SS)

Ashby, Dennis—Vice-President in charge of sales and promotion for Mercer's Bobbins, Inc. who was responsible for greatly increasing the firm's business until someone pitched him out of a window. (KNPL)

Ashby, Joan—Nee' Snyder. Former secretary at Mercer Bobbins Inc. and widow of Dennis Ashby. (KNPL)

Ashe, Leonard—Man falsely accused of Marie Willis's murder. Wolfe walked out on a subpoena and hid out from the law to acquit him. (NW)

Ashley, Clay—Manager of Kanawha Spa, West Virginia. (TMC)

Asmussen, Oaky—Player for the New York Giants during the 1952 World Series. (TWKY)

Assa, Vernon—Partner in the advertising firm of Lippert, Buff and Assa. (BM)(TMD)

Atchison, Mr.—Advertising copywriter and former boyfriend of Joan Wellman. (MBTB)

Atkinson, Brooks—Drama critic for the New York Times. He praises the way Meg Duncan uses her hands. Archie would agree. (TMCL)

Atwood, Mr.—Banker at the Thirty-fourth Street branch of the Continental Bank and Trust Company. (FH)

Aubry, Paul—Man in a bigamous marriage with Caroline Karnow. (WAMM)

Auerbach, Sergeant—NYPD officer that Wolfe reported an apparent suicide to when a suspect apparently shot himself while on the phone with Wolfe in 1951. A year later, he uses his brains on one murder to lead to the discovery of another murder. Wolfe predicts that someday he'll inherit Cramer's job. (MBTB)(PB)

Ault, Benjamin, Junior—Furniture factory owner in Evansville, Indiana. Husband of Marjorie and father of Richard. (ARTD)

Ault, Marjorie—Widow of Benjamin and mother of Richard Ault. (ARTD)

Ault, Richard—Despondent Harvard student who committed suicide in 1959 because Susan Brooke wouldn't marry him. (ARTD)

Avery, Dr. Victor—Physician for the Blount family and one of six men playing chess simultaneously against Paul Jerin. (G)

Ayers, Michael—Newspaperman for the New York Tribune and member of the League of Atonement. (LFM)

Bagby, Clyde—Owner of Bagby Answers Inc., a telephone answering service in New York City. (NW)

Bahr, Daniel—Newspaper columnist, husband of Eve Bahr and son-in-law of the deceased H.R. Landy. (OF)

Bahr, Eve—Daughter of H.R. Landy and wife of Daniel Bahr. (OF)

Bailey—Another NYPD Homicide minion. (SS)

Bailey, Miss—Adrian Evers' secretary. (TDB)

Baker, Lew—First string catcher for the New York Giants during the 1952 World Series. (TWKY)

Balar, Grudo—Boyhood friend of Wolfe in Podgorica (Titograd), Montenegro. (BKM)

Baleine, Jacques—Former chef de cuisine of the Emerald Hotel, Dublin, and deceased member of Les Quinze Maitres. (TMC)

Ballard, Cora—Executive Secretary of the National Association of Authors and Dramatists. (PIY)

Ballin, Mrs.—Witness to Molly Lauck's murder at Boyden McNair Inc. in 1936. (RDBX)

Ballou, Avery—Very wealthy President of the Federal Holding Company. After Wolfe gets him out of a jam concerning his mistress, he is able to return the favor several times in succeeding years. (DD)(FH)(PPTG)

Ballou, Minerva—nee' Chadwick of the steel and railroad Chadwicks. Mrs. Avery Ballou but her friends call her Minna. No stamina, weak memory. (DD)

Bamford, Christopher—One of the best orchid-growers in America, he joined others in an entreaty to Wolfe to solve Molly Lauck's murder. (RDBX)

Banau, Alexander—A captain at Zoller's Restaurant in New York City. Wolfe shook hands with him at their first meeting, a rare condescension. (FJP)

Banau, Anna—Mrs. Alexander Banau, what she witnessed at an Independence Day picnic forced Wolfe to solve the crime as a means of self-defense. (FJP)

Barnes, Mr. and Mrs. Nev—Some of the local color in Lame Horse, Montana. The Mrs. sells her baked goods and Nev steals some of the money to buy bootleg liquor from Henrietta. The affair culminates with wife chasing husband down the middle of the street with a leather strap. (DOD)

Barrett, Donald—Son of John P. Barrett and a junior partner in the foreign investment bankers firm of Barrett & De Russy. (OMDB)

Barrett, John P.—Senior partner in Barrett & De Russy. (OMDB)

Barrow, Cal—One of the contestants in the World Series Rodeo in 1960 and a roping contest staged at Lily Rowan's penthouse. (RM)

Barrow, Captain—New York State Police Captain who arrested Archie in Crowfield County, New York, in 1938. (SBC)

Barstow, Ellen—56, widow of Peter Oliver Barstow. Mentally fragile, possibly unstable. Once tried to shoot her husband. Offered a reward of $50,000 for her husband's killer. (FDL)

Barstow, Lawrence—27, privileged, spoiled son of Peter Oliver Barstow. One of the golfing foursome when his father dropped dead. (FDL)

Barstow, Peter Oliver—58-year-old President of Holland University who dropped dead on the golf course of the Green Meadow Club near Pleasantville, 30 miles north of New York on June 4, 1933. First murder victim of that case but the second one discovered. (FDL)

Barstow, Sarah—25, Smith graduate, daughter of Peter Oliver Barstow. Attractive. Archie likes her. (FDL) She also gave her friend Evelyn Hibbard a letter of introduction to Wolfe. (LFM)

Barth, Cora—Employee at Corrigan, Phelps, Kustin and Briggs. A virgin who wasn't worth the trouble. (MBTB)

Bascom, Del—Owner of the Bascom Detective Agency in New York City. He knows when to get out of Wolfe's way. He occasionally hires Saul, Fred and Orrie when they're not working for Wolfe but evidently his regular men are competent because Wolfe hires twenty of them for $500 a day in 1946. (LFM)(SS)(SC)(ITBF)(MAWBD)(PPTG)(DD)(AFA)

Bascom, Larry—Private detective who runs one of the best agencies in town. (TMD)

Bascomb, Lyle—Author Alice Porter's former agent. (PIY)

Bassett, Dora—Mrs. Harvey Bassett. Formerly a singer named Dora Miller, then Doremi, then Doraymee because nobody got it. Friend of Lily Rowan. (AFA)

Bassett, Harvey H.—President of National Electronics Industries, murdered following a meeting at Rusterman's Restaurant. (AFA)

Battista, Guido—Carla Wolfe's guide across the Adriatic Sea. (BKM)

Baxter, Mr.—Chief of Detectives on Long Island. (FJP)

Baxter, Tammy—Short for Tamiris. Attractive, ostensibly a fledgling actress whose landlady is Hattie Annis. Actually an undercover U.S. Secret Service agent who gets too close to a counterfeiter and becomes a murder victim. (CM)(AOAB)

Beauchamp, Mrs.—Member of the Manhattan Flower Club who brought Malcolm Vedder to Wolfe's house as her guest. (DFM)

Beebe, James M.—Stanley Karnow's attorney. (WAMM)

Beech, Mr.—A Vice-President of the Federal Broadcasting Company. (ABAV)

Bekr, Nasir ibn—A foreign screwball, terrorist bomber or Mossad? (PPTG)

Bendini, Rosa—Assistant Chief Filer in the Machinery Parts Section of Naylor-Kerr, Inc. (TMW)

Bennett, Lew—Secretary of the National Guernsey League. (SBC)

Berin, Constanza—Daughter of Jerome Berin. (TMC)

Berin, Jerome—Chef de cuisine of the Corridona in San Remo. (TMC)

Berk, Carol—Free-lance TV contact specialist and FBI informant. Despite a rocky start to their relationship, Archie dates her. (HTR)

Berman, Sergeant—NYPD officer at Homicide South in 1967. (FH)

Bert—Hired hand of Thomas Pratt. A master drink-fixer. (SBC)

Betz, Marjorie—Elaine Usher's best friend and she proves it. (CFO)

Biatti, Detective—NYPD homicide detective. Assigned to portray a reporter. (CK)

Bilic, George—Montenegrin who Wolfe and Archie try to hire to drive them 23 kilometers to Titograd. He has them taken by his rebellious son, Jube'. (BKM)

Bilic, Jube'—Son of George. He follows his father's orders but delivers Wolfe and Archie to the headquarters of the Secret Police, not his worst misjudgment. He shouldn't have given the finger to Danielo Vukcic. (BKM)

Bill—Pete Roeder's driver. (ITBF)

Billings, Ms.—Woman who searched Ellen Sturdevant's house to find a copy of Alice Porter's plagiarized manuscript. (PIY)

Bingham, Leo—Television producer and friend of Richard Valdon. (MH)

Birch, Matthew—Agent for the U.S. Immigration and Naturalization Service. He gets run over by a car and it's too good for him. (GS)

Birch, Mr.—Correspondence checker at Naylor-Kerr, Inc. An old man with a wart on his nose. (TMW)

Bischoll, Mr.—Owner of a pet shop on Third Avenue that is allied with Arnold Zeck. This alliance caused Wolfe to refuse a job for him in November of 1948. (SC)

Bissell, Al—Cab driver in Charleston, West Virginia, who took a murderer to the airport. (TMC)

Bizzaro, Angelo—Warden of the local jail in Bari, Italy. (BKM)

Black—Unnamed detective from the D.A.'s Homicide Bureau (not Cramer's men) who arrests Wolfe and Archie on material witness charges. Archie nicknamed them for their races. His partner was White. (AFA)

Blaine, Mr.—Secretary of E.D. Kimball. First name unknown. Archie calls him "Square-jaw". (FDL)

Blanc, Leon—Chef de cuisine of the Willow Club, Boston. (TMC)

Blanco, Juan—Attorney in Caracas, Venezuela, who arranges for Albert Irby to represent Eric Hagh in New York. (PB)

Blaney, Conroy—Partner and idea man in the firm of Blaney and Conroy, manufacturer of novelties. Offered to produce an orchid plant for Wolfe that would announce itself in Wolfe's voice by saying "Orchids to you!". For the first time, Wolfe fled his own office to escape the man's asininity, had him ejected from the house and refused entrance forevermore. (IOE)

Blount, Anna—Mrs. Matthew Blount and mother of Sally (Sarah). She really doesn't realize the effect her looks have on men. (G)

Blount, Helen—Friend of Althea Vail who helps her conceal her visit to Nero Wolfe. (FD)

Blount, Matthew—President of the Blount Textile Corporation and accused murderer of Paul Jerin. (G)

Blount, Sarah—Nicknamed Sally. Daughter of Matthew and girlfriend, maybe serious or maybe not, of Paul Jerin. (G)

Boas, Franz—German-American anthropologist (1858–1942). First professor of anthropology at Columbia University. Wolfe has met him and had his books autographed. (TMC)

Bodin—Wolfe's contact in Paris, France, in 1954. (BKM)

Boney—One of the domestic staff at Kanawha Spa. (TMC)

Bonino, Roy—New York City Assistant District Attorney in 1953. (GS)

Boone, Cheney—Director of the Bureau of Price Regulation who gets his head beaten in with a monkey wrench. (SS)

Boone, Mrs.—No first name given. Wife—er—widow of Cheney Boone and first cousin of General Carpenter. (SS)

Boone, Nina—Niece of Cheney Boone. (SS)

Borly, Mr.—Butler for the Whitten family. (OF)

Bosley, Adele—In charge of Public Relations for the Metropolitan Opera. (GWW)

Bottweill, Kurt—Owner of an art gallery and fiancée of Margot Dickey. Wolfe and Archie recovered some stolen tapestries for him a few months before he was murdered at his own Christmas party. (CP)

Botvinnik—Russian World Chess Champion. (G)

Boughton, Bessie—Gilbert Haight's political science teacher—and alibi. (DOD)

Bowen, Barry—Pseudonym on Leonard Dykes' list. (MBTB)

Bowen, Captain—NYPD Homicide Captain in 1947 who showed Saul Panzer the reports on Waldo Moore's death. (TMW)

Bowen, Detective—One of Inspector Cramer's minions in 1940. He had a reputation for conducting extremely thorough searches until Archie bested him by pulling a rabbit—actually a jar—out of a hat. (BE)

Bowen, Ed—District Attorney of New York County from 1952–1960. He is an old friend of Lily Rowan. (GS)(RM)(FUFM)(PB)(CFO)

Bowen, Ferdinand—Stockbroker and member of the League of Atonement. He kicked Archie in the shin once. (LFM)(TMW)

Bowen, Miss—Switchboard operator for the Rights of Citizens Committee. (ARTD)

Bowen, William R.—A man who does business with Otis Jarrell. (IDES)

Boyle, Mr.—Deputy New York City Police Commissioner. (ITM)

Bradford, Dr. Nathaniel—Old family friend of the Barstows. Initially diagnosed Peter Barstow's cause of death as a heart attack. (FDL)

Brady, Ruth—Female operative used by Wolfe. That Saul Panzer would commit a robbery with her speaks highly for her competence and trustworthiness. (SC)(ITBF)

Bragan, O.V.—Oil millionaire and owner of the Hemisphere Oil Company. (INTM)

Bram, Judith—One of 93 female taxi drivers in New York City and friend of Mira Holt. Another woman who reinforces Wolfe's opinions of women—she prattles and can't seem to speak directly to a point without circling it several times. Her one redeeming quality, aside from blind loyalty, is that she slaps Inspector Cramer resoundingly. (MTFM)

Brandt, Delia—Michael Molloy's secretary. (MAWBD)

Braunstein, Herman—New York man who owned a painting that provided a key clue to a murder. (DLAD)

Breslow, Mr.—Paper manufacturer from Denver and member of the Executive Committee of the National Industrial Association. (SS)

Brigham, Corey—Friend of the Jarrell family who beat Otis out on a business deal with inside information. (IDES)

Briggs, Frederick—Law partner in Corrigan, Phelps, Kustin and Briggs. (MBTB)

Brill, Mr.—New York City Assistant District Attorney. (MNJ)(FUFM)

Britton, William R.—Owner of a Fifth Avenue travel agency and Wolfe's son-in-law—sort of. In 1939 he married one of his employees, Carla Lovchen, who was Wolfe's adopted daughter. Britton died of a heart attack in 1950. (BKM)

Broadyke, Frank—Industrial designer. (BFO)

Brod, Clement—Poet and playwright. (AOAB)

Brodell, Edward Ellis—Owner-publisher of the St. Louis Star-Bulletin and father of Phillip Brodell. (DOD)

Brodell, Phillip—Son of Edward Brodell who made headlines in a different way than his father. (DOD)

Bronson—NYPD Detective Lieutenant. (WTAW)

Bronson, Howard—A blackguard, and a dumb one. The combination got him killed when he ignored Wolfe's advice. (SBC)

Brooke, Dolly—Mrs. Kenneth Brooke, formerly Dolly Drake. Ex-stage actress and voice impersonator. Women like her are the justification for Wolfe's preference for male companionship. (ARTD)

Brooke, Kenneth—Engineer and brother of Susan Brooke. (ARTD)

Brooke, Susan—Young lady with a star-crossed love life who has more rights than she realizes. (ARTD)

Brovnik, Pero—Man that Nero Wolfe left his adopted daughter with in Zagreb in 1921. He and his wife were arrested as revolutionaries and shot when she was eight years old. (OMDB)

Brown, Cynthia—She was about to hire Wolfe to expose a murderer when she was strangled in Wolfe's office in front of his desk. She mentioned her knowledge of his previous work for Dazy Perrit which should have given some indication of her character. She was mentioned in a case several years later. (DFM)(SAM)

Brown, Hyacinth—One of the domestic staff at Kanawha Spa. (TMC)

Brown, Percy—Con man and accomplice of Cynthia Brown. (DFM)

Browning, Amory—Vice-President in charge of programming for Continental Air Network. (PPTG)

Browning, Phyllis—Mrs. Amory Browning. (PPTG)

Bruce, Sergeant Dorothy—Secretary in 1943 in the U.S. Army's New York office of Military Intelligence. A jenny ass with streaks of brilliance, in Wolfe's estimation. (BT)

Brucker, Jay Luther—President of Softdown, Inc. (PB)

Brundage, Bill—Television newscaster who reports a murder in one of Wolfe's cases. (IDES)

Bruner, Lloyd—Deceased building magnate. (TDB)

Bruner, Mrs. Lloyd—Widow of Lloyd Bruner who is being harassed by the FBI. (TDB)

Bruno—Waiter at Rusterman's Restaurant who needs to be careful when he does and doesn't recognize Archie. (IDES)

Bryant, Mr.—Sheriff of Rockland County, New York, in 1939. I wouldn't be surprised if he lost the next election to his deputy Lon Chambers. (WTAW)

Bua—Murderer, torturer and the man who tried to stick a knife in Wolfe, almost successfully. (BKM)

Buchman, Mr.—Man at the theatrical agency that supplied the women hired to serve at the 1958 dinner of the Ten for Aristology. (PA)

Buff, Oliver—Partner in the advertising firm of Lippert, Buff and Assa. A good front man. (BM)

Buhl, Frederick—Physician in Mount Kisco, New York, who pronounced Bertram Fyfe dead from pneumonia. (WFD)

Bundy, Captain—NYPD Homicide in 1953. (GS)

Bupp, William O.—Feed store owner in Ottumwa, Iowa. (OMDB)

Bupp, Pansy—Daughter of William O. Bupp who significantly broadened her horizons until she lied to Nero Wolfe about it. (OMDB)

Buratti, Phil—Private detective with the Southwest Agency in Los Angeles. Archie gives him the world's easiest tailing job. (MBTB)

Burger, Detective—New York City Homicide Detective. (ZC)

Burke, Detective—One of Inspector Cramer's minions in 1936. (RDBX)

Burke, Jimmy—NYPD officer who is Inspector Cramer's driver in 1960. He and Archie are friendly enough to wave. (TMCL)

Burkhardt, Claire—Stenographer at Corrigan, Phelps, Kustin and Briggs. (MBTB)

Burnham, Lt.—NYPD officer who tried to help Wolfe when no help would do. (AFA)

Burr, Jimmie—Clubhouse boy for the New York Giants during the 1952 World Series. (TWKY)

Burton, Anne—Mrs. Loring A. Burton. (LFM)

Burton, Loring A.—Doctor, member of the League of Atonement and murder victim. (LFM)

Busch, Andrew—Secretary of Mercer's Bobbins, Inc. He proposed to a lady both in Wolfe's office and the South Room. (KNPL)

Butterfield, William—A young man who wanted to marry Rachel Abrams. (MBTB)

Byne, Austin—Nicknamed "Dinky", for God's sake. Louise Robilotti's nephew who invites Archie to a murder. (CFO)

Bynoe, Millard—Billionaire philanthropist, 55, who produced a flamingo pink *Vanda* orchid that Wolfe coveted. (EP)

Bynoe, Mrs. Millard—Wife of the billionaire philanthropist, 20 years his junior, and murder victim. Her wearing one of his rare orchids to an Easter parade led to the solution of her murder. (EP)

Byron, Edwin Robert—Magazine editor and member of the League of Atonement. (LFM)

Cabot, Mr.—Attorney with power of attorney over Edwin Frost's estate. (RDBX)

Cabot, Nicholas—A tough lawyer, in Archie's estimation, and member of the League of Atonement. (LFM)

Caldecott, Mr.—He accepted a $20,000 donation from James Sperling to the Committee of Progressive Businessmen in 1949. They promote Henry A. Wallace for president. (SC)

Camembert, Clarence—Archie's first suggestion for an alias for Wolfe to go undercover in the Stock Department of Naylor-Kerr, Inc. (TMW)

Campbell, Mrs.—English secretary to Prince Peter Donevitch. She took custody of Wolfe's adopted daughter from an institution after the Brovnik's were killed. (OMDB)

Carlisle, Homer N.—Executive vice-president of North American Foods Company. (DFM)

Carlisle, Mrs. Homer N.—Wife of Homer N. Carlisle who attended a flower show in Wolfe's home and discovered a body in the office. (DFM)

Carlos—Waiter at Ribiero's Brazilian Restaurant on Fifty-Second Street. (SS)

Carmel, Deputy—Deputy Sheriff in the Putnam County Sheriff's Office, sent by Inspector Cramer to arrest a man who had sent a bomb to Wolfe's office. (MC)

Carpenter, Lieutenant General—Head of Army Intelligence (G-2) and one of Archie's commanders in Washington, D.C., during World War II. He is also a first cousin of Mrs. Cheney Boone. Due to the suspension of time in the Wolfe series, he may also have been the anonymous three-star general in the Pentagon that Archie uses for access to military records in 1968. (BT)(HWM)(IOE) (SS)(CK)

Carruthers, Mr.—Member of the Gambit chess club. (G)

Carter, Evelyn—Alias once used by Cynthia Brown in Paris, France. (DFM)

Cartright, Mr.—Owner of Consolidated Products. Prior to 1954, he was being gypped, hired Wolfe, was very satisfied with the outcome and paid his $12,000 bill without a squeak. He holds a somewhat unique status in that when he tried to hire Wolfe again in 1954, Archie tried to get Wolfe to take his case when the bank balance was very healthy to dissuade him from embarking on another case. Archie was memorably unsuccessful. (BKM)

Casado, Anna—One of the cowgirls attending the World Series Rodeo in 1960. (RM)

Casey—NYPD officer. (PB)

Chack, Pearl O.—Grandmother of Ann Amory. (NQDE)

Chaffee, Ross—Artist and resident of 29 Arbor Street. One of his paintings was an integral clue to the mystery. (DLAD)

Chambers, Lon—Industrious and very competent deputy sheriff in Rockland County, New York. (WTAW)

Chaney, Mr.—Assistant to Angela Wright at the Association for the Aid of Displaced Persons. (GS)

Chapin, Dora—Mrs. Paul Chapin, nee' Dora Ritter. She indulges in self-mutilation and kidnapping, both at Wolfe's expense. (LFM)

Chapin, Paul—Writer crippled in a hazing incident at Harvard and the object of pity from the League of Atonement. (LFM)

Chatwin, Dale—A good bridge player on the make. (TMC)

Cheney—Skinny stenographer for Westchester County. (ITBF)

Chesterton, Dora—A lady in the Chesterton-Best case, an unrecorded case occurring prior to 1946 in which a guy burgled his own house and shot a weekend guest in the belly. Archie struck up an acquaintance with her but he's saving the details for his autobiography. (SS)

Chisholm, Emil—Oil millionaire and part-owner of the New York Giants at the time of the 1952 World Series. He provided the ticket for Wolfe, Pierre Mondor and Archie to attend a game of that series because of Wolfe's successful handling of a case for him several years earlier. (TWKY)

Choade, Freetham—Name Archie made up to illustrate the futility of trying to find real people who matched the pseudonyms on Leonard Dykes' list. (MBTB)

Choate, Peggy—One of the so-called Hebes, a group of a dozen young women hired to serve at the annual dinner of the Ten for Aristology in 1958. (PA)

Christy, Max—Henchman of Arnold Zeck and, for a short time, Archie's cellmate. (ITBF)

Clark, Miss—Archie's high school geometry teacher. She always had his number. Blanche Irwin reminds him of her. (CFO)

Clay, Mr.—A man who does business with Otis Jarrell. (IDES)

Claymore, Beth—Witness to Molly Lauck's murder at Boyden McNair Inc. in 1936. (RDBX)

Cliff, Leonard—Vice-president of Products and Beverages Corporation and a suspect in one of the vilest crimes imaginable, putting quinine in Wolfe's liver pate'. (BE)

Clifford, Mr.—A lawyer whose case was refused by Wolfe because Clifford had dandruff. Another of Archie's facetious *bon mots* for the lengths Wolfe will go to avoiding work. (ABAV)

Clivers, Marquis of—English lord with a distinctly un-noble past. (RB)

Coburn, Missy—Reporter for the New York World-Telegram. (BM)

Cody, Oscar—Pseudonym on Leonard Dykes' list. (MBTB)

Coffey, Sergeant—NYPD Homicide officer in 1957. (IDES)

Coffey, William—House detective at the Churchill Hotel who is trusted by Archie. (TDB)

Coggin, Daniel F.—New York City Assistance District Attorney. The first words Wolfe ever spoke to him were a lie. (AFA)

Coleman, James N.—Alias "Rubber" Coleman. His nickname came from the way he bounced back up when knocked down. His gang in 1895 Silver City, Nevada, adopted the name "The Rubber Band." (RB)

Colihan, Joseph—Denver resident and guest at Bill Farnham's dude ranch in Lame Horse, Montana. (DOD)

Collard, Fillmore—Textile mill owner and member of the League of Atonement. Judge William Harrison died at his estate. (LFM)

Collinger, Mr.—Boyden McNair's attorney. (RDBX)

Collins, Mike—Taxi driver who helps Archie on stakeouts and tails. (TMCL)

Colt, Sally—Private detective for Dol Bonner. (TMD)(IDES)

Colvin, Jasper—District attorney in upstate New York. (IMTM)

Congreve—In 1957, Archie attends a dinner for a home for unwed mothers and tells Wolfe it allows disadvantaged girls to sit on chairs made by Congreve. Wolfe points out that Congreve didn't make chairs. William Congreve (1670–1729) was an English dramatist. (CFO)

Cook, Ben—Chief of Police, White Plains, New York. A Neanderthal who itches to put his hands officially on Archie but is restrained, probably to the benefit of both. (FDL)

Copes, Dennis—Young man who has ambitions to rise within Continental Air Network but not the talent to match. He has interesting in-laws. (PPTG)

Cora—Maid and female wrestler (in Archie's estimation) who guards Madeline Fraser's door. (ABAV)

Cora—Maid for the Koven household. (SAM)

Corbett, H.R.—Investigator for the Westchester County District Attorney. Pushy. (FDL)

Corbett, Judge—Judge at Leonard Ashe's trial. He issued arrest warrants for Wolfe and Archie but was forced to quash them. (NW)

Corbett, Sally—One of Dol Bonner's operatives. Referred to as Sue Corbett in 1968. (PIY)(MH)(FH)

Corcoran, Miss—Minerva Ballou's secretary. (DD)

Correla, Phillip—Cook at Rusterman's Restaurant and Pierre Duco's best friend. (AFA)

Corrigan, James A.—Senior partner of Corrigan, Phelps, Kustin and Briggs. (MBTB)

Corwin, Mr.—Assistant to Albert Hyatt in his wiretapping inquiry in 1956. (TMD)

Costigan, Brownie—Another of Arnold Zeck's henchmen. (ITBF)

Courbet, Felix—Maitre d'hotel at Rusterman's Restaurant. He was enlisted by Lily Rowan to cook blue grouse for her rodeo guests in 1960. Was a witness in the murder of Kenneth Faber. (FJP)(PA)(RM)(MC)

Courtney, Richard—Official of the American Embassy in Rome, Italy, in 1954. He asked for and got Wolfe's autograph. (BKM)

Coyne, Lawrence—Chef de cuisine of The Rattan, San Francisco. (TMC)

Coyne, Lio—Lawrence Coyne's fourth wife. Her asking her husband to kiss her finger gave Wolfe an important clue to solve a murder. (TMC)

Cox, Frances—Receptionist for Mercer's Bobbins, Inc. (KNPL)

Crabtree, Mr.—One of the domestic staff at Kanawha Spa. (TMC)

Cragg, H.R.—A member of the elite Social Register, he and his wife were present at Boyden McNair Inc. when Molly Lauck was murdered. (RDBX)

Crisler, Mr.—Fountain pen magnate who was stoned while on the bridle paths of Kanawha Spa. (TMC)

Cross, Captain Albert—U.S. Army Military Intelligence officer who approached Wolfe about taking an assignment in early 1942 and was rebuffed. The following summer, he was murdered by being pushed from a twelfth floor window of the Bascombe Hotel. (NQDE)(BT)

Cullen. Daniel—Cattleman who attempted to forestall Thomas Pratt's plans to barbecue a champion bull for advertising. (SBC)

Cushing, Mr.—Vice-President of Naylor-Kerr, Inc. (TMW)

Cutler, Dr. Frederick M.—Physician who treated Mrs. Floyd Whitten for knife wounds and reluctantly informed Archie of same. (OF)

Dacos, Sarah—Former stenographer at the Bruner Corporation, currently secretary to Vice-President Thompson. (TDB)

Daggett, Mr.—One of the domestic staff at Kanawha Spa. (TMC)

Dahlmann, Louis—Promising young idea man with the advertising firm of Lippert, Buff and Assa. One of his bright ideas got him killed. (BM)

Damiano, Pete—One of Lon Cohen's best men at the Gazette. (PPTG)

Darby, John H.—Gilbert Irving's attorney. (MTFM)

Darrow, Lina—Sarah Rackham's secretary. (ITBF)

Darst, Bill—Sausage-maker in Hackettstown who Wolfe regards as the best sausage maker west of Cherbourg. His sausage will bring tears to your eyes. (ITBF)

Darst, Carl—Taxi driver who brought a man to Wolfe's house just before the man was murdered. (TMW)

Darst, Detective—NYPD Homicide detective sent to Michigan on an investigation. (ABAV)

Darst, Johnny—House detective at the Waldorf-Astoria Hotel. (SS)

Dart, Adrian—Hollywood actor and member of the Ten for Aristology. (PA)

Darth, Sidney—Chairman of the North Atlantic Exposition Board. (SBC)

Daumery, Bernard—Nephew of Jean Daumery and heir to his uncle's share in Daumery and Nieder. (MA)

Daumery, Helen—Deceased wife of Jean Daumery. (MA)

Daumery, Jean—One of the founding partners of Daumery and Nieder. (MA)

Davis, Eugene—Lawyer with Dunwoodie, Prescott & Davis. (WTAW)

Dawson, Earl—A jealous drunk. (WTAW)

Dawson, Luther—Defense attorney for Harvey Greve in Montana. (DOD)

Decker, Barry—Director of Clinical Psychiatry at San Francisco General Hospital and pioneer in crisis intervention. (PPTG)

Deffand, Mimi—Lily Rowan's maid and cook. (DOD)(DD)(FH)(AFA)

Degan, Patrick A.—Head of the Mechanics Alliance Welfare Association. (MAWBD)(IDES)

Delancey, Mrs.—Her husband owns a chain of restaurants, is twice her age and she cheats on him. (TMCL)

Delaney, James R.—District Attorney on Long Island. (FJP)

Dell, Nate—Sheriff in upstate New York. (IMTM)

Dell, Raymond—One of Hattie Annis' roomers. A has-been actor reduced to occasional television roles. (CM)(AOAB)

Della—Maid for Bernard Quest who is sent to see if the piece of cord he intended to strangle Priscilla Eads with was still on his dresser. (PB)

Demarest, Henry R.—Attorney and executor of Paul Nieder's estate. (MA)

Denovo, Amy—A wealthy orphan looking for her roots. (FH)

Denovo, Elinor—Mother of Amy. Camera-shy, strong-willed, vice-president of Raymond Thorne Productions who made her daughter a new star. (FH)

Derwin, Mr.—Chief Assistant District Attorney, Westchester County, New York. Obstinate but realized he was out of his depth in the first case. (FDL)

Devlin, Della—Buyer of novelties for out-of-town stores. Her ears are too big and her expression looks like she's always being imposed upon. (HTR)

Devore, Captain—NYPD Captain dumb enough to question an English lord without consulting headquarters first. No doubt severely limited his career opportunities and was never heard from again in the series. (RB)

Dexter, Solomon—Former Deputy Director of the Bureau of Price Regulation. (SS)

Dexter, Thomas—President of Title House publishers and member of the Joint Committee on Plagiarism of the National Association of Authors and Dramatists and the Book Publishers of America. (PIY)

Dickerson, Mr.—Head of the Correspondence Checking Section at Naylor-Kerr, Inc. (TMW)

Dickey, Margot—Contact woman for and fiancée of Kurt Bottweill. She induced Bottweill to propose to her with a marriage license bearing her name next to Archie Goodwin's, a paper that Archie also put to good use with Wolfe. (CP)

Dickinson, Arthur and Louise—Sylvia Venner was their house guest in Katona the weekend of a murder. (PPTG)

Dickson, George—An alias for a murderer. (MA)

Dietz, Mr. and Mrs. Herman—Dinner guests of Otis Jarrell. (IDES)

Dill, Wade G.—Partner in Rucker and Dill's seed and nursery company and president of the Atlantic Horticultural Society. (BO)

Ditson, Cuyler—One of the best orchid-growers in America, he joined others in an entreaty to Wolfe to solve the murder of Molly Lauck. (RDBX)(SBC)

Dixie—A man who runs an eatery on 170th Street who knows how to make chili. (NW)

Dixon, Captain—NYPD Captain assigned to an experiment with candy in 1936. (RDBX)

Dobbs, Mr.—Butler for the Kalmus household. (G)

Dobbs, Mrs. Robert—Former landlady of Vincent Tuttle and Bertram Fyfe. (WFD)

Dolman, Ferdinand—Private detective with the Southwest Agency in Los Angeles. He calls Wolfe "the old fatty" but not to his face. (MBTB)

Donahue, William A.—A man who used various aliases to hire various detectives for wiretapping jobs in 1955 that eventually cost him his life. (TMD)

Donaldson, Mr.—Attorney, executor of Sigmund Keyes' estate and former fiancée of Dorothy Keyes. (BFO)

Dondero, Sue—Emmett Phelp's secretary at Corrigan, Phelps, Kustin and Briggs. (MBTB)(BKM)

Donevitch, Peter—Prince of Yugoslavia. (OMDB)

Donevitch, Stefan—Crown Prince of Yugoslavia, son of Peter. (OMDB)

Donevitch, Vladanka—Princess of Yugoslavia and wife of Prince Stefan Donevitch. (OMDB)

Donofrio, Pasquale—Chef de cuisine at the Eldorado, Madrid, Spain. Deceased before 1937. (TMC) He used a sauce originated by Wolfe for his grilled kidneys. (IMTM)

Donovan, Detective—Another of Inspector Cramer's minions. (MC)

Donovan, Jimmy—Leonard Ashe's defense attorney. (NW)

Donovan, Sergeant—NYPD Desk Sergeant at the Medical Examiner's Office in 1954–56. (BKM)(MAWBD)

Donovan, T.R.—Member of the League of Atonement. (LFM)

Donvaag, Ed—Victor Lindquist's nearest neighbor in Plainview, Nebraska, in 1935. A good neighbor. (RB)

Dora—Nurse at Grantham House. (CFO)

Douglas, Roy—Keeps a pigeon loft on the roof of Miss Leeds' building. (NQDE)

Dowd, Homer—Owner of Dowd's Roofing Company in Lame Horse, Montana. He was to provide the tar to tar and feather Phillip Brodell. (DOD)

Dowd, Vera—Lucy Valdon's cook. (MH)

Doyle, Bill—An operative used by Wolfe in one case, supervised by Saul Panzer. One of his odder duties was to grab a cop's cap off his head and make him chase him trying to retrieve it. He did it without a second's hesitation, earning him Archie's undying love. (HTR)

Doyle, Detective—New York City Homicide Detective as early as 1940. In 1952, he handcuffs and searches Archie on orders from Lt. Rowcliff. (IOE)(BE)(PB)

Doyle, Mr.—Cornwall and Mayer Detective Agency's best man in 1944. Murder victim. Shot in the back near 73rd and Madison while acting as a bodyguard for Ben Jensen. (HWM)

Doyle, Mr.—New York City Assistant District Attorney under District Attorney Skinner in 1957. (EP)

Drake, Inspector—NYPD Inspector blackmailed by Arnold Zeck. (SC)

Draper, Charles—Vice-President of the Women's Nature League in Los Angeles. The President is Gertrude Frazee. (BM)

Draper, Special Agent—FBI agent investigating a kidnapping of the husband of one of Wolfe's clients. (FD)

Drescher, Miss—A superintendent at the factory of Softdown, Inc., and an intended member of the future all-female Board of Directors. (PB)

Drew, Carl—Business Manager for Alec Gallant Incorporated. Archie introduced himself to Drew as "John H. Watson." (MNJ)(FUFM)

Dreyer, Eugene—Art dealer, member of the League of Atonement and victim of nitroglycerin poisoning. (LFM)

Driscoll, Nathaniel—Fat, rich exporter/broker and a fencing student, he reported the theft of some diamonds from Miltan's studio, then changed his mind. (OMDB)

Drogo, Giuseppe—The man Geoffrey Hitchcock deals with in Rome in 1954. (BKM)

Drossos, Anthea—Pete Drossos' mother. (GS)

Drossos, Pete—A twelve-year-old boy who probably holds the record for hiring Wolfe with the lowest retainer—$4.30. (GS)(MAWBD)

Drucker, Otto—Private detective in Racine, Wisconsin. (ARTD)

Drummond, Alexander—Florist and member of the League of Atonement. (LFM)

DuBois, Armand—Another Denver resident who is a guest at Bill Farnham's dude ranch in Lame Horse, Montana. (DOD)

Ducos, Leon—Pierre Ducos' father. (AFA)

Ducos, Lucile—Pierre's daughter. She feeds facts to a computer at NYU. She knew too much but hid it well. (AFA)

Ducos, Pierre—Waiter at Rusterman's Restaurant. He violated Wolfe's hospitality like no one else ever had, albeit unintentionally and much more to his detriment than Wolfe's. (PPTG)(AFA)(TDB)

Duday, Viola—Assistant Secretary of Softdown, Inc. A poisonous shrew and it gets her face slapped. (PB)

Duffen, Arnold—Attorney for Oliver Buff. (BM)

Duffy, Jack—Process server who sneaks in behind the cops when a client is suing Wolfe to return his fee. (FD)

Duke, Blanche—Switchboard misanthrope at Corrigan, Phelps, Kustin and Briggs. She can't hold her liquor. (MBTB)

Dunbar, Paul Lawrence—Son of escaped slaves, poet and novelist (1872–1906). Wolfe makes a telling impression on young Paul Whipple by quoting Dunbar. (TMC)

Duncan, Amy—Niece of Arthur Tingley and Leonard Cliff's secretary. Her visit to Wolfe was fortuitous considering he had just vowed to do for free what she wanted to hire him for. (BE)

Duncan, Meg—Actress and scratch-cat who left something personal in the Yeager lovenest. (TMCL)

Dunn, Andrew—Son of John and June Dunn, brother of Sara. Lawyer with Dunwoodie, Prescott & Davis. (WTAW)

Dunn, John Charles—Husband of June and U.S. Secretary of State in 1939. (WTAW)

Dunn, June—nee' Hawthorne, the eldest Hawthorne daughter, sister of Noel, wife of John Charles Dunn and mother of Andrew and Sara. (WTAW)

Dunn, Sara—Daughter of John and June Dunn. Her photography hobby solved a case. (WTAW)

Dunning, Ellen—Wife of Roger Dunning. She made an anonymous call that cost Archie fourteen hours in jail. (RM)

Dunning, Roger—Promoter of the World Series Rodeo in New York in 1960. (RM)(DOD)

Durkin, Beaky—Scout for the New York Giants who discovered Nick Ferrone. No relation to Fred—I think. (TWKY)

Dykes, Ben—Head of the Westchester County detectives 1949–61. (DTD)(SC)(ITBF)(FD)

Dykes, Leonard—Confidential clerk in the law offices of Corrigan, Phelps, Kustin and Briggs. Fledgling author. He should have stayed a clerk. (MBTB)

Eads, Nathan—Deceased son of the founder of Softdown, Inc. and father of Priscilla Eads. (PB)

Eads, Priscilla—Divorced runaway little rich girl. She tried to rent the South Room for $50 a day for a week. Wolfe kicked her out, one of his most regrettable decisions. (PB)(BKM)

Eaton, Flora—Big-boned widow who does laundry and housework at the Bar JR Ranch in Lame Horse, Montana. (DOD)

Eber, James L.—Otis Jarrell's secretary before he was fired. (IDES)

Echols, Richard—Author who was sued for plagiarism by Simon Jacobs. (PIY)

Edey, Frank—55-year-old attorney, partner (27%) in the law firm of Otis, Edey, Heydecker and Jett. A brilliant idea man but rarely makes appearances in court. (EMMM)

Egan, Lawrence—Nicknamed "Lips." New York scam artist. Archie shoots a gun out of his hand. (GS)

Eggers, Lawrence H.—Business associate of Otis Jarrell. (IDES)

Ehrlich, Sol—Clerk for lawyer Nathaniel Parker. (BM)

Eisenstadt, Detective—Another of Cramer's minions but a college graduate who nevertheless presented Archie with no challenges when questioning him. (WAMM)

Eisler, Wade—Chief backer of the World Series Rodeo held at Madison Square Garden in 1960. His technique with women was a little rough and he had the effrontery to call Wolfe "Nero" but neither of those *faux pas* were what made him a murder victim. (RM)

Elga—The Vails' maid. (FD)

Elkus, Leopold—Surgeon and member of the League of Atonement. (LFM)

Emerson, Connie—Wife of Paul Emerson. She gets in a tussle with Archie trying to destroy evidence and loses. (SC)

Emerson, Paul—News commentator on WPIT radio, sponsored by the Continental Mines Corporation. He is one of the newsmen that Wolfe usually cuts off with his desk button. (SC)

Emil—The Vails' chauffeur. (FD)

Ennis, Jack—Expert diemaker and inventor. He was one of the people waiting to see Leo Heller when Heller was murdered. (ZC)

Enright, Albert—High ranking member of the Communist Party of the USA in 1949. (SC)

Epps, Beatrice—Employee of Quinn and Collins real estate who hopes to make money off of horsehair buttons. (MH)

Ernest—Hungarian or Polish waiter at Rusterman's Restaurant who tilts things. (AFA)

Ernst, Mrs. David A.—Scarsdale resident who owned the car used to run over Elinor Denovo. (FH)

Erskine, Edward Frank—Son of Frank Thomas Erskine. (SS)

Erskine, Frank Thomas—President of the National Industrial Association. (SS)

Erskine, Roland—Actor and member of the League of Atonement. (LFM)

Evers, Adrian—Head of Evers Electronics, Inc., a firm with government contracts. (TDB)

Ervin, Mortimer—Petty New York hood. Archie shoots a gun out of his hand, too. (GS)

Estey, Jean—Personal secretary of Angela Wright at the Association for the Aid of Displaced Persons. (GS)

Eston, Joe—New York Giants third baseman during the 1952 World Series. (TWKY)

Evarts, Tim—Assistant house dick (security officer to you) at the Churchill Towers. (WFD)(WAMM)(BM)

Evers—The second of two full-time deputies for the Monroe County, Montana, Sheriff's Office. (DOD)

Ewing, Adam—Black public relations specialist for the Rights of Citizens Committee. (ARTD)

Faber, Charlotte—Madeline Odell's secretary. (PPTG)

Faber, Dr.—Assistant Medical Examiner in New York City. (BKM)

Faber, Fern—One of the so-called Hebes, a group of a dozen young women hired to serve at the annual dinner of the Ten for Aristology in 1958. (PA)

Faber, Kenneth—Deliveryman for Duncan McLeod. Killed in the alley behind Rusterman's Restaurant before he could deliver Wolfe's corn. (MC)

Faber, Rudolph—Nazi agent who had no chin so Archie hit him in the eye instead. (OMDB)

Fabian, Mr.—New York City gangster and another competitor of Dazy Perrit. (BID)

Faison, Cass—Black fund-raiser for the Rights of Citizens Committee. (ARTD)

Falk, Mr.—Advertising executive who's smart enough to know when he's lost an argument. (BM)

Falk, Theodore—A director of Continental Air Network and Peter Odell's best friend. (PPTG)

Farnham, William T. "Bill"—Owner-operator of a dude ranch in Lame Horse, Montana. (DOD)

Farquhar, James—Banker. Mr. and Mrs. Amory Browning were guests on his yacht the weekend of a murder. (PPTG)

Farrell, Augustus—Architect, member of the League of Atonement and part-time errand boy for Wolfe. (LFM)

Farrell, Mr.—Assistant District Attorney in New York City. (CP)

Farrow, Morton—Nephew of Mrs. Matthew Blount and messenger at Paul Jerin's fatal multiple chess game. An egotistical mooch. (G)

Feder, Sol—Owner of the Feder Paper Company at 535 West Seventeenth Street. He helped one of Wolfe's clients dodge a tail once. (GWW)

Felix—see Felix Courbet

Fenner, Tom—Janitor in Louis Rony's apartment building. (SC)

Fenster, Julia—Acquitted after being tried for espionage. (TDB)

Ferguson, Emmet—Abrasive lawyer on the Board of Directors of Naylor-Kerr, Inc. He's on Archie's list of the people who have called him a liar. (TMW)

Ferris, Gwynne—Stenographer at Naylor-Kerr, Inc. A perfect bitch, according to a co-worker, but Archie finds out she isn't (perfect or a bitch). (TMW)

Ferris, James Arthur—Lobbyist for a syndicate of five large oil companies. He and Archie played pool to keep from burning to death. (INTM)

Ferris, Noel—Unemployed actor and roomer in Hattie Annis' house. (CM)(AOAB)

Ferrone, Nick—Rookie second baseman for the New York Giants during the 1952 World Series. He was replaced because someone beat him to death with a baseball bat just before the start of the seventh game of the series. (TWKY)

Fickler, Joel—Owner of the Goldenrod Barber Shop, located in the basement of an office building on Lexington Avenue in the upper 30s, where Carl and Tina Vardas worked. (CK)

Fife, General Mortimer—One of Archie's commanders in Washington, D.C., during World War II. A professional soldier. (HWM)(NQDE)(BT)

Finch, James P.—Member of the Charity Funds Investigating Committee and one of the aliases used by William A. Donahue to obtain wiretapping services from private detectives in New York City in 1955. (TMD)

Finch, Walter—Fictional literary agent in California portrayed by a private detective. (MBTB)

Finkle, Sergeant—Fictional NYPD officer created by Archie in a phone call to Wolfe to bluff Donald Barrett successfully. (OMDB)

Fisler, William—Night doorman at Sarah Jaffee's apartment building. He's a dope and a poor liar. (PB)

Fiore, Anna—About 20, skin like stale dough, looked like she'd been scared in the cradle and never got over it, slow-witted. Lived in the same rooming house as Carlo Maffei. Witness with crucial information. (FDL)

Flanagan, William—NYPD Detective Archie was going to report for brutality for putting his hand on Orrie's shoulder. (DD)

Fleet, Celia—April Hawthorne's secretary. (WTAW)

Fleming, Barry—Husband of Stella Fleming, brother-in-law of Isabel Kerr and high school math teacher. (DD)

Fleming, Pearl—One of the operators at Bagby Answers Inc. (NW)

Fleming, Stella—Mrs. Barry Fleming and sister of Isabel Kerr. (DD)

Fletcher—Wolfe's barber on Twenty-eighth Street for many years. He retired in 1949. (CK)

Fleury, Armand—Chef de cuisine of Fluery's in Paris and Dean of Les Quinze Maitres in 1932. (TMC)

Flick, Mack—Pseudonym on Leonard Dykes' list. (MBTB)

Flick, Mark—Pseudonym on Leonard Dykes' list. (MBTB)

Flint, Ernie—House detective at the Hotel Alexander. (OMDB)

Foltz, Marie—Lucy Valdon's maid. (MH)

Foltz, Slim—Detective on New York City's Homicide Squad. In 1935 he was assigned to the D.A.'s Office. (RB)(RDBX)

Fomos, Andreas—Husband of Margaret Fomos. He's a waiter in a restaurant and resembles Hercules. Nevertheless, Archie puts him on the floor of Wolfe's office twice in 1952. (PB)

Fomos, Margaret—nee' Caselli, wife of Andreas Fomos, maid to Priscilla Eads and future director of Softdown, Inc. (PB)

Foote, Roger—Trella Jarrell's gambler brother. (IDES)

Foster, Captain—Personnel officer for the New York office of U.S. Army Military Intelligence. (BT)

Foster, Doctor—Physician who lives in the same building as Dr. Loring Burton and came to his aid. (LFM)

Foster, Harry—Gazette reporter Archie gave a scoop to in the first case. (FDL)(RB)

Foster, Sergeant—One of Inspector Cramer's minions in 1940. (BE)

Fougere, Paul—Electronics technician and vice-president of Audiovideo Inc. Resident of James Neville Vance's building and intimate of Mrs. Martin Kirk. (BWT)

Fougere, Rita—Mrs. Paul Fougere, disenchanted with her husband and enamored of another man. (BWT)

Fox, Clara—Cable clerk for the Seaboard Products Corporation. A soft-hearted adventuress. (RB)(CFO)

Fox, Gilbert—Father of Clara Fox and former member of "The Rubber Band". (RB)

Fox, Lola—Wife of Gilbert Fox and mother of Clara Fox. (RB)

Fox, Mel—One of the contestants in the World Series Rodeo in 1960 and a roping contest held at Lily Rowan's penthouse. Also a ranch hand on her Bar JR Ranch in Montana. (RM)(DOD)

Fraser, Madeline—Widow of Lawrence Fraser, sister-in-law of Deborah Koppel and hostess of a radio show on WPIT. Cyril Orchard was poisoned during one of her broadcasts. (ABAV)

Frazee, Gertrude—Finalist in the Pour Amour perfume contest. A large, poisonous shrew. She is the same height as Archie, five feet, eleven inches. (BM)

Frazer, Tom—One of Albert Hyatt's staff during his inquiry into wiretapping in 1956. (TMD)

Freda—One of Lily Rowan's servants. (RM)

Freda—One of the Jarrell's maids. (IDES)

Free, Cynthia—Stage actress and friend of Rachel Abrams. (MBTB)

Freebling—New York Gazette reporter. (AFA)

Frenkel, Benjamin—Assistant section head at Naylor-Kerr, Inc., who hated Waldo Moore's guts. (TMW)

Frey, Annabel—Sarah Rackham's daughter-in-law. (ITBF)

Frey, Judith—Reuben Imhof's secretary who found evidence of a plagiarized manuscript in his office. (PIY)

Freyer, Albert—Attorney for Peter Hays. (MAWBD)

Friend, Al—The producer of Mortimer Oshin's new hit play. (PIY)

Frimm, Henry—Executive Secretary of the Bynoe Rehabilitation Fund. (EP)

Frisbie, Mathias R.—New York City Assistant District Attorney. Archie slapped him once for calling Wolfe crooked. (RB)(RDBX)

Fromm, Bernard—Attorney for David Althaus. (TDB)

Fromm, Damon—Deceased chemical industry multi-millionaire who left $5-20 million to his widow, Laura. (GS)

Fromm, Laura—nee' Atherton, Widow of Damon Fromm, wealthy New York socialite and philanthropist. Benefactor of the Association for the Aid of Displaced Persons. (GS)

Fromm, Miss—Louise Robilotti's secretary. (CFO)

Frost, Andrew—Senior partner in McDowell, Frost, Hovey and Ulrich. Attorney for Althea and Jimmy Vail. (FD)

Frost, Calida Buchan—Widow of Edwin Frost and mother of Helen Frost. (RDBX)

Frost, Dudley—Uncle of Helen Frost, brother of Edwin Frost, father of Llewellyn Frost, he was one of very few people who talked Wolfe into a frazzle in his own office. Didn't say a hell of a lot, just talked. (RDBX)

Frost, Edwin—Deceased (1916) father of Helen Frost and husband of Calida Frost. (RDBX)

Frost, Helen—Daughter of Edwin and Calida Frost, employee of Boyden McNair who she calls "Uncle Boyd." (RDBX)

Frost, Llewellyn—Son of Daniel Frost and nephew of Calida Frost. His description of Helen Frost as his "ortho-cousin" told Wolfe something about him. (RDBX)

Furey, Leon—Resident of Miss Leeds' building. Makes a living providing her with dead hawks for a bounty. (NQDE)

Fyfe, Bertram—Older brother of David and Paul Fyfe, Louise Tuttle, brother-in-law of Vincent Tuttle and partner with Johnny Arrow in the Fyfe-Arrow Mining Corporation of Montreal. He had been tried and acquitted of his father's murder 20 years before his own murder. (WFD)

Fyfe, David R.—Head of the English Department at Audubon High School in the Bronx. Younger brother of Bertram Fyfe and older brother of Paul Fyfe and Louise Tuttle. (WFD)

Fyfe, Mr.—Father of Bertram, David and Paul Fyfe and Louise Fyfe Tuttle. Died of pneumonia 20 years before Bertram's death from the same cause. (WFD)

Gahagan—One of Lon Cohen's best men at the Gazette. (PPTG)

Gaines, Theodore—Banker and member of the League of Atonement. (LFM)

Gale, Daniel—Pharmacist and uncle of Lile Moyse. (TWKY)

Gallagher, Horny—Guy in the New York rackets who has been seen publicly with Joel Fickler. (CK)

Gallant, Alec—Iconoclastic fashion designer. (MNJ)(FUFM)

Gallant, Flora—Sister of Alec Gallant. (MNJ)(FUFM)

Gamm, Dr. Theodore—Internist and family physician for Barry and Stella Fleming and Isabel Kerr. (DD)

Gardner, Allan W.—Member of the League of Atonement. (LFM)

Garrou, Marie—The Ducos' maid. (AFA)

Garth, Tiny—New York Giants second baseman during the 1952 World Series. He was the last minute replacement for *wunderkind* rookie Nick Ferrone. (TWKY)

Garvin, Ruth—Woman who runs Collander House, a group home in New York for women temporarily down on their luck. A very trustworthy woman. (PIY)

Gebert, Perren—Mysterious Frenchman and former terrorist. What he was mysterious about is what got him killed. (RDBX)

Geer, Jane—Former fiancee' of Captain Peter Root. She called Wolfe a mongrel bloodhound during that case but eventually changed her mind. (HWM)

Geiss, Alan—A free-lance photographer and one of several including Archie taking photos outside of an Easter service at St. Thomas's Church. (EP)

Gerley, Lord—Constanza Berin was sailing his boat around the cape without a chaperon when he fell overboard. (TMC)

Gerster, Julius—Jeweler who sold Laura Fromm the golden spider earrings. (GS)

Getz, Adrian—Friend and camp follower of Harry Koven, who calls him "The Squirt." Murder victim. (SAM)

Gibson—Private detective with the Southwest Agency in Los Angeles. A self-made ape, in Archie's estimation, he declines Gibson's services. (MBTB)

Gill, Lewis—Pseudonym on Leonard Dykes' list. (MBTB)

Gill, Louis—Pseudonym on Leonard Dykes' list. (MBTB)

Gill, Ted—A dancing student at the Miltan studio. (OMDB)

Gilliam, Arthur—Deceased production genius at Softdown, Inc. and father of Sarah Jaffee, who inherited his ten per cent of the company. (PB)

Gluck, Lieutenant—NYPD officer who authorizes the arrest of Archie for breaking and entering in 1952. (PB)

Glueckner, Winold—One of the best orchid-growers in America, he joined others in an entreaty to Wolfe to solve the murder of Molly Lauck. (RDBX)

Goheen, Fifi—Rambunctious former Park Avenue Deb of the Year. She endeared herself to Wolfe by calling him fat (twice), knocking a bowl of *Miltonias* off of his desk and pouring Scotch whiskey in his beer. He retreated to the kitchen and consoled himself with an unsullied beer, a slice of sturgeon and half of a Bursatto melon. (HTR)

Goidell, Helen—Mrs. Walt Goidell and friend of Lila Moyse. (TWKY)

Goidell, Walt—New York Giants player during the 1952 World Series. (TWKY)

Goldstein, Abe—One of the aliases Archie facetiously suggested to Wolfe when going undercover in 1957, to match the AG initials. (IDES)

Goldwyn, Daniel—Research chemist and Bess Huddleston's brother. (CITMD)

Goller, Albert—Taxi driver who helps Wolfe's clients shake tails. (TMCL)(TDB)

Goodman, Major—Officer in the New York office of U.S. Army Military Intelligence in 1943. His office is one floor above that of Major Archie Goodwin. (BT)

Goodyear—Code name to be used by Archie when trying to contact or leave messages for Dazy Perrit. (BID)

Goren, Anne—Nurse who had attended Bertram Fyfe on his deathbed. (WFD)

Gottlieb, Sergeant—Another of Inspector Cramer's NYPD minions in 1947. (TMW)

Gottschalk, Herman—Former manager of Dwyer's Lunchroom. (FH)

Gould, Harry—Gardener for Rucker and Dill's seed and nursery company. One of the models used in their woodland glade exhibit in the 1941 Flower Show at the Grand Central Palace. Former gardener and chauffeur for Lewis Hewitt before he was fired. Murder victim. In this one instance, I <u>will</u> tell you who killed him. Archie Goodwin did. (BO)

Graboff, Ed—Archie's barber for over six years as of 1951 at the Goldenrod Barber Shop. Plays the horses and had to sell his car to pay a $900 gambling debt. (CK)

Graham, Basil—He and Archie shared a cell in Crowfield County in 1938. Together they formed the Crowfield County Prisoners Union. (SBC)

Grant, Helen—Doctor Vollmer's secretary. (MAWBD)

Grant, Mr.—One of the domestic staff at Kanawha Spa. (TMC)

Grantham, Albert—Louise Robilotti's deceased first husband. Wealthy, vain and randy, three qualities that outlived him. (CFO)

Grantham, Cecil—Albert and Louise Grantham's son. (CFO)

Grantham, Celia—Albert and Louise Grantham's daughter. (CFO)

Green, Alan—The alias Archie finally settled on when going undercover in 1957. (IDES)

Green, Arnold—Executive of Best and Green publishers who provided Wolfe with a copy of an old book for research. (PIY)

Green, Dr.—An eminent neurologist hired by New York City and equipped with a court order to examine Wolfe for a nervous breakdown. (SS)

Greenberg, Hulda—Friend of Rachel Abrams. (MBTB)

Gretty—Woman who delivers an envelope to Don O'Neill at Wolfe's house. (SS)

Greve, Alma—Teenaged daughter of Harvey and Carol Greve, and an unwed mother. (DOD)

Greve, Carol—Mrs. Harvey Greve, mother of Alma. (DOD)

Greve, Harvey—One of the contestants in the World Series Rodeo in 1960 and a roping contest at Lily Rowan's penthouse. Eight years later, he's in jail for murder in Montana. (RM)(DOD)

Grier, Detective—One of Cramer's minions. (WTAW)

Griffin, H.L.—Food and wine importer who supplied exotic items for Rusterman's Restaurant and Wolfe's own table. (FJP)

Griffin, Mr.—A crook who tried to frame Doctor Vollmer on a malpractice suit in 1941. (SS)

Griffin, Sergeant—NYPD officer in the Tenth Precinct in 1953. (GS)

Grimes, Elise—An unprofitable source of gossip at Naylor-Kerr, Inc. (TMW)

Groll, Joe—Factory foreman for Blaney and Poor, novelties manufacturers. (IOE)

Groom, Leon—Captain and Chief of Detectives for the Albany Police. He arrested Wolfe and Archie as material witnesses in 1956. (TMD)

Grove, Rupert—Alberto Mion's manager although there was no love lost between them. (GWW)

Gruber, Eleanor—Louis Kustin's secretary. Formerly she was Con O'Malley's secretary. (MBTB)

Grummon, Miss—Buyer for a jewelry wholesaler who spotted the golden spider earrings. (GS)

Guilfoyle, Adonis—Another of the aliases Archie facetiously suggested to Wolfe to match his initials when going undercover in 1957. (IDES)

Gumpert, Mrs.—Fashion reporter for the New York Herald Tribune. (MA)

Gunther, Alex—Alias adopted by Archie for the trip home from Montenegro. (BKM)

Gunther, Carl—Alias adopted by Wolfe for the trip home from Montenegro. (BKM)

Gunther, Phoebe—Cheney Boone's confidential secretary. Brains, looks and a sense of humor, Archie is quite taken with her. (SS)

Gurran, Mr.—Assistant District Attorney for Westchester County in New York. He's a much better investigator than his boss, Cleveland Archer, but he didn't get to prove it. (SC)

Guthrie, Lena—Lucy Valdon's best friend. (MH)

Gyger, Dr.—Medical Examiner of Rockland County, New York. (WTAW)

Hackett—The Robilotti's butler. (CFO)

Hackett, H.H.—Retired architect hired for $100 a day (because of his physical resemblance) to impersonate Wolfe when his life was threatened in 1944. An unsurpassed nincompoop with the manners of a wart hog, in Wolfe's opinion. But then, he later became more than he seemed to be initially. (HWM)

Haft, Julian—Head of Parthenon Press, Richard Valdon's publisher. (MH)

Hagh, Eric—Ex-husband of Patricia Eads and, arguably, heir to half of her impending fortune. (PB)

Hahn, Willard K.—Banker present at the meeting at Rusterman's Restaurant after which Harvey Bassett was murdered. (AFA)

Haight, Gilbert—Son of Morley Haight and gas station attendant. He wanted and still wants to marry Alma Greve. (DOD)

Haight, Morley—Sheriff of Monroe County, Montana. (DOD)

Halloran, Mr.—Bronx Assistant District Attorney. (PIY)

Halloran, Detective—NYPD Homicide Detective following Andreas Fomos in 1952. (PB)

Halloran, Tom—Employee at the garage on Tenth Avenue where Wolfe keeps his car. He drives, delivers and even helps Archie elude FBI agents tailing him. (TDB)(AFA)

Hammond, Dana—A vice-president of the Metropolitan Trust Company, he is Sarah Rackham's banker. (ITBF)

Handsome—Archie's nickname for an anonymous recruiting-poster-type FBI agent who probably finished his career patrolling federal reservations out of Anchorage, Alaska. His partner was nicknamed Skinny. (TDB)

Hank—Chauffeur at Wolfe's garage on Tenth Avenue. (CFO)

Hannah, Paul—Off-Broadway actor and resident of Hattie Annis' house. (CM)(AOAB)

Hansen, Rudolph—Lawyer. (BM)

Harding, Hattie—Assistant Director of Public Relations for the National Industrial Association. (SS)

Harriet—Cook for the Huck family. (ITM)

Harriton, Dolly—Lawyer at Corrigan, Phelps, Kustin and Briggs. (MBTB)

Harris, Nathan—Private detective with the Southwest Agency in Los Angeles who impersonates Walter Finch for Archie. (MBTB)

Harrison, William R.—Federal judge from Indiana and member of the League of Atonement before he went off a cliff in June of 1934. (LFM)

Harry—One of Arnold Zeck's praetorian guard. (ITBF)

Hart, Alice—One of the operators for Bagby Answers Inc. (NW)

Hartig, Carl—Deceased father of Madeline Odell. (PPTG)

Harvey, Jerry—High ranking member of the American Communist Party in 1949. (SC)

Harvey, Phillip—Author of *Why The Gods Laugh* and Chairman of the Joint Committee on Plagiarism of the National Association of Authors and Dramatists and the Book Publishers of America. (PIY)

Haskins, Bud—Night man in a garage where Archie, Saul, Fred and Orrie have a gunfight and torture suspects. (GS)

Haskins, Detective—One of Inspector Cramer's minions in 1936. (RDBX)

Haskins, Mr.—A man who raises chickens specially fed on blueberries for Wolfe's table. On one of Wolfe's few personal undercover forays, they are almost worth blowing his cover for. (ITBF)

Hatch, Emil—"Pet wizard" for Kurt Bottweill. (CP)

Hatten, Doris—Friend of Cynthia Brown who was strangled to death in October of 1949. Ms. Brown's intent to solve her murder is what led to her own. (DFM)

Hausman, Ernst—Wealthy retired broker, a founder of the Gambit Chess Club and messenger at Paul Jerin's fatal multiple chess game. (G)

Hawthorne, April—Sister of June Dunn and May Hawthorne. She is an actress who tried unsuccessfully to take Wolfe's office by storm. (WTAW)

Hawthorne, Daisy—Noel's widow. Accidentally shot in the face with an arrow by her husband in 1933, she is never seen without a veil obscuring her disfigured face. She also has the talent of being in two places at once. (WTAW)

Hawthorne, May—Sister of Noel, June and May. Very brainy President of Varney College. (WTAW)

Hawthorne, Noel—Eldest of the Hawthorne clan and second in command of the Daniel Cullen Wall Street firm. He went hunting a hawk with a shotgun but the hawk got him first. (WTAW)

Hays, Peter—Copywriter who couldn't answer Wolfe's ad in the Gazette because he was in jail for murdering Michael Molloy. (MAWBD)(G)

Hazen, Barry—Wealthy public relations man and murder victim. His wealth stemmed from his nasty habit of blackmailing people which got him shot in the back. (DOAD)

Hazen, Lucy—Unhappy wife of Barry Hazen who opens her case with Wolfe by deciding not to shoot her husband, thus reinforcing Wolfe's opinion that all women at dotty, devious or both. (DOAD)

Heath, Henry Jameson—Wealthy, pudgy and crowding 50. One of the chief collectors and providers of bail money for indicted communists in the early 1950s. (HTR)

Heath, Sergeant—One of Cramer's best men in 1935, he and a Detective named Steve tried to bum's rush their way into the brownstone and were both forcibly ejected by Archie. (RB)

Heath, Charlie—NYPD Detective who escorts Neya Tormic away from the brownstone on Wolfe's orders. (OMDB)

Hebe—Doberman pinscher, Nobby's mother. (ITBF)

Heery, Ellen—Wife of Talbott Heery. (BM)

Heery, Talbott—Head of Heery Products. (BM)

Heim, Leopold—Alias for Saul Panzer when he impersonated a displaced person. (GS)

Hefferan, Officer—NYPD Mounted Patrol officer whose beat is Central Park. (BFO)

Heller, Leo—Mathematician, probability prognosticator and murder victim. Wolfe thought him a charlatan but changed his mind after he was murdered. (ZC)

Helmar, Perry—Attorney for Softdown Inc. as well as Priscilla Eads' legal guardian and trustee of her estate until her twenty-fifth birthday. (PB)

Henchy, Thomas—Executive Director of the Rights of Citizens Committee. (ARTD)

Henny—Cook for Mr. and Mrs. Loring Burton. (LFM)

Henrietta—Halfbreed bootlegger in Lame Horse, Montana. (DOD)

Henry—Soda jerk at Daniel Gale's pharmacy. (TWKY)

Herold, James R.—Hardware wholesaler from Omaha, Nebraska. Father of Paul Herold. (MAWBD)

Herold, Paul—Estranged son of James Herold. A man who seems to be making a habit of being wrongly accused. (MAWBD)(G)

Herrick, Joseph—Photographer for the Gazette, one of several people including Archie taking pictures of an Easter service outside St. Thomas's Church. (EP)

Hettinger, Perry—Man who answered Wolfe's ad in the Gazette. (MAWBD)

Hewitt, Lewis—Millionaire and orchid grower with a Long Island estate and a hundred-foot-long orchid house. Creator of the Black Orchids in 1941. His influence with Wolfe is such that Archie considers using him to appeal to Wolfe to stop training to join the army at the beginning of World War II. Wolfe buys ten dozen plants from him in 1945. Member of the Ten for Aristology (the science of dining) who arranged for Fritz to cook their annual dinner in 1958. He dines with Wolfe at least twice yearly. (SS)(NQDE)(DTD)(EP)(PA)(BFO)(BO) (SC)(IDES)(CFO)(PIY)(TMCL)(G)(TDB)(FH)

Heydecker, Miles—47-year-old attorney and partner (22%) in the law firm of Otis, Edey, Heydecker and Jett. (EMMM)

Heydt, Carl—Couturier who makes very expensive clothing for women. Lily Rowan is among his customers. He gave Sue McLeod her first modeling job. His name was written in Kenneth Faber's notebook. (MC)

Hibbard, Mr.—Attorney on the legal staff of Clock magazine. (BM)

Hibbard, Andrew—Psychology Instructor at Columbia University and member of the League of Atonement. (LFM)

Hibbard, Evelyn—Niece of Andrew Hibbard and friend of Sarah Barstow. (LFM)

Higgam, Mr.—A banker at the Metropolitan Trust Company who will obtain financial reports on suspects for Wolfe. (LFM)

Hildebrand, Byram—Artist who helps draw the cartoon strip Dazzle Dan. (SAM)

Hinckley, Marian—Staffer at Tick-Tock Magazine and fiancée of Morris Althaus. (TDB)

Hirsh, Ludlow—Chemist who works on the tenth floor of a building on 43rd Street and occasionally performs laboratory tests on objects for Archie, like identifying human blood on a tie. (BWT)

Hirsh, Nathan—Forensic scientist at Hirsh Laboratories on 43rd Street who does forensic analyses for Wolfe. (MH)

Hitchcock, Ethelbert—Private investigator Wolfe uses in London, England. Archie considers it the all-time low for a snoop's name. (RB)(RDBX)(OMDB)

Hitchcock, Geoffrey—Wolfe's contact in London in 1954. Possibly related to Ethelbert? (BKM)

Hoag, G.M.—Horticulturist Wolfe phones for help (along with Lewis Hewitt) when his plant rooms are destroyed by Mr. X in 1949. (SC)

Hobart, Clark—District Attorney of Westchester County, New York, in 1961. (FD)

Hoff, Sumner—Civil engineer at Naylor-Kerr, Inc. He and Archie don't get along, to put it mildly. (TMW)

Holcomb, Arthur—A non-existent man who was asked for at Doc Vollmer's house by an unknown man. This provided Wolfe with a significant clue. (MAWBD)

Holcomb, Mr.—One of the contestants in the World Series Rodeo in 1960. (RM)

Holland, Governor—Governor of New York in 1955. (IMTM)

Hollis, Art—CBS Television newsman foolish enough to send a crew to Wolfe's house in 1974 for an interview without prior permission. They were not admitted. (AFA)

Holt, Mira—Fashion model also known as Mrs. Waldo Kearns. Still uses her own name because she doesn't want to be married to Mr. Kearns but he refuses to allow her a divorce. (MTFM)

Holt, Phillip—Director of Organization for the United Restaurant Workers of America union. For several years, he had been unsuccessfully pursuing Fritz to join his union. Pursuing women with the same zeal, it led to his demise as a murder victim. (FJP)

Hombert, Mr.—New York City Police Commissioner in 1935. Wolfe considers him a disagreeable noise and thinks he should go back to diapers. (RB)(RDBX)(WTAW)(SS)

Hopp, Lieutenant—New York State Police officer in upstate New York. (IMTM)

Horan, Claire—Mrs. Dennis Horan, former movie actress. (GS)

Horan, Dennis—Attorney for the Association for the Aid of Displaced Persons. (GS)

Horan, Phillip—Salesman for Mercer's Bobbins, Inc. (KNPL)

Horgan, Phillip—Another man who answered Wolfe's ad in the Gazette. (MAWBD)

Horne, Ann—Wife of Norman Horne and daughter of Margaret Savage. (WAMM)

Horne, Norman—Husband of Ann (Savage) Horne and son-in-law of Margaret Savage. (WAMM)

Horowitz—One of Cramer's NYPD minions. (SS)

Horrocks, Francis—Nephew and attendant of the Marquis of Clivers. (RB)

Horrocks, Mrs. Jervis—She received a note telling her that Dr. Alan Brady had prescribed the wrong medicine for her daughter before she died from tetanus. (CITMD)

Horrocks, Helen—Daughter of Mrs. Jervis Horrocks. Scratching her arm on a nail in a riding stable led to her agonizing death from tetanus. Dr. Alan Brady treated her and Maryella Timms was a close friend. (CITMD)

Hoskins, Mr.—Bess Huddleston's butler. (CITMD)

Hotchkiss, Mortimer M.—Vice-President of the Thirty-fourth Street branch of the Continental Bank and Trust Company who is always eager to please a five-or-six figure depositor like Wolfe. (FH)

Hough, Austin—Assistant Professor of English Literature at NYU. Very literate but a lousy actor. (TMCL)

Hough, Dinah—Mrs. Austin Hough, another interested visitor to the Yeager lovenest. (TMCL)

Howell, Arthur—Employee of Beck Products Corporation in Basston, New Jersey. Murder victim and amateur smoker. (IOE)

Howell, Mr.—Customer in the Goldenrod Barber Shop. (CK)

Howie, Mr.—Man who sends Wolfe special sausage. (FD)

Huck, Beryl—Sister of Herman Lewent, wife of Theodore Huck and executor of the family fortune until her death from ptomaine poisoning, later proven to be a murder. (ITM)

Huck, Theodore—Crippled brother-in-law of Herman Lewent, husband of Beryl Huck and executor of the family fortune following her death. (ITM)

Huddleston, Bess—The most successful party-arranger that New York had ever had. In 1939 she tried to hire Wolfe to play detective in a murder game. He refused, naturally, but two years later, he solved her real murder after she died from tetanus. Wolfe said he had never heard of a more objectionable way of committing murder. He sent eight black orchids to her funeral. (CITMD)

Huddleston, Lawrence—Nephew of Bess Huddleston and another of her assistant party arrangers. (CITMD)

Hutchins, Dr.—Coroner of Monroe County, Montana. (DOD)

Hutchins, Judge—Crowfield Count Judge who issued a material witness warrant for Archie in 1938. (SBC)

Hutchinson, Pete—Friend of Thomas Pratt. Wolfe turned him down on a domestic job in 1936. (SBC)

Hyatt, Albert—Attorney and special deputy to the New York Secretary of State for an inquiry into wiretapping in 1956. (TMD)

Iacono, Helen—One of the so-called Hebes, a group of a dozen young women hired to serve at the annual dinner for the Ten for Aristology in 1958. (PA)

Ide, Harland—Owner of a private detective agency in New York City. He has a reputation for high standards. (TMD)

Igoe, Benjamin—Electronics engineer present at the meeting at Rusterman's Restaurant after which Harvey Bassett was murdered. (AFA)

Imbrie, Neil—Butler, chauffeur and handyman for Joseph G. Pitcairn. (DTD)

Imbrie, Vera—The Pitcairn household cook and wife of Neil Imbrie. (DTD)

Imhof, Reuben—President of the Victory Press publishing house and member of the Joint Committee on Plagiarism of the National Association of Authors and Dramatists and the Book Publishers of America. (PIY)

Ingalls, F.L.—Travel bureau owner and member of the League of Atonement. (LFM)

Ingalls, Peter—Summer worker at the Bar JR Ranch in Lame Horse, Montana. Also a postgraduate student in paleontology at the University of California, Berkeley. (DOD)

Ingalls, Ralph—Friend of Guy Unger, Bella Velardi and Helen Weltz. (NW)

Innes, Iris—Photographer for the magazine Senorita and former fiancée of Henry Frimm. One of a group of people including Archie taking photos of an Easter service outside of St. Thomas's Church. (EP)

Irby, Albert M.—New York City lawyer representing Eric Hagh. (PB)

Irving, Gilbert—Friend of Mira Holt although he is actually enamored with her. He has an excellent right uppercut. (MTFM)

Irving, L.M.—Social worker and member of the League of Atonement. (LFM)

Irving, Mrs. Gilbert—Wife of Gilbert Irving. (MTFM)

Irwin, Blanche—Matriarch of Grantham House home for unwed mothers. (CFO)

Irwin, Thomas L.—Printing company executive and another of Michael Molloy's theater companions. (MAWBD)

Irwin, Fanny—Mrs. Thomas Irwin and Another of Michael Molloy's theater companions. (MAWBD)

Jackson, Amy—See Julie Jaquette. (DD)

Jacobs, Simon—Author who sued Richard Echols for plagiarism. (PIY)(DD)

Jacobs, Mrs. Simon—Not an especially bright woman but at least she has a memory for faces. (PIY)

Jaffee, Sarah—Daughter of Arthur Gilliam, widow of Dick Jaffee, oldest and best friend of Priscilla Eads. (PB)

Jaffee, Richard—Deceased husband of Sarah Jaffee, killed in the Korean War. (PB)

James, Clara—Gifford James's daughter. (GWW)

James, Gifford—Baritone for the Metropolitan Opera. He had hurt Alberto Mion's larynx with a blow to the throat shortly before Mion's death. (GWW)

Jameson, Doctor—Physician summoned to the 1958 dinner of the Ten for Aristology to treat Vincent Pyle for arsenic poisoning. (PA)

Jaquette, Julie—Stage name of a night club singer named Amy Jackson. Best friend of Isabel Kerr. She gives Wolfe a solo performance in the office and is rewarded with a stay in the South Room. She is only the second woman Archie has heard call Wolfe "Nero" and the first time was a gag. (DD)

Jaret, Nora—One of the so-called Hebes, a dozen young women hired to serve at the annual dinner of the Ten for Aristology in 1958. (PA)

Jarrell, Lois—Otis Jarrell's daughter by his first marriage. (IDES)

Jarrell, Otis—Capitalist or so he's listed in *Who's Who*. (IDES)

Jarrell, Susan—Wyman Jarrell's wife. Otis thinks she's a snake. (IDES)

Jarrell, Trella—Otis Jarrell's "marital affliction."(IDES)

Jarrell, Wyman—Otis Jarrell's son by his first marriage, Lois's brother and Susan's husband. (IDES)

Jarrett, Adele—nee' Baldwin, Mrs. Eugene M. Jarrett. (FH)

Jarrett, Cyrus M.—Omnipotent, omni-wealthy, reclusive and irascible retired Chairman of the Board of Seaboard Bank and Trust Company. Although more respectable, he is probably second only to Arnold Zeck in the powerful men Wolfe has bent to his will. (FH)

Jarrett, Mrs. Cyrus M.—Died of cancer in November of 1943. (FH)

Jarrett, Eugene M.—Son of Cyrus and a vice-president of Seaboard Bank and Trust. (FH)

Jarvis, Ashley—Professional actor who bears a remarkable resemblance to Nero Wolfe. (TDB)

Jay, Laura—One of the cowgirls attending the World Series Rodeo in 1960. During one very busy day, she attacked Inspector Cramer, was going to shoot Archie in the back, and became a guest in Wolfe's south bedroom. She is one of the poorest and most prolific liars they ever encountered. (RM)

Jay, Peter—Someone important in a big advertising agency. His name was written in Kenneth Faber's notebook. (MC)

Jay, Phyllis—Friend of Robina Keane. (NW)

Jensen, Ben—A publisher, politician, poop and murder victim. Captain Peter Root offered to sell him Army information and went to prison for it. (HWM)

Jensen, Emil—U.S. Army Major in 1944 and son of Ben Jensen. (HWM)

Jerin, Paul—Chess prodigy who took arsenic with his hot chocolate. (G)

Jerome, Edith—Mrs. Perry Porter Jerome, financier for Kurt Bottweill and mother of Leo Jerome. Purley Stebbins abused her. (CP)

Jerome, Leo—Playboy son of Edith Jerome. (CP)

Jett, Gregory—36-year-old attorney and partner (11%) in the law firm of Otis, Edey, Heydecker and Jett. Former paramour of Mrs. Rita Sorrell. (EMMM)

Jessel, Herman—New York State Attorney General. (IMTM)

Jessup, Thomas R.—County Attorney for Monroe County, Montana. (DOD)

Jin—Clerk for the Secret Police in Montenegro in 1954. (BKM)

Joe—One of the majordomos at Rusterman's Restaurant and one of Marko Vukcic's heirs. (BKM)

Joffe, Detective—NYPD Detective. (CK)

Johnson, Elga—Maid who found Louis Dahlmann's body. (BM)

Johnson, Mr.—Bandleader at Grantham House's annual dinner. A man with common sense and a mind of his own. (CFO)

Jones, Mr.—A mysterious "specialist" Wolfe has used on two occasions by 1949. His specialty is unknown. (SC)

Jones, Jewel—Night-club singer who could have helped solve a murder faster if she had not concealed her husband's identity. (DLAD)

Jordan, Maud—Switchboard/receptionist volunteer for the Rights of Citizens Committee. (ARTD)

Jordan, Mrs. Arthur P.—Carol Mardus was her guest in Sarasota, Florida, in 1961. (MH)

Jordan, Mr.—Horticulturist who draws Wolfe's ire by suggesting he hybridizes *Brassavolas* in tri-generic crosses. (GS)

Jordan, Pete—Artist who helps draw the cartoon strip Dazzle Dan. (SAM)

Judd, Albert O.—Lawyer present at the meeting at Rusterman's Restaurant after which Harvey Bassett was murdered. (AFA)

Judd, Guthrie—Banking tycoon. (BE)

Kampf, Phillip—Murder victim and owner of a black Labrador retriever that helped solve his murder. (DLAD)

Kadany, Diana—Actress and house guest at the Bar JR Ranch in Lame Horse, Montana. (DOD)

Kallman, Rae—Volunteer for the Rights of Citizens Committee. (ARTD)

Kalmus, Daniel—Matthew Blount's attorney and messenger at Paul Jerin's fatal multiple chess game. (G)

Kane, Webster—Economist for the Continental Mines Corporation. (SC)(ITBF)

Karlin, Nan—One of the cowgirls attending the World Series Rodeo in 1960. (RM)

Karn, Naomi—Stenographer/secretary at Dunwoodie, Prescott & Davis. A very poor judge of men. (WTAW)

Karnow, Caroline—A widow (she thought) when her husband Stanley Karnow was reported killed in the Korean War. She then married Paul Aubry but Stanley wasn't dead…yet. (WAMM)

Karnow, Stanley—Husband of Caroline Karnow who survived the Korean War and had to come home to New York City to die. (WAMM)

Karp, Judge—Judge who set $30,000 bond (each) on Archie and Wolfe on material witness charges in 1974. The D.A. wanted it at $50,000 but offended the judge with a threat. (AFA)

Kates, Alger—Statistics man in the Research Department of the Bureau of Price Regulation. (SS)

Kauffman, Bernard—Deceased owner of the Kauffman Management Company. One of thousands of dead ends (no pun intended) in Archie's career. (FH)

Keane, Robina—Mrs. Leonard Ashe who gave up her stage career to marry him. She is one of the few women known to have accomplished the feat of throwing her arms around Wolfe with good intentions. (NW)

Kearns, Waldo—Starving artist with money and estranged husband of Mira Holt. (MTFM)

Kees, Dorothy—Daughter of Sigmund Kees and inheritor of his fortune. (BFO)

Keith, Ramsey—Chef de cuisine at the Hotel Hastings, Calcutta. (TMC)

Kelefy, Adria—Wife of Ambassador Theodore Kelefy. Wolfe found out what it took to light up her eyes when Archie couldn't and she knocked a phone out of his hand when he did. (IMTM)

Kelefy, Theodore—Ambassador to the United States from an unnamed country. (IMTM)

Kelly, Police Commissioner—Friend of Otis Jarrell. (IDES)

Kent, Beverly—Diplomatic errand boy at the United Nations and guest at Grantham House's annual dinner. (CFO)

Kent, Nora—Stenographer to Otis Jarrell. (IDES)

Kerner, Ralph—Representative of Town House Services Incorporated giving Archie an estimate for damages to Wolfe's home. (AFA)

Kerr, Isabel—Showgirl who cost Orrie ten days in jail and almost cost him a lot more. (DD)(AFA)

Kerr, Jay—Owner of a private detective agency in New York City that specialized in domestic or marital cases. (TMD)

Keyes, Sigmund—Top-drawer industrial designer and father of Dorothy Keyes. Shot to death while horseback riding in Central Park. (BFO)

Khaldah, Ferid—Chef de cuisine of the Cafe' de l'Europe, Istanbul. (TMC)

Khoury, Jules—Inventor who pays Barry Hazen at least $2000 a month. Archie introduces himself to Mr. Khoury with a kidney punch. (DOAD)

Kirby, Dale—Professional actor who bears a resemblance to Archie although half an inch shorter. (TDB)

Kieran, John—John Francis Kieran, American journalist. In 1947, Archie tells Lon Cohen that Kieran is a blank page compared to him. (TMW)

Kiernan, Alfred—Business manager for Kurt Botweill. (CP)

Kimball, E.D.—Boyhood friend of Peter Oliver Barstow and one of the golfing foursome when Barstow dropped dead. The third murder victim in FDL. The first murder victim in the series that Wolfe could probably have prevented his murder but did not. In fact, Wolfe took steps that increased his chances of being murdered and did not intervene to stop it. Wolfe alleged his actions would have interfered with a deserved destiny but Archie thought it was just so he wouldn't have to get off his fat ass go to court in White Plains. (FDL)

Kimball, Manuel—Argentinean son of E.D. Kimball and one of the golfing foursome when Peter Barstow dropped dead. (FDL)

Kinney, Art—New York Giants manager during the 1952 World Series. (TWKY)

Kirk, Jimmie—Wolfe's barber for two years in 1951. He has expensive tastes for a barber. (CK)

Kirk, Martha—20, attractive, unemployed actress now studying ballet and rooming in Hattie Annis' house. (CM)(AOAB)

Kirk, Martin—Age 33. (BWT)

Kirk, Mrs. Martin—Nee' Bonny Sommers, formerly a secretary and currently beautiful and promiscuous, both of the latter contributing factors to her murder. (BWT)

Knapp, Gerald—President of Knapp and Bowen, publishers and member of the Joint Committee on Plagiarism of the National Association of Authors and Dramatists and the Book Publishers of America. (PIY)

Knudsen,—Senior editor of Clock magazine. (BM)

Kommers, Arthur—Sales manager and member of the League of Atonement. (LFM)

Koppel, Deborah—Manager and sister-in-law of Madeline Fraser. After what happened to her brother, you'd think she'd be more careful about what she ate. (ABAV)

Koppel, Lawrence—Late husband of Madeline Fraser and brother of Deborah Koppel who died from cyanide poisoning in 1942. (ABAV)

Korby, Flora—Daughter of James Korby. (FJP)

Korby, James—President of the United Restaurant Workers of America union. (FJP)

Kosor, Stan—Montenegrin patriot who keeps watch on an old Roman fort near the Albanian border to keep an eye on the Albanian and Russian Communists. (BKM)

Koven, Harry—Creator of the cartoon strip Dazzle Dan who hires Wolfe to recover his stolen gun. (SAM)

Koven, Marcelle—Wife of Harry Koven. (SAM)

Krasicki, Andrew—Horticulturist for Joseph G. Pitcairn who was to replace Theodore Horstmann during Horstmann's absence to care for his ill mother. Formerly employed for three years by Lewis Hewitt. His talents as a prodigious hybridist caused Wolfe to leave the brownstone to recruit him and ask to shake his hand, two highly unusual compliments. The highest compliment, however, was when he was placed in charge of reconstructing Wolfe's destroyed plant rooms in 1949. (DTD)(SC)

Kreis, Emil—Chairman of the Board of Codex Press, book publishers, and member of the Ten for Aristology. (PA)

Kretzmeyer, Mr.—Butcher from whom Wolfe buys two pounds of pig chitlins in 1941. (CITMD)

Krug, Willie—Richard Valdon's literary agent. (MH)

Kuffner, Paul—Unpaid public relations expert for the Association for the Aid of Displaced Persons. (GS)

Kurtz, Mrs.—Housekeeper for Mr. and Mrs. Loring Burton. (LFM)

Kustin, Louis—Partner in the law firm or Corrigan, Phelps, Kustin and Briggs. (MBTB)

Laghi, Tony—Cook at the Gambit Chess Club. (G)

Laidlaw, Edwin—Book publisher and guest at Grantham House's annual dinner. (CFO)

Lake, Emmett—Ranch hand on the Bar JR Ranch in Lame Horse, Montana, and one of Henrietta's best customers. (DOD)

Lake, Sam—Sheriff of Crowfield County in 1936. (SBC)

Lambert, Mr.—Assistant District Attorney for New York County in 1956. (TMD)

Lamm, Nils—Doorman in the building where Leo Heller lived and worked. (ZC)

Lamont, Mrs.—Employee of Boyden McNair Inc. and witness to Molly Lauck's murder. (RDBX)

Landry—One of Lon Cohen's best men at the Gazette. (PPTG)(AFA)

Landry, H.R.—Founder of the Ambrosia chain of restaurants. (OF)

Landry, Jerome—33, partner in a real estate firm and son of H.R. Landy. (OF)

Landy, Mortimer—31, son of H.R. Landy, entrepreneur in radio and show business and had an unsuccessful turn at running his deceased father's business before he bought some wormy lamb meat. (OF)

Landy, Phoebe—24, daughter of H.R. Landy and Vassas graduate. The strongest of her father's children, she had a dinner date with Archie. (OF)

Lang, Sidney—Realtor and member of the League of Atonement. (LFM)

Lanzetta, Mr.—New York City Assistant District Attorney. Acquired a deep dislike of Wolfe during the Fairmont case in 1933. (RDBX)

Laszio, Dina—Wife of Phillip Laszio, ex-wife of Marko Vukcic and daughter of Domenico Rossi. A special kind of woman. (TMC)

Laszio, Phillip—Chef de cuisine at the Hotel Churchill in New York City. Husband of Dina Laszio. A man who made many enemies, one of who murdered him. (TMC)

Lasher, Rose—A critical witness to the murder of Harry Gould. (BO)

Lasker—Albert Davis Lasker (1880–1952). U.S. advertising executive. The late Louis Dahlmann's creative genius is compared to his. (BM)

Latham, Mrs.—The Jarrell's housekeeper. (IDES)

Lauck, Molly—Employee of Boyden McNair Inc. who died in their offices on March 23, 1936. She died because she liked to play tricks on people. (RDBX)

Lauer, Dini—Nurse of Mrs. Joseph G. Pitcairn and fiancée of Andy Krasicki. Murder victim. (DTD)

Lavery, Tim—Bess Huddleston's stableman. (CITMD)

Lawson, Lieutenant Kenneth—a Junior. Senior was a tycoon with Eastern Products Corporation which probably contributed to Junior's position with U.S. Army Military Intelligence in 1943. (BT)

Lawson, Ruby—Alias given to the police by Rose Lasher to match the initials on her handbag. Archie tracked her down anyway. (BO)

Leach, Albert—Special Agent, United States Secret Service. His telephone number is REctor 2-9100. (CM)(AOAB)

Leach, Benjamin—Llewellyn Frost's attorney. (RDBX)

Leacraft, Harvey M.—Corporation lawyer and member of the Ten for Aristology. (PA)

Leamis, James E.—Managing editor of the Racine Globe in Wisconsin. (ARTD)

Leconne, Marie—Owner of a snooty beauty parlor on Madison Avenue. Subscriber to Cyril Orchard's Track Almanac. (ABAV)

Leddegard, Ormond—Labor/management relations expert. (HTR)

Leeds, Calvin—Sarah Rackham's cousin. (ITBF)

Leeds, Cora—Lady who owned the building at 316 Barnum Street in New York City. She died, ostensibly of heart failure, on December 9, 1941. Wolfe later proved her death a murder. (NQDE)

Leeds, Miss—Daughter of Cora Leeds. (NQDE)

Leeson, David M.—Assistant Secretary of State and murder victim. (IMTM)

Leeson, Sally—Wife of David Leeson. (IMTM)

Leggett, Arthur M.—Member of the Charity Funds Investigating Committee and one of the aliases used by William A. Donahue to obtain the wiretapping services of a private detective in New York City in 1955. (TMD)

Leo—Headwaiter at Rusterman's Restaurant and one of Marko Vukcic's heirs. (BKM)

Leonard, Phillip—Member of the League of Atonement. (LFM)

Lercari—Jewelry manufacturer who made the golden spider earrings. (GS)

Lesser, William—Delia Brandt's fiancée'. (MAWBD)

Levine, Bernard—Partner in a clothing store in Newark, New Jersey. He sold a suit and hat to a murderer. (GS)

Levinson, Mr.—Customer in the Goldenrod Barber Shop. (CK)

Levstik—Secret Policeman in Montenegro in 1954. (BKM)

Levy, Detective—One of Inspector Cramer's minions. (DFM)

Lewent, Herman—Undisciplined brother of Beryl Huck. Having lived for 20 years in New York and France on the forbearance of the family fortune, he had to come home to be murdered. (ITM)

Liggett, Raymond—Manager and part-owner of the Hotel Churchill in New York City. (TMC)

Lindquist, Hilda—Daughter of Victor Lindquist. (RB)

Lindquist, Victor—Nebraska farmer and former member of "The Rubber Band". (RB)

Lindstrom, Mr.—New York Assistant District Attorney. (CM)

Lippert, Mr.—Deceased (in 1945) partner in the advertising firm of Lippert, Buff and Assa. (BM)

Lippin, Marjorie—Deceased author whose estate was sued for plagiarism by Jane Ogilvy. (PIY)

Lipscomb, Vincent—Publisher of the magazine Modern Thought who published a series of articles on displaced persons for Laura Fromm. (GS)

Liss, Portia—Filing clerk at Corrigan, Phelps, Kustin and Briggs. (MBTB)

Littauer, H. Ernest—Attorney for Benjamin Ault. (ARTD)

Livsey, Hester—Mr. Rosenbaum's secretary at Naylor-Kerr, Inc. and the late Waldo Moore's fiancée'. (TMW)

Lloyd, Dr. Nicholas—Physician who performed the operation on Alberto Mion's larynx after it was damaged by a blow from Gifford James. (GWW)

Loedenkrantz, Detective—NYPD officer who searched (very poorly) Wolfe's plant rooms with Lieutenant Rowcliff in 1935. (RB)

Loftus, Sergeant—New York City Police officer who specializes in handling dogs. (DLAD)

Lopez, Mr.—One of the contestants in the World Series Rodeo in 1960. (RM)

Losseff, Nicholas—The world's foremost expert on buttons. (MH)

Lovchen, Carla—A dancing and fencing instructor in Nikola Miltan's studio. She is also Wolfe's adopted daughter. He adopted her in Yugoslavia in 1921 when she was three years old. (OMDB)(BKM)

Lowell, Patricia—Agent, manager and promoter for Harry Koven, creator of the cartoon strip Dazzle Dan. (SAM)

Lozano, Duke of—Ex-husband of April Hawthorne. (WTAW)

Lucile—Black female janitor for the Midtown Home Service Corporation. (PPTG)

Ludlow, Percy—Fencing student murdered at the Miltan studio. He was a British agent. (OMDB)

Lugos, Helen—Amory Browning's secretary at Continental Air Network. (PPTG)

Lurick, Bill—Reporter for the New York Gazette. (BM)

Macklin, Mr.—District Attorney of New York in 1960–61. (CM)

Macy, Arline—College girlfriend of Paul Herrold. (MAWBD)

Maddox, James Albert—Attorney for Maddox and Welling, counsel for Mr. and Mrs. Damon Fromm and executor of Laura Fromm's estate. (GS)

Maffei, Carlo—Older [by two years] brother of Maria. The first known murder victim in the first published case. Attempted to blackmail the suspect. (FDL)

Maffei, Maria—Friend of Fanny [Mrs. Fred] Durkin. Younger sister of Carlo Maffei. Original client in the first case. (FDL)

Magee, Bert—Wrangler on Bill Farnham's dude ranch in Montana. (DOD)

Magnus, William—NYU student who arranges a civil rights meeting for the Rights of Citizen Committee. (ARTD)

Mahany, Zoltan—Chef at Rusterman's Restaurant. After being enlisted by Wolfe as an undercover lover, he broke the murder case of Vincent Pyle. While on a cigarette break, he also discovered the dead body of Kenneth Faber in the alley behind Rusterman's. (PA)(MC)

Malfi, Alberto—First assistant chef at the Hotel Churchill. (TMC)

Mandel, Mr.—New York Assistant District Attorney 1960–62. William Baring-Gould is of the opinion that ADA Mandelbaum shortened his name to Mandel. (DOAD)(CM)(MC)(BWT)(FD)(MH)(ARTD)

Mandelbaum, Irving—Assistant District Attorney in New York City from 1952–59. (ITM)(NW)(WAMM)(GS)(PB)(MAWBD)(IDES)(CFO)(PIY)

Manzoni, Salvatore—Waiter at Sardi's Restaurant and formerly at Tufitti's Restaurant in 1944. He has a phenomenal memory for his customer's faces. (FH)

Marcy, Sylvia—Nurse to Beryl and Theodore Huck. (ITM)

Mardus, Carol—Fiction editor for Distaff magazine and ex-wife of Willis Krug. (MH)

Maresco, Phillip—Member of the Charity Funds Investigating Committee and one of the aliases used by William A. Donahue to obtain wiretapping services from private detectives in New York City in 1955. (TMD)

Martin, Alec—Orchid-grower with 40,000 plants at Rutherford. Wolfe disdains him because he splits bulbs. If his name had been included among a group signing an entreaty to Wolfe to solve the murder of Molly Lauck, it would have been the perfect excuse for Wolfe to throw the document away and refuse the case. (RDBX)

Martin, Felix—Maitre d'hotel at Rusterman's Restaurant and one of Marko Vukcic's heirs. His name is changed to Felix Mauer in the last novel, A Family Affair. (BKM)(FJP)(IDES)(PPTG)(AFA)(TDB)

Martin, Helen—Attorney James Beebe's secretary before Vera O'Brien. Now moved to South Carolina as Mrs. Arthur Rabson. (WAMM)

Martin, Jerry—Alias used by Perren Gebert to try to avoid the law's questions. (RDBX)

Martingale, Joseph—Harvard professor and fellow gourmet of Wolfe's acquaintance, on sufficiently intimate terms that Wolfe felt compelled to notify him immediately by special delivery upon discovering that pig chitlins was the perfect ingredient for corned beef hash. (CITMD)

Marvel, Herbert—Private detective Archie nicknamed "Skinny." Started his association with Archie as an adversary and ended it as an ally. (DFM)

Maslow, Max—Fashion photographer. His name was written in Kenneth Faber's notebook. (MC)

Maturo, Susan—Registered nurse who worked at the Montrose Hospital when an explosion and fire killed 302 people there. Also one of the people waiting to see Leo Heller when he was murdered. She pleased Wolfe when she accepted his offer of beer and licked her lips when finished. She later lost whatever ground she had gained when she pounded her hands on his desk. (ZC)

Mauer, Felix—See Felix Martin. (AFA)

McCray, Bertram—Vice-President of Seaboard Bank and Trust Company. (FH)

McCue, Lawrence—Pseudonym on Leonard Dykes' list. (MBTB)

McCue, Mark—Pseudonym on Leonard Dykes'list. (MBTB)

McFarland, Oliver—Extensive mining and banking interests in Montana who has influence with that state's Attorney General. (DOD)

McGee, Julia—Thomas Yeager's secretary and even more of a scratch-cat than Meg Duncan, as Fred Durkin learned the hard way. (TMCL)

McKenna, Wallace—Illinois congressman and member of the League of Atonement. (LFM)

McKinney, Mr.—Senior partner in Daniel Kalmus's law firm. (G)

McLeod, Duncan—Putnam County farmer (60 miles north of New York City) who sells freshly picked sweet corn to Wolfe every Tuesday between July 20 and October 5 from 1957 until 1961. (MC)

McLeod, Susan—Duncan McLeod's daughter and one of the more popular models in New York. She caused Archie to be arrested once. (MC)

McMillan, Monte—One of a group of cattlemen trying to dissuade Thomas Pratt from barbecuing a champion bull for advertising purposes. (SBC)

McNab, Bill—Garden editor for the Gazette. (DFM)

McNair, Anne Crandall—Mrs. Boyden McNair, she died in childbirth on April 2, 1915. (RDBX)

McNair, Boyden—Owner of Boyden McNair Inc., he left The Red Box to Wolfe in his will. (RDBX)

McNair, Glenna—Daughter of Boyden McNair and future wife of Llewellyn Frost. She is also a friend of June Hawthorne Dunn which leads to another matter. (RDBX)(WTAW)

McNair, Isabel—Sister of Boyden McNair in Camfirth, Scotland. (RDBX)

McNeil, Mr.—Attorney from Montreal who probated the will of Bertram Fyfe. (WFD)

Meade, Sinclair—Pseudonym on Leonard Dykes' list. (MBTB)

Meadows, Bill—"Stooge and feeder" on the Madeline Fraser radio show. (ABAV)

Meegan, Richard—A commercial photographer from Pittsburgh and one of the residents of 29 Arbor Street. He tried to hire Wolfe to locate his estranged wife. (DLAD)

Meeker, Thumbs—New York City gangster and archenemy of Dazy Perrit. Given his nickname from his favorite method of getting information from reluctant persons (in which he used both thumbs). A cave man. (BID)

Meer, Kenneth—Amory Browning's chief assistant at Continental Air Network. (PPTG)

Megalech, Mr.—New York City District Attorney in October 1952. (TWKY)

Mercer, John—President of Mercer's Bobbins, Inc. (KNPL)

Meyer, Mister—A man living in Boston who was the last to see Judge William Harrison alive before his body was found at the base of a cliff. (LFM)

Michaels, Dr.—Gynecologist, blackmail victim and subscriber to Beulah Poole's newsletter. (ABAV)

Michaels, Hilda—Wife of Dr. Michaels. She reinforced Wolfe and Archie's opinions about marriage. (ABAV)

Mike—Female sergeant who acts as Cerberus for Meg Duncan. (TMCL)

Milhaus, Frank—Country doctor in Montana. (DOD)

Miltan, Jeanne—Nikola Miltan's wife and co-owner of his fencing and dancing studio. (OMDB)

Miltan, Nikola—Owner of a dancing and fencing studio in New York City. (OMDB)

Mion, Alberto—Opera singer, husband of Peggy Mion, alleged suicide but actually a murder victim. Top tenor at the Metropolitan Opera for the past five or six years. (GWW)

Mion, Margaret "Peggy"—Paramour, or at least enamored, of Frederick Weppler and widow of Alberto Mion, opera singer. (GWW)

Mister—Bess Huddleston's playful chimpanzee. If Archie had remembered to bring a gun, he would have been the late Mister. (CITMD)

Mitchell, Lee—Man sent from Boston to represent Fillmore Collard and Theodore Gaines in a meeting of the League of Atonement at Wolfe's house. (LFM)

Mitchell, Mr.—Banker who runs financial checks for Archie and Wolfe in 1950. (ITBF)

Mitchell, Thelma—Employee of Boyden McNair Inc. and witness to Molly Lauck's murder. (RDBX)

Mollen, William—Member of "The Rubber Band" who used the alias "Turtleback." (RB)

Mollew, Sandy—New York City private detective. (RDBX)

Mollison, Archibald—Professor and member of the League of Atonement. (LFM)

Molloy, Michael M.—Real estate broker and husband of Selma Molloy. Peter Hays was convicted of his murder. (MAWBD)

Molloy, Selma—Widow of Michael Molloy, fourteen years his junior and unhappily married. (MAWBD)

Mondor, Marie—Wife of Pierre Mondor. (TMC)

Mondor, Pierre—Owner and Chef de cuisine of Mondor's Restaurant in Paris, France. While Wolfe's house guest, his desire to see a World Series baseball game led Wolfe into a murder during the 1952 World Series. (TMC)(TWKY)

Montrose, Delia—One of Inspector Cramer's unsolved homicides from 1947 that Wolfe solves three years later. (ITBF)

Moore, Mabel—Typist at Corrigan, Phelps, Kustin and Briggs. (MBTB)

Moore, Waldo Wilmot—Correspondence checker at Naylor-Kerr, Inc. Jasper Pine hired Wolfe to dispel rumors that Moore's hit-and-run death was murder. (TMW)

Morley, Dick—Assistant District Attorney in New York City. Once willing to take part of a $10,000 bet from Wolfe. (FDL)(LFM)(RB)

Morley, Dr. Nicholson—Psychiatrist who offered to solve a murder for Cramer and then Wolfe. Both turned him down. (DFM)

Morrison, Mr.—FBI Agent Archie has had dealings with on a couple of occasions. (TDB)

Mort—Jailer for the Monroe County, Montana, Sheriff's Office. (DOD)

Morton, Mr.—Assistant to Waldo Kearns. (MTFM)

Moses—Bess Huddleston's pet alligator. Archie tripped over him and scratched his hand. It proved to be fortuitous in the solution of Bess Huddleston's murder. (CITMD)

Moulton, Mr.—One of the domestic staff at Kanawha Spa. (TMC)

Moyse, Lila—Mrs. William Moyse. Her reaction the Giants losing the last game of the 1952 World Series provided Archie with a vital clue to the mystery. (TWKY)

Moyse, William—Second string catcher for the New York Giants during the 1952 World Series. (TWKY)

Muecke, Siegfried—Professional gambler who spent a lot of time with Eric Hagh in South America. (PB)

Muir, Ramsey—Senior Vice-President of the Seaboard Products Corporation. A dirty old man *par excellence*. (RB)

Muller, Ernst—Out on bail for conspiring to transport stolen property across state lines, Archie might have broken his arm. (TDB)

Murdoch, Captain—NYPD Captain assigned to investigate the destruction of Wolfe's plant rooms in 1949, a hopeless task given that Wolfe didn't share much information with him. He must have acquitted himself fairly well because Wolfe allowed him to dine with him. (SC)

Murphy, Aloysius—Law partner of Louis Rony. (SC)

Murphy, Angelina—True name of the woman hired by Dazy Perrit to impersonate his daughter. Murder victim. (BID)
Murphy, Ann—Employee at Naylor-Kerr, Inc. that complains on Archie. (TMW)
Murphy, Carrie—Gwendolyn Yates' assistant at Tingley's Tidbits. (BE)
Murphy, Detective—Another of Inspector Cramer's minions. He was one of the men assigned to tail Paul Chapin in 1934. (LFM)(DFM)(BO)
Murphy, Jimmy—Taxi driver in Carmel, New York, who gives directions to a lost Archie. (PIY)
Murphy, Joe—Head of the D.A.'s Homicide Bureau in 1974. (AFA)
Murphy, Lieutenant—Officer in NYPD's Missing Persons Bureau in 1956. (MAWBD)
Murphy, Timothy—New York City Homicide Detective. (ZC)
Nagle, Florence—English lady who is the best breeder of Irish wolfhounds in the world, not that Archie really needed to know. (DD)
Nash, Bernard—Steward at the Gambit Chess Club. (G)
Naylor, George—Chairman of the Board of Naylor-Kerr, Inc. They deal in engineering equipment and supplies. (TMW)
Naylor, Kerr—Head of the Stock department at Naylor-Kerr, Inc. Also son of George Naylor, brother of Cecily Pine and brother-in-law of Jasper Pine. He eats weeds. (TMW)
Neary, Deputy Commissioner—NYPD Deputy Police Commissioner in 1953. (GS)
Negron, Jimmy—Owner of a chicken farm in Lame Horse, Montana. He was to provide the feathers to tar and feather Phillip Brodell. (DOD)
Neill, Nat—New York Giants center fielder during the 1952 World Series. (TWKY)
Nesbitt, Mrs. James R.—A former patient of retired nurse Ellen Tenzer. (MH)
Nichols, Janet—Bess Huddleston's assistant party arranger. Archie took her dancing at the Flamingo. (CITMD)
Nieder, Cynthia—Niece and heir of Paul Nieder as half-owner of Daumery and Nieder, garment manufacturers. (MA)
Nieder, Paul—One of the founding partners of Daumery and Nieder. A man with the distinction of dying twice; once by allegedly committing suicide by jumping nude into a geyser in Yellowstone National Park and once, not allegedly, as a murder victim. (MA)
Nobby—Doberman pinscher whose stabbing death provides a major clue to a murder. (ITBF)

Noel—Employee at Rusterman's Restaurant fired by Marko Vukcic, not because he stole a goose but because he lied about it. The moral is that stolen property is replaceable but stolen trust is not. (AFA)

Noonan, Con—Lieutenant, New York State Police. A stinker, free with his fists and, in Wolfe's words, a uniformed blackguard. He wanted to put Wolfe and Archie in jail for material witness to a homicide but settled for running them out of the county. But that lasted about seven months before they were back. He tried it again, equally ineffectually. (DTD)(SC)(ITBF)

Norris, Paul—Author Richard Echols' agent. (PIY)

Northrup, Bill—NYPD Detective with a good memory for names and faces. (RDBX)

O'Brien, John R.—New York City policeman who wants to make sure that he gets credit for Archie's arrest on a Westchester County warrant. (ITBF)

O'Brien, Vera—Secretary who replaced Helen Martin for attorney James Beebe. (WAMM)

O'Connor—Alias Fred Durkin uses to get in over his head in 1953. (GS)

O'Garro, Patrick—Partner in the advertising firm of Lippert, Buff and Assa. He could sell a hot water bottle to a man on his way to hell. (BM)

O'Gorman, T.M.—One of the best orchid-growers in America, he joined others in an entreaty to Wolfe to solve the murder of Molly Lauck. (RDBX)

O'Grady, Detective—He has the honor (or the frustration) of being the first member of the NYPD Homicide Squad to visit Wolfe. Cerebrally an oaf, according to Wolfe. (FDL)

O'Hara, Deputy Commissioner—NYPD Deputy Commissioner who never forgave Archie for being clever once. He's a nincompoop, Wolfe said so and Archie told him. (ABAV)(TMW)

O'Keeffe, Georgia—American artist (1887–1986) who paints semi-abstract depictions of natural subjects. Elinor Denovo has five of her prints in her apartment. O'Keeffe's husband, Alfred Stieglitz, is known as the father of modern photography and his best-known work is a 400-print series of his wife's paintings. (FH)

O'Leary, Detective—Manhattan West Homicide Detective. In 1957, Archie won $3.12 from him in gin rummy while under arrest. (IDES)

O'Neill, Roger—Name Archie makes up to check an alibi. (PPTG)

O'Shea, Cassie—Widow and housekeeper for Beryl and Theodore Huck. (ITM)

Odelette—Herman Lewent's mistress (one of three) in Toulouse, France, who tried to poison him in a jealous rage. (ITM)

Odell, Frank—Man convicted of fraud due to an article by Morris Althaus. (TDB)

Odell, Gershom—House detective at Kanawha Spa, West Virginia. (TMC)

Odell, Madeline—Mrs. Peter Odell, daughter of Carl Hartig and a director of Continental Air Network. (PPTG)

Odell, Peter—Vice-President in charge of development for Continental Air Network who made an explosive discovery. (PPTG)

Odom, Bert—Janitor in James Neville Vance's building. (BWT)

Ogilvy, Jane—Author who sued Marjorie Lippin's estate for plagiarism. (PIY)

Ogilvy, Mrs.—Jane Ogilvy's mother. Archie doesn't do her any favors. (PIY)

Oglethorpe, Lister—An employee of Paul Chapin's publisher. (LFM)

Ohrbach, Mr.—Owner of Town House Services Incorporated, the company repairing damages to Wolfe's home. (AFA)

Olga—Maid of Sarah Jaffee. She's a Valkyrie. (PB)

Oliver, Mrs. Victor—60-year-old widow of a millionaire broker who pays Barry Hazen $2000 a month. (DOAD)

Oliver, W.B.—Editor of the New York Gazette in 1939. He dines with Wolfe once a month. (WTAW)

Olmstead, Captain—NYPD Captain in Manhattan Homicide West who questions Archie after his second arrest on the same case. (PB)

Olsen, Mr.—.Janitor of the house at 29 Arbor Street. (DLAD)

O'Malley, Conroe—Former partner in Corrigan, Phelps, Kustin and Briggs before he was disbarred for bribing a juror. (MBTB)

O'Neil, Daphne—Stylist for Softdown, Inc. who is trying to get to the top through corporate bedrooms. Priscilla Eads intended to fire her when she took over the company. (PB)

O'Neill, Don—President of O'Neill and Warder Inc., member of the National Industrial Association and Chairman of the Dinner Committee at the Waldorf dinner where Cheney Boone was murdered. (SS)

Orbelian, Stephen—Author of one of Woody Stepanian's favorite quotes—"I love my country because it is mine." (DOD)

Orchard, Cyril—publisher of The Track Almanac, a tip sheet on horses, who was poisoned during his interview on Madeline Fraser's radio show. (ABAV)(ITBF)

Orwin, Eugene—Attorney and son of Mimi Orwin. (DFM)

Orwin, Mimi—Member of the Manhattan Flower Club. (DFM)

Osborn, Mrs. James Frank—Scion of the Baltimore ships and steel Osborns. (TMC)

Oscar—Retainer and man-Friday to Cyrus M. Jarrett. (FH)

Osgood, Clyde—Brother of Nancy Osgood. A $10,000 bet got him killed before he could collect. (SBC)

Osgood, Frederick—Rancher, cattleman and archenemy of Thomas Pratt. (SBC)

Osgood, Marcia—Mrs. Frederick Osgood. (SBC)

Osgood, Nancy—Sister of Clyde Osgood. Another of the few women privileged to drive Wolfe. (SBC)

Oshin, Mortimer—Playwright and member of the Joint Committee on Plagiarism of the National Association of Authors and Dramatists and the Book Publishers of America. (PIY)

Oster, Harold R.—Black lawyer for the Rights of Citizens Committee. He demands equality from Wolfe, gets it and doesn't like it. (ARTD)

Ostrow, Dr. Irwin—Psychiatrist friend of Dr. Vollmer. (PPTG)

Otis, Lamont—75-year-old senior partner (40%) in the law firm of Otis, Edey, Heydecker and Jett. (EMMM)

Otto—Doorman at Rusterman's Restaurant. (AFA)

Owen, Fred—In charge of public relations for the Starlite Company. (ABAV)

Page, Beulah—Dazy Perrit's daughter. Another one who succumbs to a dinner date with Archie. (BID)

Paige, Ann—Associate attorney in the law firm of Otis, Edey, Heydecker and Jett. Fiancée of Gregory Jett. Climbed out of a window to escape Wolfe's locked front room. (EMMM)

Palmer, Delbert—Corn deliveryman who replaced Kenneth Faber. (MC)

Palmer, Lewis—Employee of the Federal Housing Administration and member of the League of Atonement. (LFM)

Papps, Spiros—Friend and retainer of Ambassador Theodore Kelefy. (IMTM)

Pasic, Josip—Montenegrin whose message brought Wolfe halfway around the world. (BKM)

Peacock, Sam—Wrangler, on Bill Farnham's dude ranch in Montana who found Phillip Brodell's body. (DOD)

Peckham—Laura Fromm's butler and, no, he didn't do it. (GS)

Pemberton, Agnes—Fashion reporter for Vogue Magazine. (MA)

Perazzo, Jim—Head of Licensing Services for New York State. The man who grants or ungrants private detective's licenses. (TDB)

Perdis, Ambrose—Shipping magnate who pays Barry Hazen over $40,000 a year. Archie meets him by kicking him in the stomach. In spite of his wealth, Mr. Perdis was evidently a slow learner because, after a break between rounds and a strip search that left him in his underwear, he placed Archie in the position of having to throw him nine feet across a room. (DOAD)

Perez, Cesar—Superintendent/janitor of the building where the Yeager lovenest was. (TMCL)

Perez, Felita—Mrs. Cesar Perez and mother of Maria. (TMCL)

Perez, Maria—Chaste but nosy daughter of Cesar and Felita Perez. One of the three most beautiful women Archie's ever seen. (TMCL)

Perlman—One of Lon Cohen's best men at the Gazette. **(PPTG)**

Perlman, Nina—Stenographer at Corrigan, Phelps, Kustin and Briggs. (MBTB)

Perrit, Dazy—New York City's King of the Black Market. Renowned gangster and killer. Due to his occupation and lifestyle, many expected Dazy to end his days as a murder victim, it didn't happen as anyone expected. (BID). He also served as a reference of sorts for Cynthia Brown. (DFM)

Perrit, Violet—Alias used by Angelina Murphy while posing as Dazy Perrit's daughter. (BID)

Perry, Anthony D.—Multi-millionaire Director of Wolfe's bank, the Metropolitan Trust Company and President of the Seaboard Products Corporation. (RB)

Pete—Employee in the garage where Wolfe's car is kept. (NW)

Pettigrew, Sam—Sheriff of Marlin County, West Virginia. (TMC)

Phelps, Emmett—Partner in Corrigan, Phelps, Kustin and Briggs. (MBTB)

Phillips—A forensics expert for the NYPD. (SS)

Pickerel, Percy—Archie's second suggestion for an undercover alias for Wolfe as a stock clerk in Naylor-Kerr, Inc. (TMW)

Pierce, Oliver A.—New York State assemblyman, enamored of Lina Darrow. (ITBF)

Pincus, Danny—Owner of Danny's Bar and Grill and Matthew Birch's bookie. (GS)

Pine, Cecily—Mrs. Jasper Pine, daughter of George Naylor and sister of Kerr Naylor. She tries to set Archie up in his own detective business, independent of Wolfe. (TMW)

Pine, Jasper—President of Naylor-Kerr, Inc. He hires Wolfe to dispel rumors in his company that Waldo Moore's hit-and-run death was murder. He reads three times as fast as Wolfe ever does. (TMW)

Pinelli, Lila—Lady who works at a secretarial service on Eighth Avenue and supplements her income as a Notary Public. (MC)

Piotti, John—Owner of a restaurant on 14th (or 13th) Street near Second Avenue that occasionally has a special table wired for sound. (PA)(G)

Pitcairn, Belle—Wife of Joseph G. Pitcairn, mother of Donald and Sybil. (DTD)

Pitcairn, Donald—Son of Joseph Pitcairn. Had he chosen to surrender his virginity during his sojourns through four colleges, the result might have been less traumatic for all concerned. (DTD)

Pitcairn, Joseph G.—Owner of an estate near Katonah in northern Westchester County, New York, and employer of Andrew Krasicki. (DTD)

Pitcairn, Sybil—Daughter of Joseph Pitcairn. Her taunting effrontery of calling Wolfe by his first name was what made him finally decide to forgo the comforts of home to solve the murder of Dini Lauer. (DTD)

Pitkin, Oliver—Fiercely anti-feminist Secretary-Treasurer of Softdown, Inc. (PB)

Pizzi, Augustus—Photographer for Allover Pictures Inc. and one of a group of people including Archie taking photos outside of an Easter service at St. Thomas's Church. (EP)

Plehn, Raymond—Horticultural expert for Ditson and Company, and one of the best orchid-growers in America. He joined others in an entreaty to Wolfe to solve the murder of Molly Lauck. He helped Wolfe solve a case in 1939 with information on the availability of wild roses in New York. He visited Wolfe's house with W.G. Dill before March of 1941. He offered Lewis Hewitt $10,000 (futilely) for one of the black orchids. Archie considers using him to appeal to Wolfe to stop training to join the army at the beginning of World War II. (RDBX)(WTAW)(BO)(NQDE)(SBC)

Poggett, Frederick—Bank officer at the Madison Avenue branch of the Continental Trust Company. (TMD)

Pohl, Ferdinand—Business partner of Sigmund Keyes. (BFO)

Polk, William—Deceased superintendent of a building at Ten East Thirty-Ninth Street in New York. (FH)

Pompa, Virgil—Former chef and mentor of Marko Vukcic at Mondor's Restaurant in Paris, France. At 30 the best sauce man in France. Became the second-in-command to H.R. Landy and helped create the Ambrosia chain of restaurants. (OF)

Poole, Beulah—Publisher of a sheet giving advance information on political and economic affairs, murdered in 1948. (ABAV)

Poor, Eugene R.—A partner in the firm of Blaney and Poor, manufacturer of novelties like exploding cigars, one of which blew his face off. Murder victim. (IOE)

Poor, Martha—Formerly Martha Davis, an employee of Blaney and Poor until she married Eugene Poor. (IOE)

Porter, Alice—Author who sued Ellen Sturdevant for plagiarism. (PIY)

Posner, Al—Co-owner of Posart Camera Exchange who installs a camera in a baby carriage for Archie. (MH)

Postel, Titus—Father of Mrs. Barry Hazen. He committed suicide in 1955. (DOAD)

Potter, Clarence—Brother-in-law of Leonard Dykes. He's a bubblehead. (MBTB)

Potter, Peggy—Leonard Dykes' sister and Mrs. Clarence Potter. An extraordinary woman and something of a natural detective. Archie may marry her when her bubbleheaded husband dies. (MBTB)

Pratt, Bill—Reporter for the New York Courier newspaper who Archie gave a scoop the first time he was arrested in New York City. (NQDE)

Pratt, Caroline—Niece of Thomas Pratt. She rescued Wolfe from a bull. One of the few people who has driven Wolfe besides Archie. (SBC)

Pratt, George R.—Politician and member of the League of Atonement. (LFM)

Pratt, Jimmy—Nephew of Thomas Pratt and brother of Caroline Pratt. (SBC)

Pratt, Thomas—Restaurant chain mogul. (SBC)

Pratt, W.R.—Executive of the Owl Press who provided Wolfe with a copy of an old book for research. (PIY)

Prentiss, Con—New York Giants shortstop during the 1952 World Series. He had an appreciation for Mrs. William Moyse. (TWKY)

Prince, Anita—Fitter and designed for Alec Gallant Incorporated. (MNJ)(FUFM)

Pritchard, Del—Head of a New York City private investigations firm. He was called in to solve Molly Lauck's murder but failed. (RDBX)

Prescott, Glenn—Senior partner of the New York law firm of Dunwoodie, Prescott & Davis. (WTAW)

Proctor, Al—New York Gazette reporter. (G)

Promm, Nyura—In the Diplomacy Club business, she was the best example Archie ever saw of Wolfe squeezing a sponge dry. (FDL)

Prosch, Carl—Owner of an artist studio. (MTFM)

Protic, Stefan—Another Montenegrin who saves Wolfe's feet by driving him around the countryside but more genial than Jube' Bilic. (BKM)

Purcell, Ralph—Althea Purcell/Tedder/Vail's brother. (FD)

Purvil, Bill—NYPD Detective who followed Saul on an assignment once. (RB)

Putti, Lisette—Ramsey Keith's niece, perhaps. (TMC)

Putz, Jonas—The man Archie was tailing when he ran into Flora Gallant. (FUFM)

Pyle, Vincent—Theatrical agent, womanizer, heel and murder victim, in that chronological order. (PA)(TDB)

Qarmat, Armad—Arab terrorist cell leader? (PPTG)

Quayle, Detective—A NYPD Homicide minion sitting on Wolfe's stoop waiting to serve warrants on him. (SS)

Quayle, Timothy—A senior editor at Tick-Tock Magazine. (TDB)

Quest, Bernard—Vice-President of Softdown, Inc. He unsuccessfully begged Nathan Eads for a one-third share of the company. (PB)

Quinn, Marjorie—One of the Hebes, a group of a dozen young women hired to serve at the annual dinner for the Ten for Aristology in 1958. (PA)

Quinee, Mr. and Mrs.—Julia McGee's alibi during a murder. (TMCL)

Quon, Cherry—Receptionist for Kurt Bottweill. She tried to blackmail Wolfe into manufacturing evidence to frame Margot Dickey for murder. (CP)

Rackell, Arthur—Communist sympathizer and murder victim. (HTR)

Rackell, Benjamin—Owner of Rackell Importing Company and uncle of Arthur Rackell. (HTR)

Rackell, Pauline—Mrs. Benjamin Rackell, aunt of Arthur Rackell. (HTR)

Rackham, Barry—Sarah Rackham's sponging second husband. When she cuts off the money, he makes arrangements for his own income but from someone far less forgiving than the Mrs. (ITBF)

Rackham, Sarah—Wealthy, ugly and much put-upon, she deserved better than she got from everyone except Wolfe. (ITBF)

Rago, Paul—Sauce chef at the Churchill Hotel. (FJP)(AFA)

Randall, Detective—NYPD Homicide detective in 1952–53. (GS)(PB)

Randall, Richard—Man who rented a safe deposit box at the Metropolitan Safe Deposit Company. He could afford it. (MAWBD)

Rattner, Mr.—An operative used by Wolfe in one case, supervised by Fred Durkin. (HTR)

Reade, Belinda—She was at the Miltan studio when Percy Ludlow lost his last fencing match. She thinks Archie's pretty. (OMDB)

Regan, B.A.—District Attorney of Rockland County, New York. (WTAW)

Reid, Oggie—Mike Ayers' boss at the New York Tribune. (LFM)

Rennert, Kenneth—Playwright who sued Mortimer Oshin for plagiarism. (PIY)

Rentner, Dr. Abraham—Physician at Mount Sinai Hospital who had an appointment with Alberto Mion the day he died. (GWW)

Reyes, Ella—Mr. and Mrs. Thomas Irwin's maid. Johnny Keems bribed her but it didn't work out like either of them figured. (MAWBD)

Reynolds, William—The alias of a man who was Member Number 128-394 in the American Communist Party. (SC)

Ricci, Mrs.—Landlady of Carlo Maffei and Anna Fiore (FDL)

Ricco, Doris—A singer who, whenever anything goes wrong, just walks out and calls a press conference. Archie compares Wolfe to her in one of his sedentary genius stages. (PIY)

Richards, Mr.—A Vice-President of the Federal Broadcasting Company and former client who provides information to Wolfe when he is preparing to solicit a case from Madeline Fraser. (ABAV)

Riff, Dorothy—Secretary to Beryl and Theodore Huck. (ITM)

Riley, Mr.—New York City Assistant District Attorney in 1957. (IDES)

Riley, William A.—E.D. Kimball's caddy on the day Peter Barstow died. (FDL)

Riordan, Al—Reporter for the Associated Press. (BM)

Ritchie, Mr.—Employee of the Cosmopolitan Trust Company and executor of Noel Hawthorne's will. (WTAW)

Ritter, Miss—Secretary to Westchester County Assistant District Attorney Derwin. (FDL)

Robbins, Mrs. James—One of the Directors of Grantham House. (CFO)

Robert—One of the people assisting Felix Courbet in preparing a dinner of blue grouse at Lily Rowan's penthouse. (RM)

Robertson, Mr. and Mrs. Blair—Neighbors and dinner guests of the Barstows. (FDL)

Robilotti, Louise—Robert Robilotti's wife, Albert Grantham's widow and primary benefactor of Grantham House, a home for unwed mothers. Old money. Wolfe recovered a million dollars worth of her jewelry in 1956. (CFO)

Robilotti, Robert—Louise Grantham's second husband. Kept man. (CFO)

Roca, Detective—New York City Homicide Detective. He described the positions of the eight pencils and eraser on Leo Heller's desk to Wolfe that amounted to The Zero Clue. (ZC)

Rochefoucauld—Francois, Duc de La Rochefoucauld (1613–1680). French writer. Wolfe disagrees with his maxim that we should only affect compassion and carefully avoid having any. (MAWBD)

Roeder, Pete—Another of Arnold Zeck's henchman but he has worked his way up to a "D" and is a master of disguise. (ITBF)

Rogers, Stanley—Attorney in Albany, New York. Nathaniel Parker worked through him to get Wolfe and Archie out of jail on material witness charges in 1956. (TMD)

Rollins, Harold—History professor and finalist in the Pour Amour perfume contest. (BM)

Romeike, Ed—Southpaw pitcher for the New York Giants during the 1952 World Series. (TWKY)

Rony, Louis—Shady lawyer in Murphy, Kearfot and Rony. He has poor judgement and worse luck. He does business with Arnold Zeck, courts Gwenn Sperling, gets mugged by Saul Panzer and run over by Archie in Wolfe's car—well, almost. (SC)(ITBF)

Rookaloo—Pet monkey in the Koven household. Would have been a murder victim if it were possible to murder a monkey. (SAM)

Rooney, Audrey—Victor Talbott's secretary prior to being fired. (BFO)

Root, Peter—U.S. Army Captain who tried to sell confidential information to Ben Jensen in 1944. He was court-martialed and sentenced to three years in prison in Maryland. (HWM)

Root, Thomas—Father of Peter Root, very proud of his son. (HWM)

Roper, Ward—Paul Nieder's assistant at Daumery and Nieder. (MA)

Rose—Maid for Mr. and Mrs. Loring Burton. (LFM)

Rose—One of the Jarrell's maids. (IDES)

Rosenbaum, Mr.—Head of the Structural Metals Section at Naylor-Kerr, Inc. (TMW)

Ross, Bernard—Attorney hired by Lily Rowan for Susan McLeod. (MC)

Ross, Otis—Alias used by William A. Donahue when he hired Wolfe for a wire-tapping job. (TMD)

Rossi—NYPD officer Cramer orders to allow Archie to look at a murder file. (MBTB)

Rossi, Domenico—Chef de cuisine of the Empire Cafe, London, and father of Dina Laszio. (TMC)

Rowley, George—Alias of a young member of "The Rubber Band" who killed a man in Silver City, Nevada in 1895. (RB)

Rowley, Mrs.—Lady who lived across the street from Archie during his boyhood in Ohio and formed his conception of widows. Sarah Jaffee changed that conception. (PB)

Rowley, Sergeant—NYPD officer Archie occasionally calls upon for information. (BFO)

Rucker, Judge—Judge that Nathaniel Parker got a court order from to open a safety deposit box. (MAWBD)

Ryan, Margaret—Mrs. Richard Meegan before she ran away from him. (DLAD)

Ryder, Colonel Harold—U.S. Army Military Intelligence officer who approached Wolfe about accepting an assignment in early 1942 and was rebuffed. Before the war, he had been an attorney in Cleveland. (NQDE). His only son, serving with the Army Air Corps, was killed in the summer of 1943 after shooting down four German planes. The next week, Colonel Ryder also gave his life for his country in a more unusual manner for that conflict, murdered by a fellow American. (BT)

Sackett, Doctor—Physician who first examined the body of Clyde Osgood. (SBC)

Safford, Wayne—Owner of a riding stable in Central Park. (BFO)

Salzenback, Mr.—Man who butchers fresh kids for Wolfe in Garfield. (RDBX)

Sam—Bartender at Wellman's bar on 8th Street who knows Fred Durkin. (WTAW)

Sam—Doorman at Phoebe Gunther's apartment building at 611 East Fifty-Fifth Street in New York City. His attention to duty cost him $19.75. (SS)

Sam—Soda jerk in a drugstore at 54th Street and Eighth Avenue who heard about Wolfe's client's death at the same time as Archie. (FD)

Sam—Janitor for the Midtown Home Service Corporation. (PPTG)

Samek, Michael—Cook for O.V. Bragan at his upstate New York lodge. (IMTM)

Sampson, Sinclair—Pseudonym on Leonard Dykes' list. (MBTB)

Samuels, Alan—Member of the Charity Funds Investigating Committee and one of the aliases used by William A. Donahue while procuring wiretapping services from several private detectives in New York City in 1955. (TMD)

Sandler, Jack—Mortimer Oshin's former agent who found a copy of the play by Kenneth Rennert that was the basis for his plagiarism lawsuit. (PIY)

Santini, Enrico—Art expert in Mantegna from Florence, Italy. (LFM)

Saunders, Captain—Captain in the New York State Police who finds another dead body near White Plains with a connection to Wolfe. (FD)

Savage, Margaret—Stanley Karnow's aunt and mother of Richard Savage and Ann (Savage) Horne. (WAMM)

Savage, Mr.—Public Relations counsel for the Seaboard Products Corporation. (RB)

Savage, Richard—Son of Margaret Savage and brother of Ann (Savage) Horne. (WAMM)

Savarese, F.O.—Italian-American mathematics professor who was the guest who survived his interview on Madeline Fraser's radio show. (ABAV)

Schane, Morton—Fiancée of Beulah Page. He makes one of the most memorable exits from Wolfe's office. (BID)

Schipple, Mr.—New York Assistant District Attorney in 1962. (G)

Schrebenwelder, Mrs.—Fictitious married woman Archie tries to tell Wolfe he's having an affair with in 1957. Pfui. (IDES)

Schriver, Benjamin—Shipping magnate, member of the Ten for Aristology and host for their 1958 banquet at his home. (PA)(TDB)

Schultz,—Associate editor of Clock magazine. (BM)

Schuster, Paul—Promising young corporation lawyer and guest at the Grantham House's annual dinner. (CFO)

Schwab, Officer—New York City policeman sent to guard a bomb sent to Wolfe's house. (MC)

Schwartz—Another of Arnold Zeck's praetorian guard. (ITBF)

Schwartz, Sergeant—St. Louis, Missouri, policeman sent to Montana to bring back a murder suspect. (DOD)

Scott, Pitney—Harvard-educated taxi driver and member of the League of Atonement. He and Archie shared a Mickey Finn once. (LFM)

Scovil, Harlan—A weather-beaten plainsman who survived the Old West but was gunned down on the mean streets of New York City four decades later with Wolfe's name written down in his pocket. (RB)

Seaver, Ronald—An alias that intruded on one of Wolfe's areas of ignorance although, as a Mets fan, it was transparent to Archie. (PPTG)

Sebor, Dorothy—Another in a long line of extraordinary women that Archie runs into in his line of work. (FH)

Servan, Louis—Chef de cuisine of the Kanawha Spa, West Virginia. (TMC)

Seymour, John Morton—Attorney for Thomas Yeager. (TMCL)

Shanks, Charles E.—One of the best orchid-growers in America, he joined others in an entreaty to Wolfe to solve the murder of Molly Lauck. (RDBX). He later incurred Wolfe's enmity by refusing to trade albinos with him. (SBC)

Shanks, Mabel—Receptionist at Dunwoodie, Prescott & Davis. She has a good eye for flowers. (WTAW)

Shattuck, John Bell—U.S. Congressman chairing a committee in Washington, D.C., investigating misuse of industrial secrets during World War II. Godfather to Colonel Harold Ryder's son. (BT)

Shepherd, Al—Nancylee Shepherd's father. (ABAV)

Shepherd, Nancylee—Elusive sixteen-year old pest around Madeline Fraser's radio show who provided some vital information to Wolfe—eventually. (ABAV)

Shiff, Oscar—Pseudonym on Leonard Dyke's list. (MBTB)

Shuvalov, Dmitri—One of the three top Russians in Albania in 1954. He would not survive meeting Wolfe. (BKM)

Sievers, George—Lieutenant with the Evansville, Indiana, Police. (ARTD)

Skinner, Commissioner—New York City Police Commissioner in 1952–1958. (TWKY)(GS)(PB)(MAWBD)(CFO)

Skinner, William "Bill"—New York City District Attorney in 1935–39. He has been demoted to Assistant DA by 1945 but rises back to District Attorney by 1957. (RB)(RDBX)(WTAW)(BFO)(SS)(EP)

Skinner, Mr.—Manuel Kimball's airplane mechanic. (FDL)

Skinny—Archie's nickname for an anonymous FBI agent with a limited vocabulary. His performance under stress probably made him a security guard at the Watergate Hotel, if he could pass the IQ test. His more presentable partner was nicknamed Handsome. (TDB)

Small, Mr.—The Barstows' butler. (FDL)

Smalley, Dave—Hired hand of Thomas Pratt. (SBC)

Smith, John—Blatantly unimaginative alias of an anonymous lawyer representing the National Industrial Association who tries to bribe Wolfe with $300,000 to frame someone, anyone, connected with the Bureau of Price Regulation for a murder. (SS)

Smith, Sally—Alias used by Angelina Murphy on a rolling and cleaning charge in Salt Lake City that she had jumped bond on when Dazy Perrit picked her to impersonate his daughter. (BID)

Soffer, Horton—Team doctor for the New York Giants during the 1952 World Series. (TWKY)

Sol—New York City Homicide Detective. (SAM)

Sopko—Hired Wolfe to get his son out of a jam. Later loaned Archie a boat to seduce a witness. (PPTG)

Sorrell, Rita—Nee' Rita Ramsey prior to her marriage to wealthy Martin Sorrell. Beautiful former Broadway actress. She said she thinks Archie is very handsome but she may have had ulterior motives for her compliments. She ended up in Wolfe's lap. (EMMM)

Sperling, Gwenn—Youngest daughter of James Sperling and romantic interest of Louis Rony. (SC)

Sperling, James U.—Chairman of the Board of Continental Mines Corporation. (SC)

Sperling, James U., Junior—Son of James Sperling, brother of Madeline and Gwenn. (SC)

Sperling, Madeline—Widowed eldest daughter of James Sperling and sister of Gwenn Sperling. (SC)

Spero, G.G.—FBI agent in the New York office. (SS)

Stahl, Janet—Manicurist in the Goldenrod Barber Shop. Pretty but her mental processes are a perfect example of the reason for Wolfe's attitudes toward women. (CK)

Stahl, Special Agent—FBI agent who persists in reading parts of the United States Code to Wolfe. Sixteen years later, Wolfe shakes hands with him and even allows him to search his house without a warrant. (OMDB)(BKM)

Stapleton, Mr.—Someone who fields phone calls for Jasper Pine. (TMW)

Stara, Alex—Archie's alias in Montenegro. (BKM)

Stara, Tone'—Wolfe's alias in Montenegro. (BKM)

Stauffer, Osric—"Ossie." Directly under Noel Hawthorne in the foreign department of Daniel Cullen and Company. (WTAW)

Steck—Butler for the Jarrell's. (IDES)

Stepanian, Woodrow—"Woody," a traveling department store named after a series of Presidents and owner of the Woodrow Stepanian Hall of Culture in Lame Horse, Montana. (DOD)

Steve—Attendant at the Tenth Avenue garage where Wolfe keeps his cars. He gave a drugged Archie a ride in 1934. (LFM)

Steve—Unnamed NYPD Detective whose only contribution was being thrown out of the brownstone by Archie along with Sergeant Heath. (RB)

Stevens, Mr.—Third from the top in the American Communist hierarchy in 1949. (SC)

Stevens, Harold—Alias used by Archie to introduce himself to Beulah Page. (BID)

Stritar, Gospo—Head of the local Secret Police in Titograd, Montenegro, in 1954. (BKM)

Strong, Tully—Secretary of the Sponsor's Council for Madeline Fraser's radio show. (ABAV)

Sturdevant, Ellen—Author who was sued by Alice Porter for plagiarism. (PIY)

Sturgis, Detective—One of Inspector Cramer's minions in 1936. Not a skilled interrogator. (RDBX)

Sturtevant, Mr.—Pilot who leases his plane out of the Crowfield County Airport. (SBC)

Sullivan, Detective—NYPD Detective. (CK)

Swing, Raymond—Radio news broadcaster. (SS)

Tabb, Jerome—President of National Association of Authors and Dramatists. Wolfe has read four of his books and they are all A's. (PIY)

Tabby—Alias of a petty thief who owed Archie a favor and sold his talents to Wolfe to steal an orchid spray from Mrs. Millard Bynoe. (EP)

Talbot, Anne—Wife of Henry Lewis Talbot who pays Barry Hazen $2500 a month. Their introduction consisted of Archie strip-searching a group of people of whom Mrs. Talbot was by far the most attractive. (DOAD)

Talbott, Victor—Salesman for Sigmund Keyes' firm. (BFO)

Talento, Victor—Attorney and resident at 29 Arbor Street. (DLAD)

Tassone, Henri—Chef de cuisine of Shepheard's Hotel, Cairo. (TMC)

Teague, Mr.—Secretary of the American Embassy in Rome, Italy, in 1954. (BKM)

Tedder, Margot—Althea Vail's daughter by her first marriage. (FD)

Tedder, Noel—Althea Vail's son by her first marriage. A twenty-three-year-old brat. (FD)

Telesio, Paolo—Wolfe's contact in Italy in 1954. They go way back. Thirty years earlier, he knifed two Fascists to death who had Wolfe cornered. (BKM)

Tenzer, Anne—Employee of Quinn and Collins real estate who wears horsehair buttons on her blouse. (MH)

Tenzer, Ellen—Anne Tenzer's aunt, a retired nurse and maker of horsehair buttons. (MH)

Tescher, Susan—Researcher for Clock magazine and finalist in the Pour Amour perfume contest. (BM)

Thales, Milton—A fairly transparent blackmailer. (DD)

Thayer, Paul—Failed musician and nephew of Theodore Huck. (ITM)

Thomas, Mr.—Member of the Board of Directors of Naylor-Kerr, Inc. (TMW)

Thompson, George—Another working alias of Archie's. It didn't last long. (MBTB)

Thompson, Mr.—Nat Driscoll's attorney. (OMDB)

Thompson, Mr.—The best hybridizer in England. Wolfe is willing to go to Lewis Hewitt's Long Island estate to meet him for a few hours. (CP)

Thorne, Emmy—In charge of contacts and promotion for Alec Gallant Incorporated. (MNJ)(FUFM)

Thorne, Raymond—Owner of Raymond Thorne Productions, television producer and boss of Elinor Denovo. (FH)

Tiger, Beth—Black stenographer for the Rights of Citizens Committee. (ARTD)

Tillotson, Henrietta—Wife of Albert Tillotson. (ZC)

Timms, Maryella—Bess Huddleston's secretary. She is the only known woman to be accorded to dual honor of touching Wolfe without his flinching or drawing away and not only allowed to invade the sanctity of the kitchen but actually participate in the preparation of meals. (CITMD)

Tingley, Arthur—Owner of Tingley's Tidbits and uncle of Amy Duncan. (BE)

Tingley, Phillip—Adopted son of Arthur Tingley but the relationship is much more convoluted than that. (BE)

Tingley, Thomas—Arthur Tingley's father, deceased. (BE)

Tinkham, Colonel—formerly some type of gumshoe for a New York bank, he became an officer in the New York office of U.S. Army Military Intelligence in 1943. (BT)

Tite, Mr.—Head of Clock magazine. (BM)

Tolman, Barry—Prosecuting attorney of Marlin County, West Virginia. (TMC)

Tom—If you called LIncoln 6-3232 between 7 and 10 A.M. in October of 1946, asked for Tom and used Dazy Perrit's name, you might be able to order some meat in spite of the Great Meat Shortage. (BID)

Tony—Cab driver who assisted Archie with a surveillance in 1948. (ABAV)

Toracco, Phillip—A barber in the Goldenrod Barber Shop. Had a nervous breakdown in 1945 and spent a year in an asylum. (CK)

Tormic, Neya—A dancing and fencing instructor at Nikola Miltan's studio. She is introduced to Wolfe as his daughter. For once he was speechless and his eyes popped out to a new record. (OMDB)

Townsend, Mr.—Employee of Corliss Holmes who brought a wide variety of golf clubs for Wolfe to inspect and educated him in their use. (FDL)

Tracy, Anne—Stenographer in Rucker and Dill's seed and nursery company, used as a model in their woodland glade exhibit in the Grand Central Palace Flower Show in 1941. Another one Archie fell in love with at first sight. She eventually spent the night in his room at Wolfe's house but it's not what you might think. (BO)

Traub, Nathan—Advertising executive who handles the accounts of three of Madeline Fraser's radio sponsors. (ABAV)

Travis, Special Agent—New York City FBI agent who freely admits that Wolfe is his superior at interrogation. (SS)

Treble, Gus—Assistant gardener for the Pitcairn family, assistant to Andy Krasicki. (DTD)

Tremont, Mrs.—A client of Wolfe's in an unrecorded case in June of 1946. Arnold Zeck tried to intimidate Wolfe into limiting his efforts on her behalf. (ABAV)

Troy, Helen—Get it? Stenographer at Corrigan, Phelps, Kustin and Briggs. Niece of Frederick Briggs. (MBTB)

Truett, Peggy—Friend of Sam Peacock's. (DOD)

Truett, Peter—The alias Archie selected when he went undercover at Naylor-Kerr, Inc. after Wolfe refused the job. (TMW)

Trumbic—Secret Policeman in Montenegro in 1954. (BKM)

Tufitti, Giuseppe—Former owner of Tufitti's Restaurant. (FH)

Turner—The Hawthorne's butler. (WTAW)

Turtle-back—Alias of William Mollen. (RB)

Tuttle, Louise—Wife of Vincent Tuttle and younger sister of Bertram, David and Paul Fyfe. (WFD)

Tuttle, Richard M.—Employee of a boy's school and member of the League of Atonement. (LFM)

Tuttle, Rose—Unwed mother at Grantham House's annual party. (CFO)

Tuttle, Vincent—Husband of Louise Tuttle and brother-in-law of Bertram, David and Paul Fyfe. (WFD)

Unger, Dorothy—Stenographer at the New York office of the Bureau of Price Regulation. A fiction within a fiction. (SS)

Unger, Guy—Friend of Helen Weltz. (NW)

Updegraff, Fred—Owner of Updegraff Nurseries in Erie, Pennsylvania. (BO)

Upson, Edith—Alias used by another woman outsmarted by Saul Panzer. (CFO)

Upton, Manuel—Editor of Distaff women's magazine and Richard Valdon's first publisher. (MH)

Urquhart, Ernest—Washington lobbyist present at the meeting at Rusterman's Restaurant after which Harvey Bassett was murdered. (AFA)

Usher, Elaine—Mother of Faith Usher. (CFO)

Usher, Faith—Unwed mother at Grantham House's annual dinner. (CFO)

Utley, Dinah—Althea Vail's secretary. (FD)

Valdon, Lucy—Widow of Richard Valdon who gets something to remember him by nine months after his death. (MH)

Valdon, Richard—Novelist who drowns accidentally in 1961 but while he lived, he made Orrie look like a monk. (MH)

Vail, Althea—nee' Tedder. Former actress, wealthy widow of Harold F. Tedder and the current Mrs. Jimmy Vail. (FD)

Vail, Jimmy—Another man who married his wife for her money. He was kidnapped for half a million dollars of it. (FD)

Vail, Maude—Widow who had poisoned two husbands, proving to Archie that physical attractiveness has no correlation with a woman's lethal capabilities. (ZC)

Valenko, Sergei—Chef de cuisine at Chateau Montcalm, Quebec. (TMC)

Vance, Elinor—Script writer for Madeline Fraser's radio show. (ABAV)

Vance, Floyd—Public relations counselor. (FH)

Vance, James Neville—Owner of the house at 219 Horn Street, landlord of Bonny Kirk. (BWT)

Vardas, Carl—Hat, coat and tie man at the Goldenrod Barber Shop which Archie patronized. Husband of Tina. (CK)

Vardas, Tina—Mrs. Carl Vardas. Manicurist at the Goldenrod Barber Shop. (CK)

Vardis, Helen—Employee of Blaney and Poor, manufacturers of novelties. (IOE)

Varr, Ethel—Unwed mother at Grantham House's annual dinner. (CFO)

Vasseult—The greatest art forger of the century. (LFM)

Vassos, Elma—Pete Vassos' daughter and a stenographer at Mercer's Bobbins, Inc. A good girl in spite of the rumors. Another one that Archie threatens to marry. (KNPL)

Vassos, Peter—Greek bootblack and murder victim in December of 1960. For over three years, he had come to the brownstone on Mondays, Wednesdays and Fridays to shine Wolfe's and Archie's shoes. (KNPL)

Vaughn, Carlotta—Originally secretary to Mrs. Cyrus Jarrett who moved on to bigger and better things. (FH)

Vaughn, Peter—Automobile salesman and hopeful fiancée of Susan Brooke. (ARTD)

Vaughn, Sam—Father of Peter Vaughn and owner of Heron Manhattan Inc. where Wolfe buys his cars. (ARTD)

Vawter, Johnny—Son of Mort and Mabel Vawter. (DOD)

Vawter, Mabel—Mrs. Mort Vawter. (DOD)

Vawter, Miss—Executive reception clerk for the Seaboard Products Corporation. (RB)

Vawter, Mort—Owner of Vawter's General Store in Lame Horse, Montana. (DOD)

Vawter, Pete—The last step in arranging for a private detective never to work again. (AFA)

Veale, Mr.—Attorney General of Montana. (DOD)

Vedder, Malcolm—An actor who attended a showing at Wolfe's home for the Manhattan Flower Club. He caught Archie's eye because of the way he lifted a flowerpot. He refused to give Archie his name when he left and he should have because Saul Panzer later placed his name and face together. (DFM)

Velardi, Bella—One of the operators for Bagby Answers Inc. (NW)

Venner, Sylvia—Former TV actress, former because Amory Browning kicked her off her show. (PPTG)

Vetter, Dick—Television personality who becomes enamored with Flora Korby at an Independence Day picnic. (FJP)

Vick, Dorian—Pseudonym on Leonard Dykes' list. (MBTB)

Vilar, Roman—Industrial security specialist present at the meeting at Rusterman's Restaurant after which Harvey Bassett was murdered. (AFA)

Vinson, Ernest—Pseudonym on Leonard Dykes' list. (MBTB)

Volk, Mr.—Member of the Board of Directors of Naylor-Kerr, Inc. (TMW)

von Rantz-Deichen, Countess—She was after Boyden McNair. (RDBX)

Voss, Colonel—Officer in U.S. Army Intelligence during World War II that Wolfe called upon for information. (HWM)

Voss, Bianca—Traitor, blackmailer and murder victim. (MNJ)(FUFM)

Vukcic, Danielo—Marko Vukcic's nephew in Montenegro. (BKM)

W-J—Private detective. True name unknown as this was just Archie's nickname for him which stood for "Wrestler-Jockey" because of his odd physical build. (DFM)

Waddell, Mr.—District Attorney of Crowfield County in 1938. (SBC)

Wade, Deputy Commissioner—NYPD Deputy Commissioner helping to question the employees of Softdown, Inc. in 1952. (PB)

Waldron, Clara—The mother everyone is hunting for in The Mother Hunt. (MH)

Wallen, Jacob—Murder victim and NYPD Detective, 20th Precinct, stabbed in the back with a pair of scissors in the Goldenrod Barber Shop. (CK)

Waller, Jake—Caretaker at the Vail's country home. Slow on the draw. (FD)

Walsh, Michael—A contentious old security guard at a New York City construction site. His murder gave Wolfe one of the definitions for the case Archie called The Rubber Band. (RB)

Walsh—Name Archie makes up to check an alibi. (PPTG)

Walsh, Mr.—A forensic scientist for the Albany Police. (TMD)

Warder, Henry A.—Vice-President and Treasurer of O'Neill and Warder, Inc. He makes a belated but crucial appearance in a case in 1946. (SS)

Watson, John H.—Sidekick of another famous fictional detective and another of Archie's aliases. (MNJ)(FUFM)

Wayne, Nora—One of the witnesses to Stanley Karnow's will. (WAMM)

Weber, Hans—Member of the League of Atonement. (LFM)

Weed, Theodore—Employee of Barry Hazen who is in love with Mrs. Hazen. (DOAD)

Welch, Ed—Deputy Sheriff in Monroe County, Montana. He couldn't work for Cramer in any capacity. For Rowcliff, maybe. (DOD)

Weinbach, Mr.—Employee of the Fisher Laboratories who does forensic analyses for Wolfe in 1941 and 1949. He is apparently of foreign extraction. He hisses his esses. (CITMD)(SC)

Wellman, Joan—A reader for New York book publishers Scholl and Hanna. Reading one particular manuscript got her run over by a car. (MBTB)

Wellman, John R.—Wholesale grocer from Peoria, Illinois. Father of Joan Wellman who provided money, persistence and unflappable self-control in the hunt for her murderer. Put the icing on the case when the murderer refused to shake hands with him. (MBTB)

Weltz, Helen—One of the operators for Bagby Answers Inc. (NW)

Wenger, Arthur—Locksmith who made some keys for someone who misused them. (TMCL)

Wengert, Bill—Reporter for the New York Times. You know Archie's opinion of him if you know that he thinks of Wengert and Rowcliff at the same time. (AFA)

Wengert, Mr.—New York City FBI agent who stonewalled Archie about any involvement in the Rackell case in spite of the fact that Wolfe had come through for him on "that mercury thing." He and Archie served in Army Intelligence together during World War II. (HTR)

Weppler, Frederick—Music critic for the New York Gazette and fiancée of Peggy Mion. (GWW)

Wheelock, Carol—Finalist in the Pour Amour perfume contest. (BM)

Whipple, Art—Detective with Manhattan Homicide West who tails one of Wolfe's suspects and Archie lets him get away with it. (BM)

Whipple, Mr.—Chemist who analyzes some liver pate' for Wolfe in November of 1940. (BE)

Whipple, Dunbar—Son of Paul Whipple and volunteer worker for the Rights of Citizens Committee. (ARTD)

Whipple, Paul—One of the domestic staff at Kanawha Spa in 1937 but destined for better things. Nearly three decades later, he's an assistant professor of anthropology at Columbia University. (TMC)(ARTD)

White—Unnamed detective from the D.A.'s Homicide Bureau (not Cramer's men) who arrests Wolfe and Archie on material witness charges. Archie nicknamed them for their races. His partner was Black. (AFA)

Whitten, Floyd—Former head of public relations for the chain of Ambrosia Restaurants who married the widow of his deceased boss, H.R. Landy, although she was a dozen years his senior. In a position to control the business when he became a murder victim. (OF)

Whitten, Mrs. Floyd—Former wife of H.R. Landy and mother of Jerome, Mortimer and Phoebe Landy and Eve (Landy) Bahr. Following Mr. Landy's death, she married Floyd Whitten and became the head of the Ambrosia chain of restaurants. (OF)

Wilkes—Archie's jailer on the second floor of the Westchester County Jail in White Plains, New York, in 1950. (ITBF)

William—Elevator man in the building where Barry and Stella Fleming live. (DD)

Williamson, Burke—Father of Tommie Williamson, the victim of a kidnapping that Wolfe solved in 1929. He provided Raymond Liggett with a letter of introduction to Wolfe in 1937. (FDL)(TMC)

Williamson, Richard A.—Cotton broker and friend of Perry Helmar. He recommended Wolfe to Helmar, saying that Wolfe performed a miracle for once. (PB)

Willis, Marie—Employee of Bagby Answers Inc. until she crossed a blackmailer and became a murder victim. (NW)

Wilts—Another of Arnold Zeck's henchmen. (ITBF)

Winslow, John R.—One of the people waiting to see Leo Heller when Heller was murdered. He wanted Heller to predict how long his wealthy aunt would live. (ZC)

Winslow, Norton—John Winslow's wealthy uncle who was shot to death in a hunting accident in 1947 in Maine. (ZC)

Winston, Charles—Reporter for the New York Times. (BM)

Winterhoff, Mr.—Member of the Executive Committee of the National Industrial Association. (SS)

Witmer, Mr.—Witness who thought he could identify the driver of the car that ran over Pete Drossos. He was wrong. (GS)

Worthington, Dr. James Odell—Eugene Jarrett's physician. (FH)

Worthy, Wade—Professional author hired to write a biography of Lily Rowan's father. (DOD)

Wragg, Richard—Special Agent in Charge of the New York City FBI office. Once upon a time, anyway. (TDB)

Wright, Albert—Vice-President of Eastern Electric and member of The Harvard Club who helps Wolfe obtain a typewriter. (LFM)

Wright, Angela—Executive Secretary of the Association for the Aid of Displaced Persons. (GS)

Wyatt, Mr.—Member of the Board of Directors of Naylor-Kerr, Inc. (TMW)

Wylie, Detective—NYPD Homicide Detective used as an alibi by Archie. (EMMM)

Wynn, Amy—Author and member of the Joint Committee on Plagiarism of the National Association of Authors and Dramatists and the Book Publishers of America. (PIY)

Yaeger, Carl—Man wanted for a murder in St. Louis, Missouri, in 1962. (DOD)

Yare, Sarah—Alcoholic former Broadway actress that Archie was infatuated with in the mid-1950s after seeing her in Thumb A Ride several times. Murder victim. (MNJ)(FUFM)

Yarmack, Vincent—A senior editor at Tick-Tock Magazine. (TDB)

Yarmis, Helen—Unwed mother at Grantham House's annual dinner. (CFO)

Yates, Gwendolyn—Long-time employee of Tingley's Tidbits, factory superintendent in charge of production. (BE)

Yeager, Anne—Daughter of Thomas G. Yeager and Bennington College student. (TMCL)

Yeager, Ellen—Mrs. Thomas G. Yeager. She gave Wolfe a one dollar retainer and shouldn't have. (TMCL)

Yeager, Thomas G.—Executive Vice-President of Continental Plastic Products. His character is the epitome of the type of businessman Rex Stout despised. (TMCL)

Yeager, Thomas G., Junior—Son of Thomas G. Yeager, employed in the Cleveland, Ohio, office of his father's company. (TMCL)

Yerkes, Charles W.—Banker and messenger at Paul Jerin's fatal multiple chess game. (G)

Yerkes, David—Pseudonym on Leonard Dykes' list. (MBTB)

Yerkes, Tom—Barber in the Goldenrod Barber Shop. Served time in 1930 for assaulting a man who took advantage of his granddaughter and is known to have a quick temper. (CK)

Youmans, Deputy Commissioner—NYPD Deputy Commissioner in 1953. (GS)

Young, Mr. and Mrs. Percy—Weekend yachting guests of James Farquhar. (PPTG)

Younger, Phillip—Finalist in the Pour Amour perfume contest. (BM)

Zarella, Polly—Scissors and needle wizard for Daumery and Nieder's. (MA)

Zelota—Chef in Tarrangona, Spain. Phillip Laszio stole the secret of Rognons aux Montagnes from him. (TMC)

Ziegler, Agent—U.S. Secret Service agent. He stands by. (AOAB)

Zorka, Madame—Mysterious couturiere and dancing instructor at the Miltan studio. Wolfe penetrates her mystery and reveals a much more mundane past. (OMDB)

Zov, Peter—Secret Policeman in Titograd, Montenegro, in 1954. (BKM)

The Nero Wolfe Canon

"Before long the day will come, maybe in a year or two, possibly as many as five, when I won't be able to write any more of these reports for publication."
　　　　　　　　　　　　　　—Archie Goodwin
　　　　　　　　　　　　　　The Father Hunt
　　　　　　　　　　　　　　1967–

Rex Stout made his first money from writing when he sold a poem to a publication named *The Smart Set* in 1904 at the age of seventeen. Eight years later, he began writing full time and within a year had published several short stories including his first crime story. By the next year, he had published his first novel.

He was a prolific writer for the rest of his life. He wrote many crime, mystery and detective stories that did not feature Nero Wolfe. In fact, he didn't create Wolfe until he was forty-six years of age. He also wrote several books featuring characters from the Nero Wolfe series including Dol Bonner and Inspector Cramer. This book, however, is concerned solely with the thirty-three novels, thirty-nine novellas and two re-written novellas that feature Nero Wolfe.

By the time Stout had finished the second Nero Wolfe novel, he had been able to discipline his writing pace to produce a novel in about thirty-eight days and a novella in two weeks or less. In early 1957, he wrote the novella *Fourth-Of-July Picnic* in a mere nine days. He was able to maintain this pace, more or less, until the latter part of his life when he began experiencing increasingly frequent and serious health problems.

He usually set the stories during the same general time period in which he had written them. In the early years, he varied from this most significantly in the fourth Wolfe novella *Not Quite Dead Enough* to allow Wolfe (i.e. Stout) to express his fresh opinions about the treachery of the attack on Pearl Harbor. The timelines become somewhat skewed in the later books that took longer than usual to produce.

He produced eight of the novels before he wrote one of the shorter novellas. Where possible, the exact dates he wrote the books are noted. For the first thirteen years, these are approximations. At that point, Stout began keeping an exacting writing record that listed the precise dates he began and finished each book. The record also included the number of days he wrote and the days he took off for vacations, fishing trips, gardening or holidays along with his many other interests and obligations. By the time he began keeping the writing record, he also began writing Nero Wolfe stories exclusively and maintained that for the rest of his life.

Before being published in collections of three or four, the novellas were serialized in The American Magazine. *A Window For Death* was the last Wolfe novella featured in that publication in May of 1956, shortly before it went out of business. Others were published in the most popular magazines of the era including Look, Collier's and The Saturday Evening Post as well as Ellery Queen's Mystery Magazine.

The Nero Wolfe series was to end very much as it began. The last novella, *Blood Will Tell*, was published in 1963. The last dozen years of the series, corresponding to the last dozen years of Rex Stout's life, were finished with eight novels.

In one sense, it might be considered that there are 73 Wolfe stories because Stout wrote two versions of two of the novellas. *Murder Is No Joke* was rewritten, expanded and retitled as *Frame-Up For Murder*, and the first published version of *Counterfeit For Murder* was actually the second version of the story Stout wrote. The first, longer and considerably different version, retitled *Assault On A Brownstone*, was not published until a decade after Stout's death in 1975.

The 74 cases cover 652 days of investigation by Nero Wolfe and/or his assistants. This is figured from the initial day of Wolfe's involvement until the day the case was solved. The beginning date of the case is not necessarily the date of the first murder since some were days or weeks old before Wolfe became involved. The stories also often went several days beyond the day the case was solved so the number of the days in the settings is more than the number of days of investigation. This is an average of slightly over nine days on each case but they vary widely. Six were solved in a single day, fifteen in two days and forty-seven in a week or less, almost two-thirds of the total. The brevity of the novellas naturally lend themselves to the shorter cases. None of them lasted more than one week.

The longest-running case was the one chronicled in *In The Best Families* in 1950 when Wolfe uprooted himself and went after his personal Moriarty, Arnold Zeck. That case lasted 156 days, over five months. Only one other case, *The Mother Hunt* in 1962, lasted over one month.

The following is a chronological listing of the Nero Wolfe series. They are listed in the order they were written which is not necessarily the order in which they were set or published. They are listed in the following format:

1. **Publication Title (Novel or Novella)**
2. Original title (if different).
3. Beginning and ending dates the story was written, as nearly as can be determined. In 1946, Rex Stout began keeping a written record of the dates he wrote the stories. Prior to 1946, the dates are approximate.
4. Dates the story was set on, as nearly as can be determined. Again, some are approximations but, lacking any specific indications within the story itself, they are judged by the fact that Stout usually set the beginning date of the story within a week of when he began writing it.
5. Publication dates.
6. Remarks.

Case Chronologies

1. **Fer—De—Lance (Novel)**
Written October 18-Before Christmas, 1933.
Set on Wednesday, June 7-Saturday, June 24, 1933.
Published in The American Magazine as "Point Of Death" on October 24, 1934.
Published in book form October 26, 1934.
2. **The League Of Frightened Men (Novel)**
Written October-November 1934.
Set on Friday, November 2-Thursday, November 15, 1934.
Published August 14, 1935.
3. **The Rubber Band (Novel)**
Written Fall 1935.
Set Sunday, October 6-Wednesday, October 9, 1935.
Published in The Saturday Evening Post, December 1935.
Published in book form April 9, 1936.
4. **The Red Box (Novel)**
Written Spring 1936.
Set Monday, March 30-Monday, April 6, 1936.
Published April 15, 1937.
5. **Too Many Cooks (Novel)**
Written Spring 1937.
Set Monday, April 5-Friday, April 9, 1937.

Published in The American Magazine in March, 1938.
Published in book form August 17, 1938.

6. **Some Buried Caesar (Novel)**
Written approx. January-March 1938.
Set Monday, September 12-Thursday, September 15, 1938.
Published February 2, 1939.

7. **Over My Dead Body (novel)**
Written in the Fall of 1938.
Set on two very long days in November of 1938 (possibly a Monday and Tuesday because Marko Vukcic had dined with Wolfe the day before the case began. Although we don't know if the custom had begun by then, Vukcic eventually dined with Wolfe every Sunday).
Published in The American Magazine in September, 1939.
Published in book form in 1940.

8. **Where There's A Will (Novel)**
Written Fall 1939.
Set Friday, July 14-Sunday, July 16, 1939.
Published in The American Magazine as "Sisters In Trouble", June 1940.
Published in book form June 10, 1940.

9. **Bitter End (novella)**
Written September 1940.
Set on a Tuesday and Wednesday in November 1940.
Published in The American Magazine in November 1940.
Published in book form in December 1985 in Death Times Three.

10. **Black Orchids (Novella)**
Written in March 1941.
Set on a Monday through Friday in March 1941.
Published in The American Magazine in August 1942 as "Death Wears An Orchid."
Published in book form in Black Orchids in May of 1942.

11. **Cordially Invited To Meet Death (Novella)**
Written August 1941.
Set Monday, August 18-Friday, August 29, 1941.
Published in The American Magazine in April 1942.
Published in book form in Black Orchids in May of 1942.

12. **Not Quite Dead Enough (Novella)**
Written in August 1942.
Set on a Monday through Wednesday in early March 1942.

Published in The American Magazine in December 1942.

Published in book form September 7, 1944.

13. Booby Trap (Novella)

Written in August 1943.

Set on Monday, August 9-Tuesday, August 10, 1943.

Published in The American Magazine in August, 1944.

Published in book form in Not Quite Dead Enough, September 7, 1944.

14. Help Wanted Male (Novella)

Written in June 1944.

Set on a Tuesday through Saturday in May 1944.

Published in The American Magazine in August of 1945.

Published in book form in Trouble in Triplicate, February 11, 1949.

15. Instead Of Evidence (Novella)

Written in September 1945.

Set on a Tuesday through Saturday in October of 1945.

Published as "Murder On Tuesday" in The American Magazine in May of 1946.

Published in book form in Trouble in Triplicate, February 11, 1949.

16. The Silent Speaker (Novel)

Written March-April, 1946.

Set on Wednesday, March 27-Monday, April 8, 1946.

Published on October 21, 1946.

From this point in his career, Rex Stout began keeping a meticulous writing record. He also wrote nothing but Nero Wolfe stories from this point forward.

17. Before I Die (Novella)

Written October 12-22, 1946-11 days writing time, no days off.

Set on Monday, October 7-Monday, October 14, 1946.

Published in The American Magazine in April of 1947.

Published in book form in Trouble In Triplicate, February 11, 1949.

18. Too Many Women (Novel)

Original Title-Protect Your Woman.

Written March 19-May 2, 1947-38 days writing time, 6 days off.

Set on Monday, March 17-Saturday, April 5, 1947.

Published October 20, 1947.

19. Man Alive (Novella)

Written July 24-August 3, 1947-11 days writing time, no days off.

Set Monday, June 9-Tuesday, June 10, 1947.

Published in The American Magazine in December 1947.

Published in book form in Three Doors to Death, April 21, 1950.

20. **Bullet For One (Novella)**
Written November 17-29, 1947-11 days writing time, 2 days off.
Set on a Tuesday through Friday in October of 1947.
Published in the American Magazine in July of 1948.
Published in book form in Curtains for Three, February 23, 1951.

21. **And Be A Villain (novel)**
Written March 19-April 24, 1948-34 days writing time, 3 days off.
Set Saturday, March 13-Saturday, April 3, 1948.
Published on September 27, 1948.

22. **Omit Flowers (Novella)**
Written July 14-23, 1948-10 days writing time, no days off.
Set Tuesday, July 6-Thursday, July 8, 1948.
Published in The American Magazine in November 1948.
Published in book form in Three Doors To Death, April 21, 1950.

23. **Door To Death (Novella)**
Written December 8-19, 1948-11 days writing time, 1 day off.
Set on Tuesday, December 7-Wednesday, December 8, 1948.
Published in The American Magazine in June of 1949.
Published in book form in Three Doors To Death, April 21, 1950.

24. **The Second Confession (novel)**
Written March 16-April 23, 1949-35 days writing time, 4 days off.
Set on Thursday, June 16-Tuesday, June 28, 1949.
Published September 6, 1949.

25. **The Gun With Wings (Novella)**
Written July 16-28, 1949-10 ½ days writing time, 2 ½ days off.
Set on Sunday, August 14-Wednesday, August 17, 1949.
Published in The American Magazine in December of 1949.
Published in book for in Curtains For Three, February 23, 1951.

26. **Disguise For Murder (Novella)**
Original Title-The Scarf.
Written December 12-24, 1949-11 days writing time, 2 days off.
Set on a Monday through Wednesday in March 1950.
Published as "The Twisted Scarf" in The American Magazine in September of 1950.
Published in book form in Curtains For Three, February 23, 1951.

27. **In The Best Families (Novel)**
Written April 14-May 29, 1950-38 days writing time, 8 days off.

Set on Thursday, April 6-Friday, September 8, 1950.

Published on September 29, 1950.

28. The Cop Killer (Novella)

Original Title-Just In Time.

Written July 24-August 7, 1950-12 days writing time, 3 days off.

Set on a Tuesday in late July or early August of 1949.

Published in The American Magazine in February of 1951.

Published in book form in Triple Jeopardy, March 21, 1952.

NOTE: In accordance with Rex Stout's writing habits, this story should have taken place in 1950 but Wolfe was plotting against Zeck then. Therefore it was either set a year earlier or a year later. Since Stout never placed any of the Wolfe stories that much in the future, I have chosen 1949.

29. The Squirt And The Monkey (Novella)

Written Jan. 20-Feb. 1, 1951-12 days writing time, 1 day off.

Set on a Monday through Wednesday in January of 1951.

Published as "See No Evil" in The American Magazine in August of 1951.

Published in book form in Triple Jeopardy, March 21, 1952.

30. Murder By The Book (Novel)

Written March 29-May 23, 1951-37 days writing time, 19 days off.

Set on Tuesday, January 9-Monday, March 12, 1951.

Published on October 12, 1951.

31. Home To Roost (Novella)

Written July 27-August 10, 1951-14 days writing time, 1 day off.

Set on Tuesday, July 31-Monday, August 6, 1951.

Published as "Nero Wolfe and the Communist Killer" in The American Magazine in January of 1952.

Published in book form in Triple Jeopardy, March 21, 1952.

32. This Won't Kill You (Novella)

Written Jan. 20-Feb. 4, 1952-11 days writing time, 5 days off.

Set on Wednesday and Thursday in October of 1951.

NOTE: Baring-Gould places this story in 1952. Stout's past habits make it more likely he would have post-dated rather than pre-dated it. The only real World Series between the New York Giants and Boston Red Sox (the setting for this story) occurred in 1912 (the Sox won four games to three). The 1951 Series was between the N.Y. Yankees and the Giants (Yankees, four games to two) and the 1952 Series occurred after the story was written and published. Since Boston had only made it to the World Series once (and lost it) in the

33 years since they had traded Babe Ruth to the Yankees, maybe Rex was trying to boost their self esteem.

Published as "This Will Kill You" in The American Magazine in September of 1952.

Published in book form in Three Men Out, March 26, 1954.

33. **Prisoner's Base (Novel)**
Original Title-Dare Base
Written June 19-August 3, 1952-35 ½ days writing time, 10 ½ days off.
Set on Monday, June 23-Monday, June 30, 1952.
Published October 24, 1952.

34. **Invitation To Murder (Novella)**
Written Oct. 23-Nov. 17, 1952-13 days writing time, 13 days off.
Set on a Friday in October of 1952.
Published in book form in Three Men Out, March 26, 1954.

35. **The Zero Clue (Novella)**
Written March 11-25, 1953-10 days writing time, 5 days off.
Set on a Wednesday and Thursday In March of 1953.
Published as "Scared To Death" in The American Magazine in December of 1953.
Published in book form in Three Men Out, March 26, 1954.

36. **The Golden Spiders (Novel)**
Written May 12-July 1, 1953-34 days writing time, 17 days off.
Set on Tuesday, May 19-Friday, May 29, 1953.
Published on October 26, 1953.

37. **When A Man Murders (Novella)**
Written Sept. 27-Oct. 18, 1953-11 days writing time, 11 days off.
Set on a Tuesday and Wednesday in October of 1953.
Published in The American Magazine in May of 1954.
Published in book form in Three Witnesses, March 10, 1956.

38. **Die Like A Dog (Novella)**
Written Jan. 28-Feb. 10, 1954-10 days writing time, 4 days off.
Set on a Wednesday and Thursday in February of 1954.
Published as "The Body in the Hall" in The American Magazine in December of 1954.
Published in book form in Three Witnesses, March 10, 1956.

39. **The Black Mountain (Novel)**
Written April 5-June 22, 1954-37 days writing time, 42 days off.

Set on Thursday, March 18-Wednesday, April 28, 1954.
Published October 14, 1954.

40. The Next Witness (Novella)

Written Sept. 23-Oct. 13, 1954-13 days writing time, 8 days off.
Set on a Wednesday and Thursday in late September or early October of 1954.
Published as "The Last Witness" in The American Magazine in May of 1955.
Published in book form in Three Witnesses, March 10, 1956.

41. Immune To Murder (Novella)

Written Jan. 21-Feb. 3, 1955-12 days writing time, 2 days off.
Set on two days in the Spring of 1955.
Published in The American Magazine in November of 1955.
Published in book form in Three For The Chair, May 3, 1957.

42. Before Midnight (Novel)

Written April 14-May 20, 1955-32 days writing time, 5 days off.
Set on Tuesday, April 12-Wednesday, April 20, 1955.
Published on October 27, 1955.

43. A Window For Death (Novella)

Written August 13-30, 1955-12 days writing time, 6 days off.
Set on Tuesday, August 9-Thursday, August 11, 1955.
Published as "Nero Wolfe and the Vanishing Chair" in The American Magazine in May of 1956.
Published in book form in Three For The Chair, May 3, 1957. (NOTE: This was the last story published in The American Magazine.)

44. Too Many Detectives (Novella)

Written January 13-24, 1956-11 days writing time, 1 day off.
Set on Monday, January 9 and Tuesday, January 10, 1956.
Published in Collier's Magazine, September 14, 1956.
Published in book form in Three For The Chair, May 3, 1957.

45. Might As Well Be Dead (Novel)

Written April 16-May 23, 1956-31 days writing time, 7 days off.
Set on Monday, April 9-Monday, April 16, 1956.
Published October 21, 1956.

46. Christmas Party (Novella)

Original Title-License To Kill.
Written August 19-September 4, 1956-17 days writing time.
Set on Wednesday, December 20-Saturday, December 23, 1956?
NOTE: Baring-Gould sets this story in 1957. The year 1956 would be more correct in accordance with the time-frame in which it was written. However,

these days and dates will not coincide with 1957—only with 1939, 1944, 1950 and 1961, for those years closest to the time it was written. Your guess is as good as mine—and Rex's. Nobody's perfect.

Published in Collier's Magazine as "The Christmas Party Murder", January 4, 1957.

Published in book form in And Four To Go, February 14, 1958.

47. **Easter Parade (Novella)**

Written December 6, 1956-January 8, 1957-11 days writing time, 23 days off.

Set on Tuesday, April 16-Monday, April 22, 1957.

Published as "The Easter Parade Murder" in Look Magazine, April 16, 1957.

Published in book form in And Four To Go, February 14, 1958.

48. **Fourth—Of—July Picnic (Novella)**

Written March 9-22, 1957-9 days writing time, 5 days off.

Set on Wednesday, July 4-Thursday, July 5, 1956.

Published as "The Labor Union Murder" in Look Magazine, July 9, 1957.

Published in book form in And Four To Go, February 14, 1958.

49. **If Death Ever Slept (Novel)**

Written May 16-June 19, 1957-32 days writing time, 3 days off.

Set on Monday, May 20-Tuesday, June 4, 1957.

Published October 25, 1957.

50. **Murder Is No Joke (Novella)**

Written August 5-15, 1957-10 days writing time, 1 day off.

Set on a Tuesday and Wednesday in August of 1957.

Published in the Saturday Evening Post as "Frame-Up For Murder" in June/July, 1958.

Published in book form in And Four To Go, February 14, 1958.

50(a). **Frame—Up For Murder (Novella)**
    Rewritten and expanded version of Murder Is No Joke

Written Nov. 23-Dec. 5, 1957-11 days writing time, 2 days off.

Set on a Monday through Wednesday in August of 1957.

Published in the Saturday Evening Post on 6/21, 6/28 and 7/5/58.

Published in book form in Death Times Three, December 1985.

51. **Champagne For One (Novel)**

Original Title-Murder Of An Unmarried Mother.

Written March 1-April 24, 1958-34 days writing time, 21 days off.

Set on a Tuesday through Sunday in March 1958.

Published on November 24, 1958.

52. **Poison A La Carte (Novella)**
Written June 26-July 10, 1958-12 days writing time, 3 days off.
Set on Tuesday, April 1-Thursday, April 3, 1958.
Published in book form in Three At Wolfe's Door, April 29, 1960.
Published in Ellery Queen's Mystery Magazine in April, 1968.

53. **Method Three For Murder (Novella)**
Written Aug. 21-Sept. 3, 1958-13 days writing time, 1 day off.
Set on a Monday, September 1, and Tuesday, September 2, of 1958.
Published in the Saturday Evening Post on January 30, 1960.
Published in book form in Three At Wolfe's Door, April 29, 1960.

54. **Eeny Meeny Murder Moe (Novella)**
Written December 15, 1958-January 5, 1959-13 days writing time, 9 days off.
Set on Monday, January 5-Tuesday, January 6, 1959.
Published in Ellery Queen's Mystery Magazine, March of 1962.
Published in book form in Homicide Trinity, April, 1962.

55. **Assault On A Brownstone (Novella)**
The original longer version of Counterfeit For Murder
Written Jan.22-Feb. 11, 1959-18 days writing time, 3 days off.
Set on Monday, January 26-Tuesday, January 27, 1959.
Published in book form in Death Times Three, December 1985.

56. **Counterfeit For Murder (Novella)**
Written Mar.6-31, 1959-17 days writing time, 9 days off.
Set on Monday, January 26-Tuesday, January 27, 1959.
Published in the Saturday Evening Post as "Counterfeiter's Knife" on January 14, 21 and 28, 1961.
Published in book form in Homicide Trinity, April, 1962.

57. **Plot It Yourself (Novel)**
Written May 20-July 2, 1959-34 days writing time, 10 days off.
Set on Monday, May 18-Wednesday, June 3, 1959.
Published on October 30, 1959.
(In *Death Of A Doxy*, Archie states this case took place in 1958 but Rex Stout's writing record and the dates in the book place it as stated above.)

58. **The Rodeo Murder (Novella)**
Written September 17-October 14, 1959-17 days writing time, 11 days off.
Set on a Monday through Wednesday in late September or early October of 1959.
Published in book form in Three At Wolfe's Door, April 29, 1960.

59. Death Of A Demon (Novella)
Written January 26-February 16, 1960-18 days writing time, 4 days off.
Set on Tuesday, January 26-Wednesday, January 27, 1960.
Published in the Saturday Evening Post, June 10, 1961.
Published in book form in Homicide Trinity, April, 1962.

60. Too Many Clients (Novel)
Written May 6-June 22, 1960-35 days writing time, 13 days off.
Set on Monday, May 9-Saturday, May 14, 1960.
Published on October 28, 1960.

61. Kill Now—Pay Later (Novella)
Written December 5-29, 1960-18 days writing time, 7 days off.
Set on a Monday through Friday in December of 1960.
Published in the Saturday Evening Post, December 9, 1962.
Published in book form in Trio For Blunt Instruments, 1964.

52. The Final Deduction (Novel)
Original Title-Deduction For Death.
Written April 23-June 5, 1961-32 days writing time, 12 days off.
Set on Tuesday, April 25-Monday, May 1, 1961.
Published on October 13, 1961.

63. Murder Is Corny (Novella)
Written September 1961.
Set Tuesday, September 12-Friday, September 15, 1961.
Published in the Saturday Evening Post, 1962.
Published in book form in Trio For Blunt Instruments, 1964.

64. Gambit (Novel)
Written February 10-May 1, 1962-41 days writing time, 40 days off.
Set on Monday, February 12-Friday, February 16, 1962.
Published in October of 1962.

65. Blood Will Tell (Novella)
Written August 4-29, 1962-16 days writing time, 10 days off.
Set on Tuesday, August 7-Thursday, August 9, 1962.
Published in Ellery Queen's Mystery Magazine in December of 1963.
Published in book form in Trio For Blunt Instruments, 1964.

66. The Mother Hunt (Novel)
Written December 17, 1962-February 9, 1963-37 days writing time, 18 days off.
Set on Tuesday, June 5-Monday, July 23, 1962.
Published in August of 1963.

67. A Right To Die (Novel)
Written February 21-April 7, 1964-35 days writing time, 12 days off.
Set on Monday, February 24-Friday, March 13, 1964.
Published on October 22, 1964.

68. The Doorbell Rang (Novel)
Written December 18, 1964-February 6, 1965-40 days writing time, 11 days off.
Set on Tuesday, January 5-Monday, January 18, 1965.
Published on October 8, 1965.

69. Death Of A Doxy (Novel)
Written January 27-April 17, 1966-39 days writing time, 42 days off.
Set on Saturday, January 29-Monday, February 7, 1966.
Published in August of 1966.

70. The Father Hunt (Novel)
Written October 29-December 26, 1967-44 days writing time, 15 days off.
Set on Thursday, August 17-Friday, September 8, 1967.
Published on May 28, 1968.

71. Death Of A Dude (Novel)
Original Title-Dead Dude.
Written September 20, 1968-February 7, 1969-No writing record.
Set on Friday, August 2-Tuesday, August 13, 1968.
Published August 20, 1969.

72. Please Pass The Guilt (Novel)
Written October 31, 1969-January 26, 1972.
Set on Tuesday, June 3-Monday, June 30, 1969.
Published September 24, 1973.

73. A Family Affair (Novel)
Written November 6, 1974-January 6, 1975.
Set on Tuesday, October 29-Thursday, November 7, 1974.
Published September 8, 1975.

The final Nero Wolfe story, *A Family Affair*, was published on Monday, September 8, 1975. Exactly seven weeks later, Rex Stout died on October 27, five weeks to the day before his eighty-ninth birthday.

A long life by any standard. But not long enough for his readers.

Bibliography

Books:

Baring-Gould, William S., *Nero Wolfe Of West Thirty-Fifth Street*, The Viking Press Inc., New York, NY, 1969.

Brooks, Tim and Earle Marsh, *The Complete Directory To Prime Time Network And Cable TV Shows, 1946–Present*, Ballantine Books, New York, NY, 1995.

Goldin, J. David, *The Golden Age Of Radio*, Radio Yesteryear, 1999.

Kimes, Beverly Rae, and Henry Austin Clark Jr., *Standard Catalog Of American Cars, 1805–1942*, Third Edition, Krause Publications, Iola, WI, 1996.

Kowalke, Ron, Editor, *Standard Catalog Of American Cars, 1946–1975*, Fourth Edition, Krause Publications, Iola, WI, 1997.

McAleer, John, *Rex Stout—A Biography*, Little, Brown and Company, Boston-Toronto, 1977.

Stout, Rex, The Canon, as listed.

Van Dover, J. Kenneth, *At Wolfe's Door: The Nero Wolfe Novels of Rex Stout*, The Borgo Press, San Bernardino, CA, 1991.

Magazines:

Stout, Rex, *Why Nero Wolfe Likes Orchids*, Life Magazine, April 19, 1963.

Internet Websites:

http://nerowolfe.freeservers.com
  " www.chaparraltree.com/essays/wolfe.shtml
  " epguides.com/Nero Wolfe
  " www.nexus.hu/mic/beer
  " johnclaytonsr.com/wolfe/index.html
  " concentric.net/~Kgunby/
  " www.geocities.com/Athens/8907/nero.html
  " yahoo.com/goo/nero+wolfe/15/*
  " www.thrillingdetective.com
  " www.orchid.org

0-595-27861-2

Printed in the United States
21737LVS00001B/190

9 780595 278619